# COLLECTION

# u.s.
# architecture

## architektur der u.s.a.
## architecture des états unis

# Imprint

The Deutsche Bibliothek is registering this publication in the Deutsche Na-
tionalbibliographie; detailed bibliographical information can be found on the
internet at http://dnb.ddb.de

ISBN  978-3-03768-022-3
Copyright 2009 by Braun Publishing AG
www.braun-publishing.ch

1st edition 2009

Editorial coordination:
Annika Schulz
Editorial staff:
Megan Bunting
French version:
Marcel Saché, Berlin
Translation into German:
Joanna Zajac-Heinken
Graphic design:
Michaela Prinz

COLLECTION

Michelle Galindo

# u.s. architecture

architektur der u.s.a.
architecture des états unis

BRAUN

# CONTENTS
# INHALT
# SOMMAIRE

**WEST**

**Collection: U.S. Architecture** presents the world's largest architecture market – with a building volume in excess of one trillion USD annually, the United States is clearly ahead of Japan, whose volume is only roughly half that amount. Despite the current recession, which is affecting the residential construction market as well as all other construction sectors, when comparing continents, the vast lead of the USA places North America in second place after Europe. While this figure also includes many construction projects that do not even remotely represent "architecture," it goes without saying that the number of excellent buildings is accordingly high.

This book focuses on architecture with high esthetic value – around 157 projects from all corners of the nation present a cross-section of contemporary architecture. They include the work of globally operating stars that are active in all parts of the United States, as well as smaller offices with a more regional focus. This wide range is due to the fact that what may appear to outsiders to be uniformly "American," is in reality only a sum of many regionalisms on the one hand, and national and, more importantly international characteristics, on the other – residential buildings in Los Angeles and New York differ due to their climatic as well as historical differences. Similarly, only an inclusive look at the very diverse building types presents an approximate picture of what US American architecture is all about –a country house is just as typical as an office skyscraper, which was invented here. However, mass residential projects, whether high rises or residential estates, remain an exotic exception in American architecture, with service flats for upscale customers the only truly "architectural" projects of this kind.

Attentive observers will notice other differences from the rest of the world as well. For example, the "new elegance"(orthogonal buildings with exquisite surface materials in the tradition of the immigrated post-war modernity style of Ludwig Mies van der Rohe) dominate the US architecture much more than in other countries. Blobitecture and deconstructivism only act as exceptions to a rule and are usually conceived by the internationally operating architects. The use of natural and "raw" materials, frequently combined with characteristic large roof overhangs and the interaction of symmetric and asymmetric elements, follows the tradition of Frank Lloyd Wrights' prairie houses. These already featured the the combination of volumes and room sequences that distinguish many of the  single-family homes in this book. Yet even older traditions continue to affect residential building design.

For example, the arrangement of the individual rooms around a large living room, with a fireplace at its center, was in the late 19th century already the basis for the opening of the layout to the outside in the shingle style (which emerged from the British Queen-Anne style). To this day, this basic concept dominates room structure, even in two-floor homes. Traditions such as these are part of any vivid culture and not only outlast all economic problems but also use the exterior circumstance for new insights as long as they do not become folklore as is often the case in reviews due to cultural fixations. Therefore, **Collection: U.S. Architecture** is encouraging for the future and creates a desire for a vivid modernity that does not forget its roots.

# VORWORT

**Collection: Architektur der U.S.A.** beschäftigt sich mit dem größten nationalen Architekturmarkt der Welt: Mit einem Bauvolumen von mehr als einer Billionen USDollar pro Jahr führen die Vereinigten Staaten von Amerika deutlich vor Japan, dessen Umsatz nur etwa halb so hoch ist. Trotz der aktuellen Rezession, die den Wohnungsbau wie auch die übrigen Bauaufgaben betrifft, liegt Nordamerika beim Vergleich der Kontinente, dank des gewaltigen Vorsprungs der USA, auf Platz zwei hinter Europa. Zwar ist in dieser Bilanz auch viel „Gebautes" enthalten, das dem Begriff „Architektur" nicht einmal nahe kommt, dennoch ist die Zahl guter Bauten selbstverständlich entsprechend hoch.

Diese Architektur mit hohem ästhetischem Anspruch ist Thema dieses Buches: rund 157 Bauten aus allen Teilen des Landes, zeigen einen Querschnitt durch die zeitgenössische Baukunst. Hierunter finden sich ebenso Werke der global agierenden Stars, die in allen Regionen der USA tätig sind, wie auch der kleineren Büros mit regionalem Schwerpunkt. Denn was für den Außenstehenden als einheitlich „amerikanisch" erscheint, ist in Wirklichkeit nur die Summe aus zahlreichen Regionalismen einerseits und nationalen, wichtiger noch internationalen Tendenzen andererseits: Wohnungsbau in Los Angeles und in New York unterscheiden sich sowohl aufgrund klimatischer als auch historischer Voraussetzungen. Gleichermaßen ist es nur infolge einer gemeinsamen Betrachtung der unterschiedlichsten Baugattungen möglich, ein ungefähres Bild dessen zu bekommen, was US-amerikanische Architektur ausmacht: Das Landhaus ist gleichermaßen typisch wie der hierzulande erfundene Wolkenkratzer mit Büronutzung. Der Massenwohnungsbau – ob als Hochhaus oder als Siedlung – bleibt hingegen weiterhin eine exotische Aufgabe in der amerikanischen Baukunst und wird nur bei Serviceflats für die gehobene Klientel zu „Architektur".

Dem aufmerksamen Betrachter werden noch weitere Unterschiede zum Rest der Welt auffallen. So dominiert die „Neue Eleganz" (orthogonales Bauen mit exquisiten Oberflächenmaterialien in Nachfolge der hier eingewanderten Nachkriegsmoderne in der Art Ludwig Mies van der Rohes) die US-amerikanische Architektur weit stärker als dies sonst der Fall ist. BLOB sowie Dekonstruktivismus spielen lediglich als Ausnahme von der Regel eine Rolle und stammen häufig von den international tätigen Architekten. Die Anwendung natürlicher und „roh" belassener Materialien stellt sich – oftmals kombiniert mit charakteristischem großen Dachüberstand und dem Spiel von Symmetrie und Asymmetrie – in die Nachfolge der Präriehäuser Frank Lloyd Wrights. Diese wiesen bereits das Interesse an der Kombination von Volumina und Raumfolgen auf, die viele der Einfamilienhäuser dieses Bandes prägen. Aber auch noch ältere Traditionen zeigen im individuellen Wohnungsbau ihren Fortbestand.

So ist die Anordnung der einzelnen Wohnräume um ein großes Wohnzimmer– dessen Mittelpunkt wiederum der Kamin ist – schon im Schindel-style (aus dem englischen Queen-Anne hervorgegangen) Ende des 19. Jahrhunderts ursächlich für die Öffnung des Grundrisses ins Freie. Noch heute bestimmt diese Grunddisposition selbst bei zweigeschossigen Bauten viele Raumanordnungen. Traditionen wie diese sind Teil einer jeden lebendigen Kultur und überstehen nicht nur jede wirtschaftliche Schwäche, sondern nutzen äußere Umstände für neue Einsichten, solange sie nicht, wie dies in Rezessionen durch Kulturfixierung oft geschieht, zu Folklore werden. So macht **Collection: Architektur der U.S.A** Mut für die Zukunft und Lust auf eine lebendige Moderne, die ihre Wurzeln nicht vergisst.

# PRÉFACE

Le livre **Collection: Architecture des états unis** est consacré au plus grand marché national au monde en matière d'architecture. Les entreprises américaines de BTP réalisent un chiffre d'affaires annuel de plus d'un milliard de dollars, plaçant ainsi les États-Unis à la première place devant le Japon, où le chiffre d'affaires est moitié moins important. Au niveau des ensembles continentaux, l'Amérique du Nord occupe la seconde place derrière l'Europe en dépit de la récession actuelle qui affecte tous les secteurs de l'industrie du bâtiment, et cela grâce à l'avance considérable dont bénéficient les USA. Certes, ces chiffres tiennent compte d'un grand nombre de réalisations médiocres, mais il n'en reste pas moins qu'on trouve aux États-Unis toute une gamme de bâtiments de haute qualité architecturale.

C'est précisément à ces réalisations d'une grande valeur esthétique que s'intéresse le présent ouvrage. On y trouvera 157 exemples d'immeubles construits dans tout le pays, qui offrent ainsi un panorama de l'architecture américaine contemporaine. Il s'agit non seulement d'œuvres de stars internationales qui développent des projets dans tous les États-Unis, mais aussi de réalisations dues à des architectes d'envergure plus régionale. À y regarder de plus près, on s'aperçoit que l'architecture américaine est en fait la somme de particularismes régionaux et de diverses tendances nationales voire internationales. Les différentes approches qui existent par exemple en matière de logements entre Los Angeles et New York sont ainsi le fruit de l'Histoire autant que du climat. De même, ce n'est qu'en considérant les divers types de bâtiments qu'on peut se faire une idée de ce qu'est aujourd'hui l'architecture américaine, la maison de campagne et le gratte-ciel de bureaux — « inventé » à Chicago — étant les deux types caractéristiques du pays. Les grands projets de logements verticaux ou horizontaux restent par contre quelque chose d'exotique et se limitent à quelques réalisations destinées à une clientèle haut de gamme.

Une observation attentive du marché du BTP aux États-Unis révèle encore d'autres particularités nationales. Citons notamment la « nouvelle élégance », c'est-à-dire les bâtiments orthogonaux à enveloppe très soignée hérités de Ludwig Mies van der Rohe et des autres architectes de la seconde moitié du XXe siècle ayant émigré aux USA. Biomorphisme et déconstructivisme sont par contre des exceptions, dues la plupart du temps à des architectes étrangers. Autre particularité américaine : l'utilisation de matériaux naturels ou laissés bruts, souvent combinés à des toits débordants et à une opposition symétrie/asymétrie, ces deux éléments s'inspirant des « maisons de prairie » de Frank Lloyd Wright, qui présentaient déjà plusieurs volumes reliés entre eux tels qu'on les retrouve dans de nombreuses maisons individuelles illustrées dans le présent ouvrage.

D'ailleurs, en ce qui concerne les maisons individuelles, l'architecture américaine reste fortement ancrée dans la tradition. Rappelons que le style Schindel développé à la fin du XIXe siècle sur la base du style Queen Anne d'origine britannique se caractérisait notamment par l'agencement des pièces autour d'un grand séjour ayant lui-même une cheminée en son centre. C'est selon un schéma similaire, largement ouvert sur l'extérieur, que s'organisent de nombreuses villas modernes de plain-pied, voire à un étage. Partie intégrante de toute culture vivante, les traditions de ce genre survivent à toutes les crises et peuvent s'adapter à de nouvelles situations — dans la mesure où elles ne se fixent pas dans un folklore, comme c'est bien souvent le cas durant les périodes de récession. **Collection: Architecture des états unis** entend ainsi donner confiance en l'avenir, en une modernité vivante qui n'oublie pas ses racines.

# COLLECTION

# east

OUSE OF SWEDEN_WASHINGTON D.C._D.C._SANDER TREE HOUSE  WILMING
ON_DE_CUBE TOWER MIAMI_FL_THE VAULT MIAMI_FL_XSMALL BOSTON_MA
IG DIG BUILDING CAMBRIDGE_MA_NEIMAN MARCUS AT NATICK COLLECTION
ATICK_MA_PROVINCETOWN ART ASSOCIATION AND MUSEUM PROVINCETOWN
AVH  R-10 GHOUSE VINEYARD HAVEN_MA_LIBRARY AT MORGAN STATE UNI
ERSITY BALTIMORE_MD_BOWDOIN COLLEGE MUSEUM OF ART BRUNSWICK
E_RE-COVER RESIDENCE AMAGANSETT_NY_CC01 HOUSE ANCRAM_NY NYP
RANCIS MARTIN LIBRARY_BRONX_NY_THE BRONX MUSEUM OF THE ARTS EX
ANSION, NORTH WING_BRONX_NY_TERRY WINTERS STUDIO_COLUMBIA COUN
Y_NY_DUTCHESS  COUNTY  GUEST  HOUSE_DUTCHESS  COUNTY_NY_STON
OUSES_EASTHAMPTON, LONG ISLAND_NY_C-I HOUSE_HUDSON VALLEY_NY
VANT CHELSEA_NEW YORK_NY_MUSEUM OF ARTS AND DESIGN_NEW YORK
Y_CRISTIANO CORA STUDIO_NEW YORK_NY_CHATHAM HOUSE_NEW YORK_NY
LIFF TREE HOUSE_NEW YORK_NY_471 WASHINGTON STREET_NEW YORK_N

## WASHINGTON D.C._D.C. **HOUSE OF SWEDEN**

**ARCHITECTS:** GERT WINGÅRDH AND TOMAS HANSEN
**COMPLETION:** 2006_**TYPOLOGY:** CIVIC
**PHOTOS:** MICHAEL PERLMUTTER (13 B. L.),
PATRIK GUNNAR HELIN (13 A.)
ÅKE E:SON LINDMAN (12, 13 B. R.)

This building has seven levels, including a rooftop terrace and underground car park, and was built right up to the property boundary, except at entrance level. This lies at the highest point to which the Potomac River is ever expected to rise. A large flight of steps and a ramp along the entrance side of the building leave the pillars exposed and create a loggia in a classicistic and classically modern style (compare this with Villa Savoye). The entrance floor is the hub of all operations. The part of the building used exclusively for the embassy is on the left together with the reception area. The offices are located on the next floor. The public part of the building has its reception on the right, with a large, glazed exhibition space (the Anna Lind Hall) facing the Potomac River and with a series of multi-purpose exhibition and conference rooms leading off a lower lobby.

Das siebengeschossige Gebäude mit Dachterrasse und Tiefgarage steht abgesehen von der Eingangsebene unmittelbar an der Grundstücksgrenze. Eine großzügige Treppe und eine Rampe führen zum Eingang und schaffen mit exponierten Stützen eine Kolonnade in einem klassizistischen und klassisch modernen Stil (vgleiche mit Villa Savoye von Le Corbusier). Das Herzstück aller Aktivitäten bildet die Eingangsebene. Der von der Botschaft genutzte Teil befindet sich zusammen mit einer Empfangszone auf der linken Seite. Im Geschoss darüber sind Büros angeordnet. Der öffentliche Gebäudeteil mit Empfang liegt auf der rechten Seite. Ein verglaster Ausstellungsraum weist zum Potomac River.

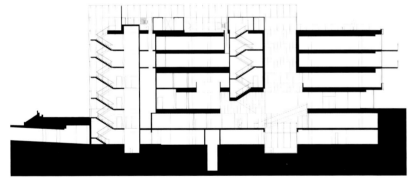

Ce bâtiment sur sept niveaux (dont le parking souterrain et la terrasse) a été construit près du Potomac, l'entrée étant située au-dessus du niveau pouvant être inondé lors des crues du fleuve. Sur la façade principale, les larges marches qui se fondent dans une rampe et les colonnes qui supportent le premier étage en porte-à-faux rappellent à la fois les édifices classiques et les réalisations modernes du début du XXᵉ siècle telles que la Villa Savoye. Le hall d'entrée permet d'accéder aux différents espaces intérieurs: à gauche, les bureaux de l'ambassade qui occupent une partie du rez-de-chaussée et le premier étage ; à droite les espaces publics, notamment la salle d'exposition dont les vitres donnent sur le Potomac, ainsi que divers espaces polyvalents.

left: Section_Lounge_Stair to upper floor_Staircase. right: Entrance view_Rooftop_General view.
links: Schnitt_Aufenthaltsraum_Treppe zum Obergeschoss_Treppenhaus. rechts: Eingangsansicht_Dachterrasse_Gesamtansicht.
à gauche: Vue en coupe_Salle et couloir_Escalier menant au premier étage_Escalier. à droite: Vue générale du côté de l'entrée_Toit en terrasse_Vue générale.

## WILMINGTON_DE **SANDER TREE HOUSE**

**ARCHITECTS:** SANDER ARCHITECTS
**COMPLETION:** 2006_**TYPOLOGY:** LIVING
**PHOTOS:** SHARON RISEDORPH PHOTOGRAPHY

The Tree House sits in a residential subdivision surrounded by century-old trees and a seasonal stream. The vertical form allows the house to sit in the trees and to have marvelous views of the canopy from the two upper floors. Horizontal windows provide select views into the landscape, while a large window in the living room provides dramatic views into the deep woods. The exterior entrance stair, cantilevered away from the façade, enters through a trio of trees and provides a view of the stream as one rises to enter the house. A spiral stair leads from the ground to the roof, where the tree canopy sits close overhead.

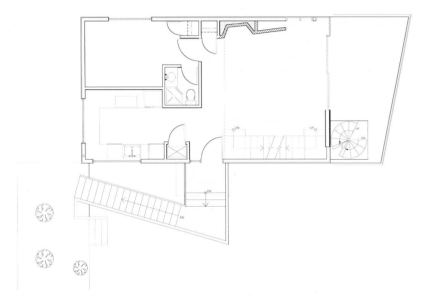

Das Baumhaus steht in einem Wohngebiet umgeben von hundertjährigen Bäumen und einem saisonal wasserführenden Fluss. Seine vertikale Form ermöglicht eine Platzierung in den Bäumen, sodass die beiden Oberge-schosse Blicke in die Baumwipfel gewähren. Horizontale Fenster gestatten ausgewählte Aussichten in die Landschaft, während ein großflächiges Fenster im Wohnzimmer eine spannungsvolle Sicht in die Tiefe der Wälder bietet. Die aus der Fassade auskragende Treppe führt durch eine Dreiergruppe von Bäumen hinauf zum Hauseingang und gestattet unterwegs einen Blick auf den Fluss. Außerdem reicht eine Wendeltreppe vom Erdboden bis zum Dach dicht unter den Baumkronen.

Cette maison a été construite dans un quartier résidentiel où se trouvent des arbres centenaires. La forme toute en hauteur du bâtiment garantit des vues magnifiques sur la forêt environnante à partir des larges fenêtres horizon-tales des étages supérieurs. Un escalier extérieur en bois, qui prend son départ au pied de trois grands arbres solitaires, dessert le premier étage. Un escalier métallique en colimaçon, lui aussi extérieur, mène jusqu'au toit en terrasse, à hauteur de la couronne des arbres.

left: Ground floor plan_Entrance stairs_Exterior view at dusk_South façade_Entrance view. right: View from east.
links: Grundriss Erdgeschoss_Treppenaufgang, Eingang_Außenansicht bei Dämmerung_Süd-fassade_ Blick auf den Eingang. rechts: Ostansicht.
à gauche: Plan du rez-de-chaussée_Vue de l'escalier extérieur_La maison au crépuscule_Façade sud_Vue de l'entrée. à droite: La maison vue de l'est.

left: Fireplace wall. right: Sketch _Living room with view to balcony_Aluminum stairs.
links: Kamin. rechts: Skizze_Wohnzimmer mit Blick auf den Balkon_Aluminiumtreppe.
à gauche: Séjour avec cheminée. à droite: Esquisse_ Vue du séjour et de sa terrasse_ Escalier en aluminium.

# MIAMI_FL **CUBE TOWER**

**ARCHITECTS:** OPPENHEIM
**COMPLETION:** UNBUILT_**TYPOLOGY:** LIVING
**RENDERINGS:** DBOX

This project represents the next frontier in urban multifamily high-rise housing. A dramatic steel infrastructure allows ultimate volumetric flexibility, letting the homeowner customize spatial prerogatives. Rising 22 stories, the building encourages occupants to design their own domain by connecting multiple cube modules vertically, horizontally, and diagonally in addition to creating double height volumes, garden voids and cantilevered living environments. Generated by desire and need rather than architectural assumption, the volumetric play of the building creates intriguing arrangements of solid and void.

Dieses Projekt repräsentiert die nächste Entwicklungsstufe beim Bau vielgeschossiger Mehrfamilienhäuser in der Stadt. Eine aufsehenerregende stählerne Infrastruktur mit höchster volumetrischer Flexibilität ermöglicht Wohnungseigentümern die Verwirklichung ihrer räumlichen Vorstellungen. Bei dem 22 Stockwerke hohen Gebäude können Bewohner ihr eigenes Heim gestalten, indem sie kubische Module vertikal, horizontal und diagonal miteinander verbinden. Auch zweigeschossige Volumen, Gärten sowie Auskragungen sind möglich. Das eher von Wünschen und Bedürfnissen als von architektonischen Vorgaben erzeugte Spiel mit Gebäudevolumen ergibt faszinierende Anordnungen fester und hohler Baukörper.

Ce projet constitue une « nouvelle frontière » en matière d'immeuble résidentiel. Un squelette en acier permet une flexibilité exceptionnelle des volumes et par conséquent des appartements qui répondent au mieux aux souhaits des propriétaires. L'immeuble, haut de vingt-deux étages, permet aux utilisateurs à concevoir eux-mêmes l'espace qu'ils entendent habiter en reliant des modules cubiques horizontalement, verticalement et diagonalement de manière à créer des duplex, des jardins suspendus et des volumes en porte-à-faux. La volumétrie, issue des besoins des occupants plus que de la théorie architecturale, génère une surprenante succession de pleins et de déliés.

left: East elevation_Sky terrace_North elevation. right: Exterior view into interior.
links: Ostansicht_Dachterrasse_Nordansicht. rechts: Blick von Außen in den Innenbereich.
à gauche: Élévation, façade est_Vue d'une terrasse_Vue de la façade nord. à droite: Vue de l'intérieur au travers de la façade transparente.

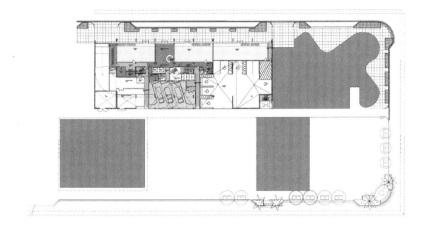

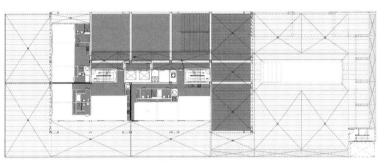

left: Cantilivered units. right: Level twelve and deck level floor plans_Pool deck.
links; Auskragungen. rechts: Grundriss zwölftes Ober- und Dachgeschoss_Sonnenterrasse mit Pool.
à gauche: Volumes en porte-à-faux. à droite: Plans du douzième et du dernier étages.

# MIAMI_FL **THE VAULT**

**ARCHITECTS:** OPPENHEIM
**COMPLETION:** 2010_**TYPOLOGY:** LEISURE
**RENDERINGS:** DBOX

The project, an iconic ten-story building, will be located on the edge of the Miami art district and next to one of the busiest highways in the city. It will serve as a state-of-the-art storage facility for valuables and art collections from museums and private collectors in Miami, as it operates as a vehicle to support and showcase local artists. The program will include storage, exhibition and work areas, offices and a luxury vehicles storage facility. It will also offer different garden areas – at the ground level and at a private elevated garden – as part of a plan to generate spaces for the exhibition of sculptures as well as the creation of spaces for art fairs and art-related events.

Das Projekt, ein symbolträchtiges zehngeschossiges Gebäude, soll am Rande von Miamis Art District und neben einer der verkehrsreichsten Autobahnen der Stadt entstehen. Als hochmoderne Lager für die Wertgegenstände und Kunstsammlungen der Museen und Privatsammler in Miami wird es lokale Künstler durch die Präsentation ihrer Werke fördern. Zum Raumprogramm zählen Magazine, Ausstellungs- und Arbeitsflächen, Büros und ein Raum für Luxusautos. Verschiedene Gartenbereiche auf Geländeniveau sowie in einem erhöhten privaten Bereich sind für die Ausstellung von Skulpturen sowie für Kunstmessen und kunstbezogene Veranstaltungen bestimmt.

Ce bâtiment de dix étages appelé à devenir emblématique de Miami doit être construit en bordure du quartier où se concentre la vie artistique, près de l'une des artères principales de la ville. Il servira à présenter et entreposer dans des conditions ultramodernes certaines collections assemblées par les musées locaux et diverses personnes privées. Il abritera également des espaces de travail, des bureaux et des garages pour véhicules de collection haut de gamme. Le musée se complètera à l'extérieur par des espaces verts et des jardins suspendus, où il sera possible d'organiser des expositions de sculpture ainsi que des salons et diverses manifestations artistiques.

left: Rooftop_General view. right: Façade covered with revolving panels of images.
links: Dachterrasse_Gesamtansicht. rechts: Fasade mit umlaufenden farbigen Wandtafeln.
à gauche: Jardin suspendu_Vue générale. à droite: Façade composée de panneaux tournants.

ATLANTA_GA **1180 PEACHTREE**

**ARCHITECTS:** PICKARD CHILTON ARCHITECTS
ASSOCIATE ARCHITECTS: KENDALL/HEATON ASSOCIATES
**COMPLETION:** 2006_**TYPOLOGY:** MIXED-USE
**PHOTOS:** COURTESY BY THE ARCHITECTS

1180 Peachtree marks the reemergence of Atlanta's skyscraper tradition. The tallest tower to be built in the city in 14 years, it rises 41 floors to a height of 197 meters. The tower is anchored by an impressive landscaped lobby and is topped with a dramatic lighted steel and glass veil. It serves as the international headquarters of King & Spalding. 1180 Peachtree is one the most advanced skyscrapers in a generation and incorporates the latest sustainable design strategies. As a pilot project for the USGBC's LEED Core and Shell certification program, it was the first high-rise office building in the world to be pre-certified for LEED-CS Silver and was ultimately awarded LEED-CS Gold.

1180 Peachtree steht für Atlantas wiederaufgelebte Hochhaustradition. Dieser Turm ist das höchste aller, in den vergangenen 14 Jahren entstandenen Gebäude der Stadt und steigt mit 41 Geschossen zu einer Höhe von 197 Metern auf. Der Turm wird wird von einer landschaftlich gestalteten Eingangslobby umgeben und von einem beleuchteten Schleier aus Stahl und Glas gekrönt. 1180 Peachtree dient King & Spalding als Weltzentrale. Als eines der fortschrittlichsten Hochhäuser seiner Generation integriert es die neuesten nachhaltigen Entwurfsstrategien. Beim LEED Zertifizierungsprogramm Core and Shell (CS) des U.S. Green Building Council war das Pilotprojekt das weltweit erste vielgeschossige Bürogebäude, das für LEED-CS Silber vorzertifiziert und schließlich mit LEED-CS Gold ausgezeichnet wurde.

Cette tour marque le renouveau de la tradition des gratte-ciel à Atlanta. Il s'agit d'un immeuble de quarante-et-un étages qui s'élève à 197 mètres de haut et constitue ainsi le plus haut bâtiment construit dans la ville depuis une quinzaine d'années. On trouve au rez-de-chaussée un hall d'entrée paysager particulièrement impressionnant, et au dernier étage une voile en acier et en verre d'aspect très audacieux. Siège de la multinationale King & Spalding, l'immeuble « 1180 Peachtree » est un des plus modernes de sa génération, notamment en matière de développement durable. Conçu comme un projet pilote de l'Agence fédérale pour les immeubles verts (USGBC), il a été le premier gratte-ciel au monde à bénéficier du label écologique LEED-CS Silver — et satisfait même aux normes nécessaires à l'attribution du label LEED-CS Gold.

left: Section_Skyline view at night_General view. right: Façade.
links: Schnitt_Blick auf die Skyline bei Nacht_Gesamtansicht. rechts: Fassade.
à gauche: Vue en coupe_Le gratte-ciel la nuit_Vue d'ensemble. à droite: Façade.

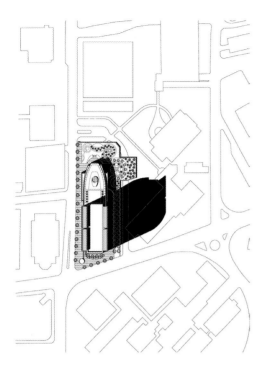

# BOSTON_MA **XSMALL**

**ARCHITECTS:** UNI
**COMPLETION:** 2006_**TYPOLOGY:** LIVING
**PHOTOS:** UNI

The final building for this larger residential compound, XSmall consists of three, rotated 16-by-22-foot boxes. Four-corner skylights provide natural light through minimum windows and maximum privacy, important since the design includes four houses on two lots that draw much attention. Finished in marine plywood, typically used in boat building for its broad and pronounced grain, XSmall creates the appearance of a huge piece of furniture. Each floor of XSmall has a different look and feel, including marble on the first floor and oak plywood on the second, but all are connected by a pared-down wooden staircase that threads through the space.

Das letzte für dieses Wohngebiet errichtete Gebäude XSmall besteht aus drei gedrehten 4,90 Meter x 6,70 Meter großen Boxen. Vier Oberlichter an den Hausecken lassen natürliches Licht in die Räume und sorgen für möglichst viel Privatsphäre. Dies ist insofern wichtig, als die vier auf zwei Grundstücken platzierten Häuser viel Aufmerksamkeit erregen. Außensperrholz, das beim Bootsbau wegen seiner breiten und ausgeprägten Maserung zum Einsatz kommt, lässt XSmall wie ein riesiges Möbelstück erscheinen. Unterschiedlich gestaltete Geschosse (mit Marmor in der ersten und Eichensperrholz in der zweiten Etage) ergeben eine jeweils andere Atmosphäre. Allen gemein ist die durchgehende schlichte Holztreppe.

Trois volumes orthogonaux de cinq mètres par sept se superposent avec un certain décalage pour former cette maison individuelle. Un nombre minimum de fenêtres assure une intimité maximale, tandis qu'un éclairage zénithal positionné aux angles laissés libres par le volume supérieur assure un bon éclairage naturel de l'intérieur. Des façades recouvertes de contreplaqué marine confèrent à l'ensemble l'aspect d'un meuble gigantesque. Chacun des étages, reliés entre eux par un escalier également habillé en bois, a une atmosphère qui lui est propre. Citons notamment l'ambiance « marbre » du rez-de-chaussée et l'ambiance « chêne » du premier étage.

## VARIATIONS

by configuration

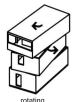  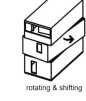

rotating    shifting    rotating & shifting

by siding material

exterior plywood    self-rusting metal    translucent polycarbonate
(Prodema)          (Corten)            (Polygal)

left: Variations_Three rotated boxes_Wooden staircase connecting all levels. right: Façade of marine plywood.
links: Variationen_Drei rotierende Volumen_Hölzerne Treppe, die alle Etagen miteinander verbindet. rechts: Fassade aus Bootsbausperrholz.
à gauche: Vues axonométriques_Volumes superposés avec un certain décalage_Escalier en bois intérieur. à droite: Volumes en contreplaqué marine.

# CAMBRIDGE_MA **BIG DIG BUILDING**

**ARCHITECTS:** SINGLE SPEED DESIGN
**COMPLETION:** 2006_**TYPOLOGY:** LIVING
**PHOTOS:** SINGLE SPEED IMAGE

Boston's ongoing Central Artery Tunnel Project is one of the largest, most complex infrastructural undertakings in American urban history. In regards to the massive amount of waste that accompanies construction on such a scale, the proposed alternative was to relocate and reuse these materials. As this recycled infrastructure offers the potential to create architecture that can withstand much higher loads than conventional systems, landscape can be easily brought to the roof and upper levels of the building, increasing useable open space, controlling runoff, and bringing natural environments closer to building users.

Bostons Tunnelprojekt für die zentrale Stadtautobahn ist eine der größten und komplexesten infrastrukturellen Maßnahmen in der Geschichte des amerikanischen Städtebaus. Die bei einem Vorhaben dieser Größenordnung anfallenden riesigen Abfallmengen legten nahe, diese Materialien an einen anderen Ort zu bringen und dort wiederzuverwenden. Architektur aus recycelter Infrastruktur kann deutlich höhere Lasten aufnehmen als herkömmliche Systeme. Daher lässt sich die Landschaft bis zum Dach und zu den Obergeschossen des Gebäudes fortführen. Auf diese Weise entsteht weiterer nutzbarer Freiraum, wird das abfließende Niederschlagswasser zurückgehalten und die Landschaft den Gebäudenutzern näher gebracht.

La construction du tunnel de Boston (« the Big Dig ») constitue le plus important et le plus complexe des projets d'infrastructure jamais réalisés aux États-Unis. La masse de matériaux excavés à cette occasion imposait de les réutiliser dans la région — notamment dans le « Big Dig Building ». Ces matériaux pouvant supporter des charges plus importantes que les produits conventionnels, il a été possible de réaliser ici un jardin suspendu qui augmente la surface habitable, a une action bénéfique sur l'environnement et permet aux occupants de se réapproprier une portion de nature.

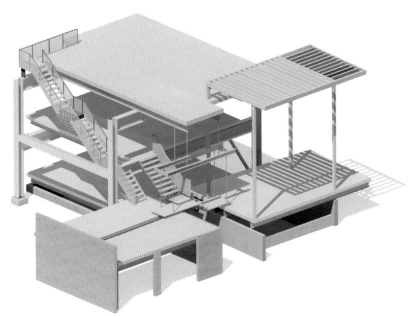

left: Elevation of lightframe stairs_Interior_Roof garden. right: Southeast façade_Northeast view_Exposed structure.
links: Ansicht der Light-frame Treppen_Innenansicht _Dachterrasse. rechts: Südostfassade_Nordostfassade_Fassadenkonstruktion.
à gauche: Axonométrie de l'escalier_Intérieur_Jardin suspendu. à droite: La maison vue du sudest_Vue du nord-ouest_Vue générale.

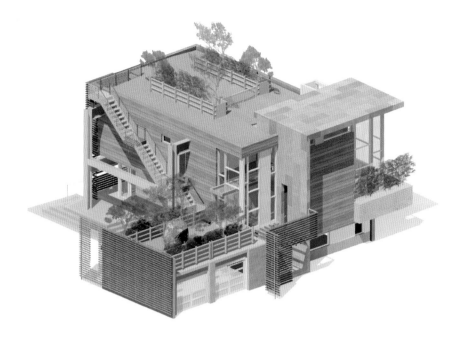

left: Stairs leading to multiple levels. right: Bird´s eye view_Interior stairs_Living room with fire-place.
links: Treppen zu mehreren Ebenen. rechts: Ansicht_Treppenhaus_Kamin im Wohnzimmer.
à gauche: Escalier desservant les différents niveaux. à droite: Axonométrie_Intérieur_Séjour avec cheminée.

# NATICK_MA **NEIMAN MARCUS AT NATICK COLLECTION**

**ARCHITECTS:** ELKUS MANFREDI ARCHITECTS
**COMPLETION:** 2007_**TYPOLOGY:** RETAIL
**PHOTOS:** BRUCE T. MARTIN

The specialty store in Natick, Massachusetts is the most unusual and unique store for a company whose business plan and corporate image requires that it creates environments specifically tailored to each business location. The design represents the style and sophistication of the Neiman Marcus product line, while also emphasizing its New England location. The undulating patterned stainless steel exterior is evocative of a silk scarf, or sophisticated fabrics from the Neiman couture line, billowing in the coastal breezes. The surrounding landscape recalls the sea grass of tidal marshes and traditional stonewalls of the region.

Das Fachgeschäft in Natick, Massachusetts ist ein höchst ausgefallener und ungewöhnlicher Laden eines Unternehmens, dessen Geschäftskonzept und Firmenimage für jede Niederlassung eine maßgeschneiderte architektonische Lösung vorschreibt. Der Entwurf repräsentiert den Stil und die Raffinesse der Produktlinie Neiman Marcus, wobei er auch den Standort des Geschäfts in New England herausstellt. Sein wellenförmiges, gemustertes Äußeres aus Edelstahl erinnert an ein von der Meeresbrise geblähtes Seidentuch oder einen raffinierten Stoff aus der Neiman Couturelinie. Die umgebende Landschaft lässt an das Seegras der Marschen und die traditionellen Natursteinmauern der Region denken.

Ce magasin de Natick, au Massachusetts, est le plus exceptionnel jamais réalisé pour une chaîne dont l'identité d'entreprise exige que chaque lieu de vente s'adapte à son environnement. Les architectes ont conçu un bâtiment dont le style et la sophistication correspondent non seulement à la marque Neiman Marcus, mais aussi à l'implantation en Nouvelle-Angleterre. La façade en acier inox forme des ondulations qui évoquent une des précieuses écharpes en soie vendues par la, qui flotterait au vent du large. Les autres éléments de l'extérieur rappellent les algues découvertes sur la plage à marée basse et les nombreux murets en pierres traditionnels qu'on trouve dans la région.

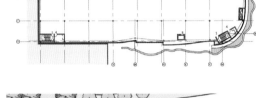

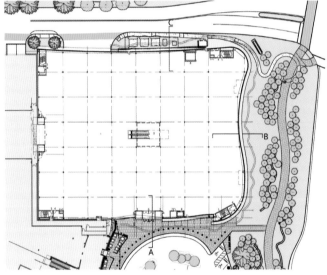

left: Plans_Exterior view at night. right: Entrance area by night.
links: Grundrisse_Außenansicht bei Nacht. rechts: Eingangsbereich bei Nacht.
à gauche: Plans_L'extérieur la nuit. à droite: La façade et l'entrée au crépuscule.

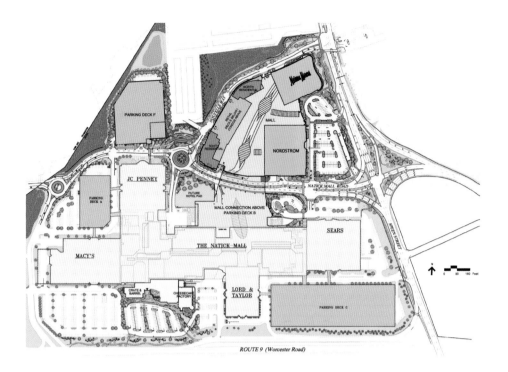

left: Undulating patterned stainless steel façade. right: Site plan_Detail façade_Exterior during the day_Entrance.
links: Gewellte Edelstahlfassade. rechts: Lageplan_Fassadendetail_Außenansicht_ Eingang.
à gauche: Ondulation de la façade en acier inox. à droite: Plan de situation_Détail de la façade_Vue générale de la façade_Entrée.

PROVINCETOWN_MA **PROVINCETOWN ART ASSOCIATION AND MUSEUM**

**ARCHITECTS:** MACHADO AND SILVETTI ASSOCIATES
**COMPLETION:** 2006_**TYPOLOGY:** CULTURE
**PHOTOS:** ANTON GRASSL / ESTO

The Provincetown Art Association and Museum (PAAM) is an organization dedicated to the exhibition and collection of art, as well as the education of the public in the arts. The renovation and expansion to PAAM created a new architectural identity for the institution, while improving PAAM's ability to display and store art. The objectives for the project included establishing a clear entry for the Museum that incorporated an existing historic structure, developing a clear sequence of gallery spaces that could be used individually or collectively, and expanding the Museum School and art storage areas.

Die Vereinigung Provincetown Art Association and Museum (PAAM) widmet sich neben dem Präsentieren und Sammeln von Kunst auch der Vermittlung von Kunstwissen. Mit dem Umbau und der Erweiterung des PAAM-Gebäudes erhielt die Institution eine neue architektonische Identität und bessere Möglichkeiten zum Ausstellen und Lagern von Kunst. Projektvorgaben waren ein deutlich artikulierter Museumseingang, der den bestehenden historischen Bau einbezieht, eine klare Raumfolge mit Galerien, die sich einzeln oder zusammen nutzen lassen sowie weitere Flächen für die Museumsschule und das Depot.

Le musée d'art de Provincetown (PAAM) est à la fois une galerie d'exposition et un centre de sensibilisation aux beaux-arts. L'annexe récemment construite et les travaux de modernisation réalisés simultanément ont renouvelé l'identité du musée en augmentant ses capacités d'exposition et de stockage. Les objectifs étaient les suivants: réaliser une zone d'entrée claire en intégrant un bâtiment préexistant ; construire des espaces d'exposition pouvant être utilisés séparément ou tous ensemble ; augmenter la surface disponible pour la réserve et les espaces éducatifs du musée.

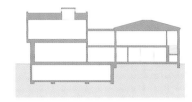

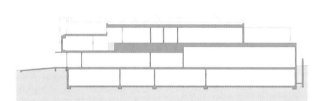

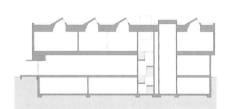

left: Sections_General view. right: Entrance_Front view_Wooden façade.
links: Schnitte_Gesamtansicht. rechts: Eingang_Vorderansicht_Holzfassade.
à gauche: Vues en coupe_Vue d'ensemble. à droite: Entrée_Façade principale_Façade avec bardage en planches.

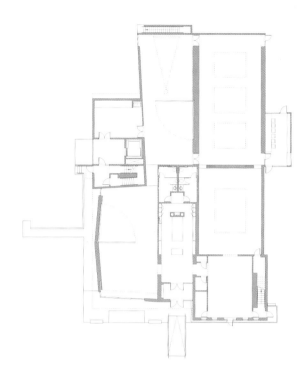

left: Gallery. right: Floor plan_Studio area_Gallery with glass wall_Workshop.
links: Galerie. rechts: Grundriss_Atelier_Galeier mit Glaswänden_Werkstatt.
à gauche: Espace d'exposition. à droite: Plan_Atelier_Espace d'exposition avec mur en verre_Atelier.

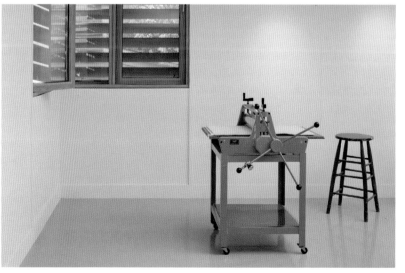

# VINEYARD HAVEN_MA **VH R-10 GHOUSE**

**ARCHITECTS:** DARREN PETRUCCI, PRINCIPAL A-I-R INC.
[ARCHITECTURE-INFRASTRUCTURE-RESEARCH INC.]
**COMPLETION:** 2007_**TYPOLOGY:** LIVING
**PHOTOS:** BILL TIMMERMAN

The VH R-10 gHOUSE is a prototype for guesthouses in the Town of Tisbury (Vineyard Haven) on the Island of Martha's Vineyard in Massachusetts. The design objective of the house is three fold: to maximize the restrictive zoning envelope; to combine contemporary building techniques with modified conventional building systems; to create a high performance design for the climatic and programmatic conditions of Martha's Vineyard. The house attempts to poetically synthesize and optimize these three objectives as an alternative to the ubiquitous Cape design.

Das VH R-10 gHOUSE ist ein Prototyp für Gästehäuser in der Stadt Tisbury (Vineyard Haven) auf der Insel Martha's Vineyard in Massachusetts. Der Entwurf des Hauses verfolgt drei Ziele: Die Geschossflächenzahl soll maximal ausgenutzt werden, moderne Bautechniken sind mit herkömmlichen, modifizierten Bausystemen zu kombinieren und für die klimatischen und programmatischen Bedingungen von Martha's Vineyard ist eine hocheffiziente Bauweise vorzusehen. Als Alternative zu der allgegenwärtigen Kap-Architektur versucht das Haus, diese drei Ziele stimmungsvoll zu vereinen und zu optimieren.

Ce bâtiment est un prototype de maison de vacances pour la commune de Tisbury/Vineyard Haven, située sur l'île de Martha's Vineyard au Massachusetts. Il poursuit un triple objectif: tirer le maximum d'un terrain faisant l'objet d'un plan de zonage restrictif, associer la technologie moderne aux techniques conventionnelles revisitées, créer un design « hautes performances » adapté aux conditions locales, notamment en matière de climat. Le bâtiment réalise une synthèse poétique optimale de ces trois objectifs afin d'offrir une alternative au style omniprésent dans la région.

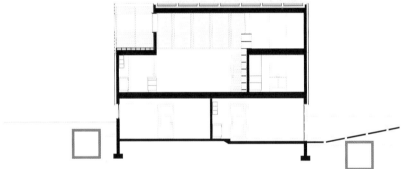

left: Sections_Planted roof_Roof deck. right: View from street_Garden view.
links: Schnitte_Bepflanztes Dach_Dachterrasse. rechts: Straßenansicht_ Blick in den Garten.
à gauche: Deux vues en coupe_Toit végétalisé_Terrasse. à droite: Le bâtiment vu de la rue_Le bâtiment vu du jardin.

left: Wooden façade. right: Basement plan_Bedroom with elaborate ceiling_Living room with shutters open_Living room with shutters closed.
links: Holzverkleidung. rechts: Grundriss Erdgeschoss_Schlafzimmer mit kunstvoller Decke_Wohnzimmer mit geöffneten Fensterläden_ Wohnzimmer mit geschlossenen Fensterläden.
à gauche: Façade avec bardage en planches. à droite: Plan de la cave_Chambre avec plafond sophistiqué_Séjour avec les stores ouverts_Séjour avec les stores fermés.

BALTIMORE_MD **LIBRARY AT MORGAN STATE UNIVERSITY**

**ARCHITECTS:** SASAKI ASSOCIATES
**COMPLETION:** 2008_**TYPOLOGY:** EDUCATION
**PHOTOS:** ROBERT BENSON

The library is multidirectional and relates to the surrounding campus in various ways. To the north, it visually connects to the core academic campus with a specific visual link to Holmes Hall, Morgan's most iconic building. To the east, the library serves to strengthen and animate the pedestrian mall with a broad glass curtain wall that lends a sense of openness and animations as well as a feeling that this new building, the most expensive in Morgan's history, is the new epicenter of the campus. The west elevation is the quietest, establishing an edge between the campus and the adjacent residential community.

Die mehrseitig ausgerichtete Bibliothek steht in verschiedener Weise zum umliegenden Campus in Beziehung. Im Norden schafft sie eine Sichtverbindung zum Mittelpunkt des Universitätscampus, wobei zur Holmes Hall, Morgans zeichenhaftestem Gebäude ein besonderer Bezug besteht. Im Osten unterstreicht und belebt sie die Fußgängerpassage mit einer breiten, gläsernen Vorhangwand. Das offene und bewegte Erscheinungsbild vermittelt das Gefühl, dass dieser in der Geschichte Morgans teuerste Neubau die neue Mitte des Campus darstellt. Die Westfassade der Bibliothek wirkt am ruhigsten. Sie bildet einen Rand zwischen dem Campus und der benachbarten Wohngemeinde.

La bibliothèque de l'université Morgan de Baltimore répond à un concept multidirectionnel qui l'intègre au tissu urbain de plusieurs manières. Vers le nord, elle est reliée visuellement au Homes Hall, bâtiment le plus célèbre du campus. Du côté de l'est, la bibliothèque renforce et anime la zone piétonne grâce à sa grande façade en verre qui ouvre le bâtiment — le plus cher jamais réalisé ici — sur les alentours et en fait le nouveau centre du complexe universitaire. La façade ouest est plus calme en ce qu'elle établit une liaison entre le campus et le quartier résidentiel voisin.

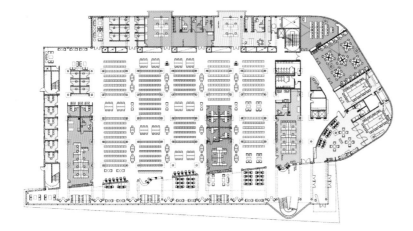

left: First floor plan_General view_Fully glazed staircase. right: Side view.
links: Grundriss erstes Obergeschoss_Gesamtansicht_Verglastes Treppenhaus. rechts: Seitenansicht.
à gauche: Plan du rez-de-chaussée_Vue générale_Cage d'escalier entièrement vitrée. à droite: Vue latérale de la grande façade en verre.

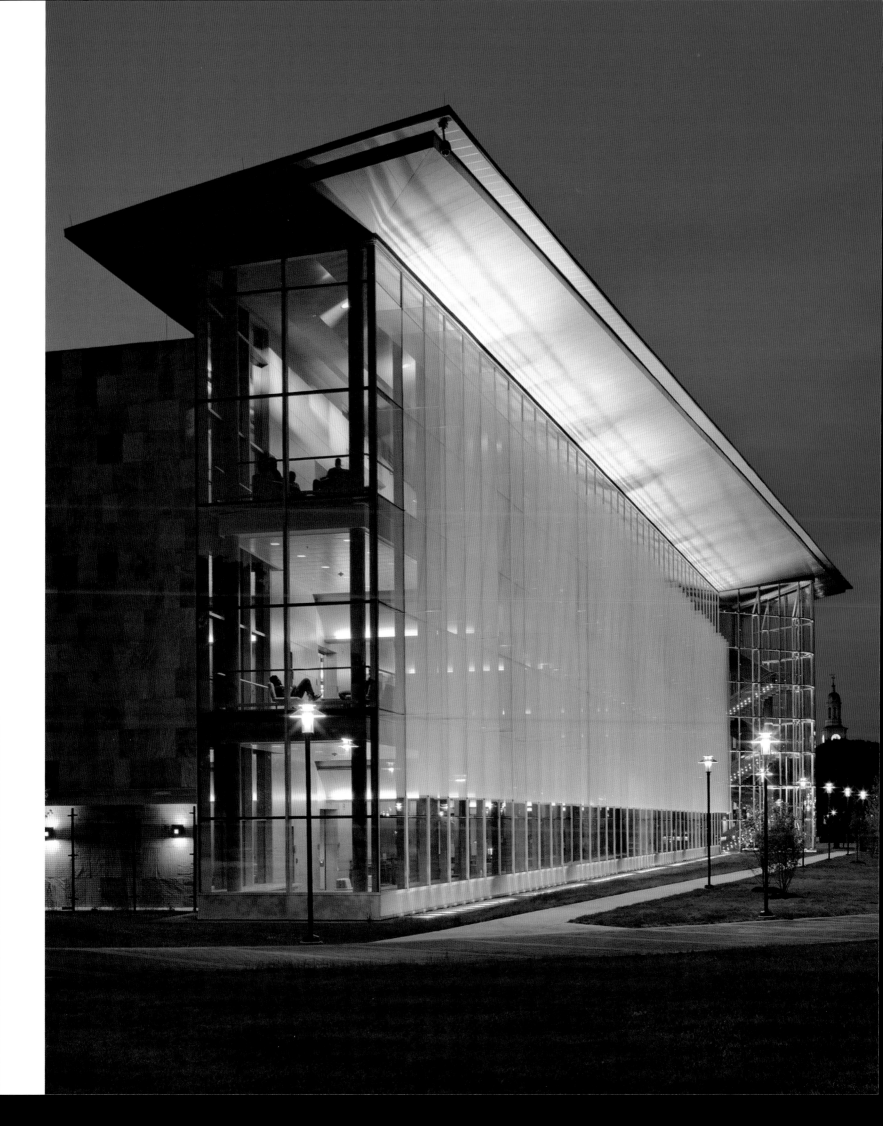

# BRUNSWICK_ME **BOWDOIN COLLEGE MUSEUM OF ART**

**ARCHITECTS:** MACHADO AND SILVETTI ASSOCIATES
**COMPLETION:** 2007_**TYPOLOGY:** CULTURE
**PHOTOS:** FACUNDO DE ZUVIRIA

Bowdoin College holds one of the oldest collegiate art collections in the country, dating back from 1811. The design addresses new program needs, necessary code and accessibility upgrades and incorporates state of the art security and climate control systems to meet current museum standards. A dramatic glass, bronze, and blackened steel pavilion on the south side of the original building provides a new entry to the expanded museum. This six hundred square foot pavilion houses a gracious new steel and stone stair and glass elevator which leads down to visitor service spaces and a new lower level gallery entrance.

Bowdoin College beherbergt eine der landesweit ältesten, bis 1811 zurückreichenden Kunstsammlungen eines Colleges. Die Gestaltung reagiert auf neue programmatische Anforderungen, eine notwendige bessere Erschließung und integriert moderne Sicherheits- und Klimatisierungssysteme, um heutigen Museumstandards gerecht zu werden. Ein Aufsehen erregender Pavillon aus Glas, Bronze und geschwärztem Stahl an der Südseite des Originalgebäudes dient als neuer Eingang zum erweiterten Museum. In diesem 183 Quadratmeter großen Pavillon führen eine elegante neue Stahl- und Steintreppe sowie ein gläserner Aufzug hinunter zu den Serviceräumen für Besucher und zu einem neuen Galerieeingang in der unteren Ebene.

Ce musée présente une collection d'œuvres d'art dont les origines remontent à 1811, ce qui en fait l'une des plus anciennes rassemblées par une université américaine. Les architectes ont été chargés d'agrandir le bâtiment et de le moderniser, tant en ce qui concerne la sécurité que la climatisation ou l'accessibilité aux handicapés. Au sud du bâtiment d'origine, ils ont notamment construit un nouveau hall d'entrée qui se caractérise par l'association remarquable du verre, du bronze et de l'acier noirci. Ce pavillon d'environ deux cents mètres carrés abrite un magnifique escalier en pierre et acier, ainsi qu'un ascenseur avec cage en verre qui mène aux salles d'exposition et aux espaces de services situés au niveau inférieur.

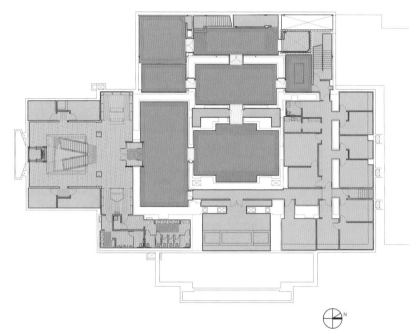

left: Lower level floor plan_Gallery_Gallery_Staircase. right: Entrance view_Fully glazed volume
General view.
links: Grundriss Untergeschoss_Ausstellung_Galerie_Treppenhaus. rechts: Eingangsansicht
Verglaster Baukörper_Gesamtansicht.
à gauche: Plan du niveau inférieur_Salle d'exposition_Autre salle d'exposition_Escalier. à droite:
Nouveau hall d'entrée du musée_Volume entièrement vitré_Vue d'ensemble.

# AMAGANSETT_NY **RE-COVER RESIDENCE**

**ARCHITECTS:** BATES MASI ARCHITECTS
**COMPLETION:** 2008_**TYPOLOGY:** LIVING
**PHOTOS:** CHRISTOPHER WESNOFSKE

Thirty-five years after the firm originally designed this vacation residence, its new owners sought to rejuvenate the house while preserving its spaces, seasoned tones, and texture. Clad inside and out almost entirely in twelve-inch wide cypress boards, the original house exuded a straightforward simplicity the owners wished to maintain. By constraining the palette of materials and reusing salvaged parts of the existing house, the line between new and old becomes nearly imperceptible, limited only to minimal inflections in finish.

Fünfunddreißig Jahre nachdem das Büro dieses Ferienhaus entworfen hatte, wünschten die neuen Eigentümer eine Modernisierung, wobei seine Räume, Patina und Textur erhalten bleiben sollten. Von dem ursprünglich innen und außen nahezu vollständig mit 30 Zentimeter breiten Zypressenbohlen verschalten Haus ging eine unmittelbare Schlichtheit aus, die beizubehalten war. Indem die Materialpalette eingeschränkt und Teile des Bestands wiederverwendet wurden, ist der Unterschied zwischen Alt und Neu kaum wahrnehmbar und betrifft lediglich minimale Veränderungen der Oberflächenausführung.

Trente-cinq ans après avoir construit cette maison de vacances, les architectes ont été chargés par les nouveaux propriétaires de la moderniser tout en conservant les textures, la répartition spatiale et les tons agréablement patinés. Le revêtement de façade et certains aménagements intérieurs réalisés en planches de cèdre de trente centimètres de large sont restés inchangés, car leur simplicité convenait parfaitement aux nouveaux propriétaires. Les architectes ont volontairement limité la gamme de matériaux et réutilisé certains composant d'origine, de sorte que les différences entre l'ancien et le nouveau sont tout juste perceptibles et se limitent à quelques nuances dans les finitions.

left: Site plan_Entrance view_Staircase and lounge_Bathroom. right: View into kitchen.
links: Lageplan_Blick auf den Eingang_Treppenhaus und Sitzecke_Badezimmer. rechts: Blick in die Küche.
à gauche: Plan de situation_Vue de l'entrée_Arrière de la maison. à droite: La cuisine vue de l'extérieur.

# ANCRAM_NY **CC01 HOUSE**

**ARCHITECTS:** LEVEN BETTS STUDIO ARCHITECTS
**COMPLETION:** 2006_**TYPOLOGY:** LIVING
**PHOTOS:** MICHAEL MORAN PHOTOGRAPHY

The CC01 House's design begins with a reading of the landscape. Long linear grooves, formed by the dimensions of machinery – the distance between tractor wheels and the frequency of the blades of a plow – are etched into the rolling hills from years of farming. Framing the topography, these lines were developed into diagrams that inform the design of all configurations of the house, from the primary organization and form to the cladding and details of the building. Additionally, the section of the house follows the contour of the land as it steps up from east to west.

Die Konzeption des CC01 House beginnt mit einer Einschätzung der Landschaft. Lange, lineare, von landwirtschaftlichen Maschinen erzeugte Rillen – ihren Abstand bestimmt die Entfernung zwischen den Traktorrädern oder den Scharen des Pflugs – sind durch die langjährige Bewirtschaftung in die hügelige Landschaft gefurcht. Diese topografischen Linien werden zu Diagrammen entwickelt, die für die gesamte Gestaltung des Hauses prägend sind, von der grundlegenden Organisation und Form bis zu der Verkleidung und den Konstruktionsdetails. Zusätzlich folgt der Schnitt des Hauses den Umrissen des Geländes, das von Ost nach West stufenförmig ansteigt.

Les architectes ont conçu cette villa en s'efforçant de l'intégrer au paysage. L'accès se fait par des sillons recouverts de dalles qui courent en parallèle et correspondent aux traces laissées par le passage des tracteurs durant des années. Ces lignes inscrites dans la topographie du terrain ont déterminé l'aspect de l'ensemble du projet, qu'il s'agisse des revêtements de façade ou d'autres détails du bâtiment. Orientée d'est en ouest, la villa suit par ailleurs les contours du terrain.

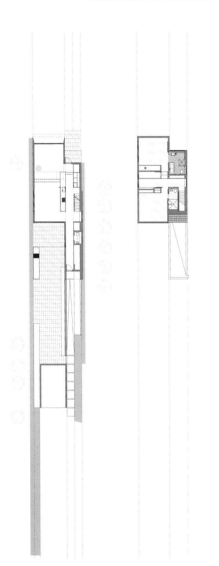

left: Floor plans_East view_Side view. right: Patio view.
links: Grundrisse_Ostansicht_Seitenansicht. rechts: Blick auf die Terrasse.
à gauche: Plans des différents niveaux_Le bâtiment vu de l'est_Façade. à droite: Vue de la cour et du bâtiment.

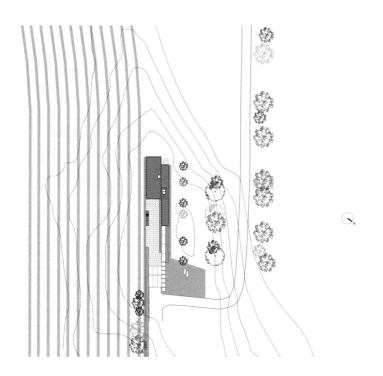

left: West view. right: Site plan_Kitchen and dining room area.
links: Westansicht. rechts: Lageplan_Küche und Esszimmer.
à gauche: Façade ouest. à droite  Plan de situation_Cuisine/salle à manger.

BRONX_NY **NYPL FRANCIS MARTIN LIBRARY**

**ARCHITECTS:** 1100 ARCHITECT
**COMPLETION:** 2008_**TYPOLOGY:** EDUCATION
**PHOTOS:** TIMOTHY FURZER

This children's reading room is designed to stimulate its users' imaginations, encouraging them to learn through form, color and layout. Bold and graphic elements with a bright palette of oranges, greens, and blues are offset by glossy white. The elevated curving façade of the library provides panoramic views that are fully realized through the new open plan configuration. The reading tables utilize the natural lighting and outside views. Reflective Barrisol undulates to form a playful ceiling, at parts folding away to reveal greater, adding openness to the space. The diagonal arrangement of the shelving allows for active spaces for the children while increasing visibility for staff.

Das Lesezimmer für Kinder soll die Fantasie seiner Nutzer anregen und sie mittels Form, Farbe und Gestaltung zum Lernen ermuntern. Auffällige grafische Elemente in leuchtendem Orange, Grün und Blau kontrastieren mit einem glänzenden Weiß. Die gebogene Fassade der Bibliothek gewährt Panoramaaussichten, die durch den neuen offenen Grundriss deutlich zur Geltung kommen. Von den natürlich belichteten Lesetischen bieten sich Ausblicke nach draußen. Reflektierendes Barrisol in Wellenform ergibt eine spielerisch wirkende Decke. Stellenweise ist sie weggeklappt, wodurch der Raum höher wird und zusätzliche Weite erhält. Diagonal angeordnete Regale schaffen Platz für Kinderaktivitäten und einen besseren Überblick für Mitarbeiter.

Les architectes ont conçu la décoration de cette bibliothèque pour enfants afin de stimuler l'imagination des jeunes lecteurs et de les encourager à apprendre par l'intermédiaire des formes et couleurs utilisées. Divers éléments graphiques et pièces d'aménagement intérieur en orange, vert et bleu s'inscrivent en contraste dans un espace ouvert où le blanc mat domine. La façade incurvée du bâtiment est percée de grandes ouvertures qui offrent des vues panoramiques sur les environs et assurent un bon éclairage naturel de l'intérieur. Le plafond a été recouvert de Barrisol réfléchissant ou laissé brut avec poutres apparentes de manière à augmenter l'impression d'ouverture qui se dégage de cet espace. La disposition en diagonale des étagères libère des zones d'activité pour les enfants et accroît la visibilité dont dispose le personnel.

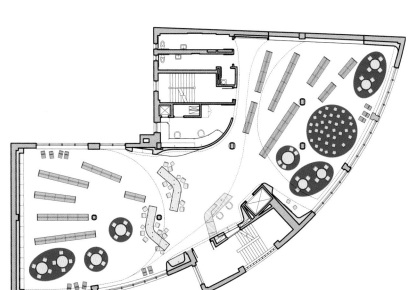

left: Second floor plan_General reading area_View from entrance. right: Curved ceiling.
links: Grundriss zweites Obergeschoss_Lesesaal_Eingangsbereich. rechts: Gewölbte Decke.
à gauche: Plan du second étage_Salle de lecture_Zone d'entrée. à droite: Plafond Barrisol incurvé.

nfluential film director,
"2001: A Space Odyssey"
FIOREL
LAGUA
He was the publisher

BRONX_NY **THE BRONX MUSEUM OF THE ARTS EXPANSION, NORTH WING**

**ARCHITECTS:** ARQUITECTONICA
**COMPLETION:** 2006_**TYPOLOGY:** CULTURE
**PHOTOS:** NORMAN MCGRATH PHOTOGRAPHY

The three-story, 16,700-square-foot museum addition emerges from the sidewalk as an irregular folded screen made of fritted glass and metallic panels. The diagonal components emphasize the depth of the crevices, where the resulting vertical zones of metal and glass, angle and twist like an architectural origami. Pedestrians can sneak a peek into the ground floor gallery through the slivers of semitransparent glass that face them as they approach from either direction. The design dramatizes the vertical dimension of the otherwise modest structure, turning it into an unexpectedly monumental surface.

Der dreigeschossige Museumsanbau mit einer Fläche von 1.550 Quadratmetern erhebt sich vom Bürgersteig als unregelmäßig gefaltete Fassade aus Fritteglas und Metallpaneelen. Seine diagonalen Komponenten unterstreichen die tiefen Klüfte der wie ein architektonisches Origami geknickten und gedrehten vertikalen Metall- und Glaszonen. Fußgänger können aus zwei Richtungen kommend durch halbtransparente Glasstreifen einen Blick in die Galerie im Erdgeschoss werfen. Der Entwurf zeigt spannungsvoll die vertikale Dimension einer ansonsten schlichten Konstruktion und macht sie dadurch einzigartig.

Cette annexe de musée, d'une superficie de 1.550 mille mètres carrés sur trois niveaux, présente une façade sur rue qui forme des plis irréguliers composés de panneaux métalliques et de plaques de verre fritté. Les composants architecturaux disposés en diagonale soulignent la profondeur des crevasses, les angles formés par les surfaces verticales en verre et métal formant ainsi un origami de la taille d'un bâtiment. Les passants peuvent jeter un coup d'œil à l'intérieur de l'annexe grâce aux panneaux en verre semi-transparents utilisés au rez-de-chaussée. Cette conception particulière met en évidence la dimension verticale d'un édifice somme toute modeste, qui acquiert ainsi une apparence monumentale.

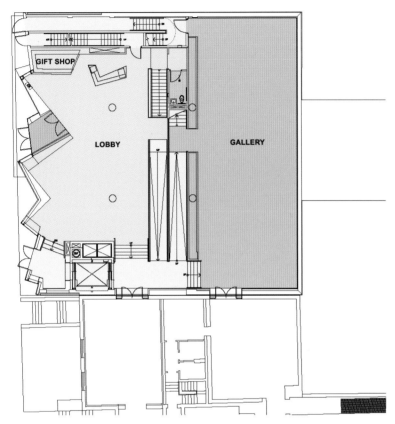

left: First floor plan_Circulation into exhibition spaces_Exhibition space. right: Semitransparent glass slivers.
links: Grundriss erstes Obergeschoss_Umlauf in Ausstellungsräume_Ausstellungsraum. rechts: Teildurchlässige Glasfassade.
à gauche: Plan du rez-de-chaussée_Espace de circulation entre les salles d'exposition_Vue d'une salle d'exposition. à droite: Bandes verticales en verre fritté semi-transparent.

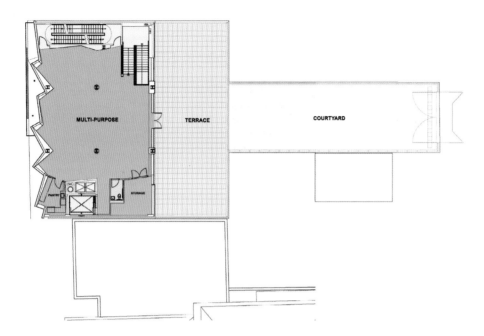

left: Main entrance. right: Second and third floor plans_Fritted glass façade and metallic panels_Front façade.
links: Haupteingang. rechts: Grundriss zweites und drittes Obergeschoss_Fassade aus Fritteglas und metalischen Paneelen_Vorderfassade.
à gauche: Entrée principale. à droite: Plans des second et troisième étages_Façade en métal et verre fritté_Autre vue de la façade.

# CHATHAM_NY **CHATHAM HOUSE**

**ARCHITECTS:** AXIS MUNDI
**COMPLETION:** 2008_**TYPOLOGY:** LIVING
**PHOTOS:** REINHOLD & CO.

The house in the heart of Shaker County provides living accommodations for a small family and is home to a private art gallery for contemporary art and design objects. The building is raised on a low concrete dais; access is via a gently inclined ramp sprouting grass. The architectural gesture is composed of two shifted rectangular volumes bisected by a 16 foot high, light-filled entrance gallery, which separates the main living space from the guest rooms. A detached studio clad in Corten steel shingles is separated from the main block, yet the entire composition is neatly held together under one continuous roof sheathed in copper.

Das Haus mitten im Shaker County dient einer kleinen Familie als Unterkunft und beherbergt eine Privatgalerie für zeitgenössische Kunst und Designobjekte. Der auf einem flachen Betonpodest errichtete Bau ist über eine sanft geneigte Rampe zu erreichen, durch die Gras wächst. Die architektonische Besonderheit besteht aus zwei erhöhten, rechtwinkligen Volumen, die durch eine fünf Meter hohe lichterfüllte Eingangsgalerie getrennt werden. Diese trennt das Wohnzimmer von den Gästezimmern ab. Das mit Schindeln aus Cortenstahl verkleidete Studio steht isoliert vom Hauptgebäude; die gesamte Komposition wird aber unter einem durchgehenden, mit Kupfer ausgekleideten Dach zusammengehalten.

Cette maison située au cœur du Shaker County abrite des pièces d'habitation pour une famille avec un ou deux enfants et une galerie d'exposition pour une collection privée d'art contemporain et d'objets design. Elle est construite sur une base en béton et on y accède par une rampe couverte d'herbe. Il s'agit d'un ensemble composé de deux parallélépipèdes séparés par un couloir d'entrée de 4,80 mètres de haut — un espace baigné de lumière qui sert également de séparation entre les principales pièces de séjour et les chambres d'amis. Le troisième élément de l'ensemble est un volume détaché avec bardage d'acier Corten. Un toit en cuivre particulièrement harmonieux assure l'unification de tous les bâtiments.

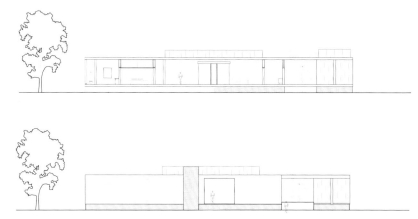

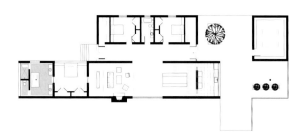

left: Elevations and floor plan_Exterior view, concrete base_Dining room. right: Entrance gallery.
links: Ansichten und Grundriss_Außenansicht, Betonfundament_Esszimmer. rechts: Eingangshalle.
à gauche: Vues en élévation et plan du rez-de-chaussée_Vue de l'extérieur avec le socle en béton
Salle à manger. à droite: Entrée/galerie d'art.

COLUMBIA COUNTY_NY **TERRY WINTERS STUDIO**

**ARCHITECTS:** MOS, MICHAEL MEREDITH, HILARY SAMPLE
**COMPLETION:** 2007_**TYPOLOGY:** LIVING
**PHOTOS:** MICHAEL VAHRENWALD

This project explores the idea of creating a space for both painting and drawing, set against an intense landscape of shale cliffs, forest, and ponds. Overlooking the hills of the Taconic State Park, this isolated site is one of several freestanding structures making up a compound for an artist and a curator/writer. The design focuses on constructing an open space uninterrupted by structure. This dictated the design of the structural system and enabled a column free interior with moment frames on each end that would serve as external porches and viewing spaces between nature and the built environment.

Dieses Projekt beschäftigt sich mit einem zum Malen und Zeichnen bestimmten Raum vor der Kulisse einer eindrucksvollen Landschaft mit Steilufern aus Schiefergestein, Wäldern und Teichen. Der abseits gelegene Bau überblickt die Hügel des Taconic State Parks und gehört auf dem Areal zu einer von mehreren freistehenden Konstruktionen für einen Künstler und einen Konservator/Schriftsteller. Da ein offener, vom Tragwerk nicht unterbrochener Raum entstehen soll, kommt ein Konstruktionssystem zum Einsatz, das einen stützenfreien Innenraum ermöglicht. Rahmentragwerke an beiden Gebäudeenden dienen als Veranden und Aussichtsdecks zwischen Natur und bebautem Raum.

Le client, un peintre-dessinateur, souhaitait disposer d'un atelier implanté dans un paysage magnifique: les collines du parc naturel de Taconic, composé de forêts, d'étangs et de falaises de schiste argileux. La maison est isolée, ses seuls voisins étant quelques pavillons occupés par d'autres artistes et écrivains. L'idée de base était de réaliser un espace habitable ouvert et ininterrompu. Les architectes ont donc conçu une structure porteuse sans piliers, que des surfaces vitrées positionnées aux deux extrémités ouvrent largement sur l'extérieur, la liaison entre l'architecture et la nature étant assurée par deux porches triangulaires.

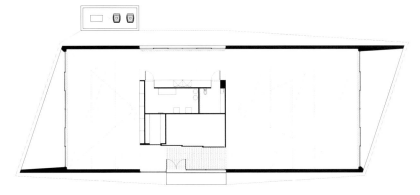

left: First floor plan_Exterior view_Rear view. right: View inside kitchen_Exterior view.
links: Grundriss erstes Obergschoss_Außenansicht_Rückansicht. rechts: Blick in die Küche Außenansicht.
à gauche: Plan du rez-de-chaussée_Porche en vue latérale_Vue de la face arrière. à droite: La cuisine vue de l'extérieur_Vue générale.

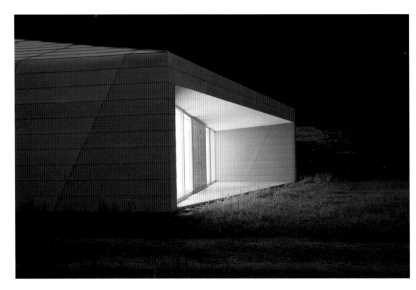

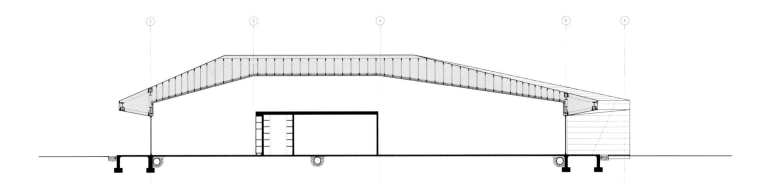

left: Open work space. right: Section_Studio with large window_Work space_Embedded cube.
links: Offener Arbeitsbereich. rechts. Schnitt_Atelier mit großen Fenstern _Arbeitsplatz_Einge-
bauter Würfel.
à gauche: Vue de l'atelier. à droite: Vue en coupe_Baies vitrées de l'atelier_Autre vue de l'atelier_
Cube fonctionnel au centre de l'espace intérieur.

# DUTCHESS COUNTY_NY **DUTCHESS COUNTY GUEST HOUSE**

**ARCHITECTS:** ALLIED WORKS ARCHITECTURE
**COMPLETION:** 2008_**TYPOLOGY:** LIVING
**PHOTOS:** JEREMY BITTERMANN (68 B.L., 69 B. R.), HELENE BINET

Allied Works was commissioned by contemporary art collectors to design a primary residence, guesthouse and private gallery on 350 acres in Dutchess County, New York. The 1,300-square -oot guesthouse was completed in 2007, the private gallery completed in 2008 and the 5,500-square-foot main house in 2009. Each of the three structures is conceived as an exploration of a specific site and material response.

Allied Works erhielten von Sammlern zeitgenössischer Kunst den Auftrag für den Entwurf eines Hauptgebäudes, eines Gästehauses und einer Privatgalerie auf einem 142 Hektar großen Areal in Dutchess County in New York. Das Gästehaus mit einer Fläche von 121 Quadratmetern wurde 2007 realisiert, die Privatgalerie 2008 und für 2009 ist die Fertigstellung des 510 Quadratmeter großen Hauptgebäudes vorgesehen. Jede der drei Konstruktionen ist als Erforschung einer spezifischen Lage und materiellen Reaktion konzipiert.

Des collectionneurs d'art contemporain ont demandé aux architectes de concevoir un bâtiment principal, un pavillon pour les invités et une salle d'exposition sur une propriété de 142 hectares du Dutchess County dans l'État de New York. Le pavillon, d'une superficie de 121 mètres carrés, a été terminé en 2007, la salle d'exposition en 2008 et le bâtiment principal, qui couvre 510 mètres carrés, en 2009. Chacun des trois éléments architecturaux de la propriété a été conçu comme moyen d'explorer le terrain à l'aide de matériaux spécifiques.

left: Site plan_Detail exterior_Fully glazed façade. right: Exterior frame construction_General view.
links: Lageplan_Detail der Außenansicht_Glasfassade. rechts: Äußere Rahmenkonstruktion Gesamtansicht.
à gauche: Plan de situation_Détail de l'extérieur_Façade entièrement vitrée. à droite: Vue de l'extérieur et des cadres métalliques_Vue d'ensemble.

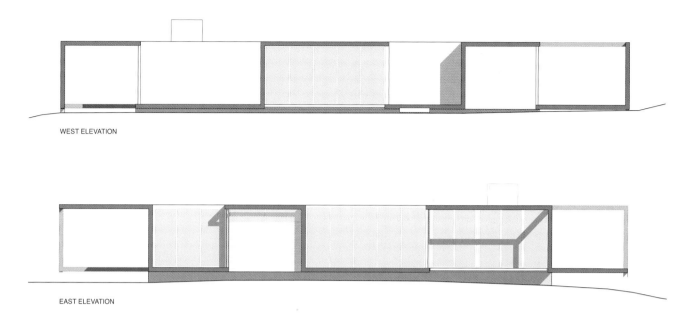

WEST ELEVATION

EAST ELEVATION

left: Detail construction. right: East and West elevation_Living room.
links: Konstruktionsdetail. rechts: Ost- und Westansicht_Wohnzimmer.
à gauche: Détails. à droite: Vue en élévation des façades est et ouest_Séjour.

# EASTHAMPTON, LONG ISLAND_NY **STONE HOUSES**

**ARCHITECTS:** LEROY STREET STUDIO
**COMPLETION:** 2004_**TYPOLOGY:** LIVING
**PHOTOS:** PAUL WARCHOL PHOTOGRAPHY

Located on a flat, twelve-acre site dotted with specimen trees and rimmed by tall evergreens, this family retreat is one block from the ocean in Eastern Long Island. Responding to the need to create three separate family residences, the program for the complex is anchored around a common courtyard. Granite walls that provided internal and external spaces and a unifying texture were introduced to create a unique sense of place and to give each home ample privacy. House I's south facing entry appears solid and private, while its north side, facing the agricultural reserve, is expansively glazed. House II is entered at its narrowest point, through a glazed hall opening to a raised court of bamboo, extending up through an opening in the long, low roof plane.

Dieses Wochenendhaus auf einem flachen, 48.560 Quadratmeter großen Grundstück mit Solitärgehölzen liegt einen Block entfernt vom Ozean im östlichen Teil von Long Island. Als Antwort auf den Bedarf an drei separaten Einfamilienhäusern ist das Programm um einen gemeinsamen Hof verankert. Granitmauern verbinden Innen- und Außenräume und schaffen eine vereinheitlichende Textur, sodass ein einzigartiges Gefühl für den Ort entsteht und jedes Haus ein Höchstmaß an Privatsphäre erhält. Der Eingang im Süden von House I erscheint solide und privat, dagegen ist seine zum landwirtschaftlichen Schutzgebiet weisende Nordseite großzügig verglast. House II wird über eine verglaste Halle erschlossen, die sich zu einem erhöhten Hof öffnet und eine Aussparung in der lang gestreckten, tiefen Dachfläche aufweist.

Cette résidence familiale est située à l'est de Long Island, sur un terrain d'environ cinq hectares bordé de grands résineux qui entourent une pelouse où se dressent quelques arbres solitaires. Elle se compose de trois unités distinctes groupées autour d'une cour commune. Des murs en granit délimitent les espaces intérieurs et extérieurs, donnent à chaque unité l'intimité qu'elle requiert, et contribuent à l'unification de l'ensemble. La Maison I présente au sud une façade d'entrée à la fois massive et intimiste, tandis qu'elle s'ouvre largement sur les champs au nord par ses vastes baies vitrées. L'accès à la Maison II se fait par un hall vitré qui mène à une cour surélevée plantée de grands bambous.

left: Elevations_Living space_Pool_Façade detail. right: Exterior with yard_General view.
links: Ansichten_Wohnraum_Pool_Fassadendetail. rechts: Außenansicht_Gesamtansicht.
à gauche: Deux vues en élévation_Séjour_Bassin_Détail de la façade. à droite: Arbre dans le parc, avec le bâtiment à l'arrière plan_Vue d'ensemble.

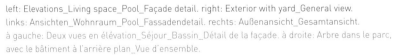

# HUDSON VALLEY_NY **C-I HOUSE**

**ARCHITECTS:** PAUL CHA ARCHITECT
**COMPLETION:** 2008_**TYPOLOGY:** LIVING
**PHOTOS:** DAO-LOU ZHA

Located in the historic Hudson Valley, the four-acre site is situated in south-ern Columbia County, bordering Duchess County to the south. Overlooking a pond, the house is surrounded by dense vegetation while commanding a vineyard view to the east and a view of the distant Black Dome Mountain to the west. Designed as a weekend retreat, the construction consists of concrete foundation/footings, supporting a wood framed enclosure with spatial layouts based upon standard modular construction dimensions. Opening sliding glass doors give access to a sun-deck, acting as an ethereal transition between the indoors and outdoors.

Das 16.000 Quadratmeter große Areal liegt im historischen Hudson Valley im Süden von Columbia County an der Grenze zu Duchess County. Von einer dichten Vegetation umgeben, überblickt das Haus einen Teich und gewährt Aussichten auf ein Weinbaugebiet im Osten und der ferne Black Dome Moun-tain im Westen. Bei dieser als Wochenendhaus konzipierten Konstruktion ist einem Fundament aus Beton ein Fachwerkbau aufgesetzt, dessen räumliche Anordnung auf den Abmessungen marktgängiger Modulbauten basiert. Zu ei-ner Sonnenterrasse geöffnete Glasschiebetüren leiten von innen nach außen über.

Cette maison est construite près d'un étang sur un terrain d'un hectare et demi dans la vallée de l'Hudson, au sud du Columbia County, c'est-à-dire près du Duchess County. Elle est bordée par un vignoble à l'est, tandis qu'on aperçoit à l'ouest la silhouette du mont Black Dome. Il s'agit d'une rési-dence de week-end avec une base et des fondations en béton surmontées d'un étage en bois, volume modulaire aux dimensions standards. Des portes vitrées coulissantes donnent accès à la terrasse, assurant ainsi la transition entre l'intérieur et l'extérieur.

left: Axonometric_Concrete foundation with wood framed enclosure_Exterior. right: Front façade.
links: Axonometrie_Betonfundament und hölzerne Ummantelung_Außenansicht. rechts: Vorderfassade.
à gauche: Axonométrie_Socle en béton et étage en bois_Vue latérale. à droite: Façade principale.

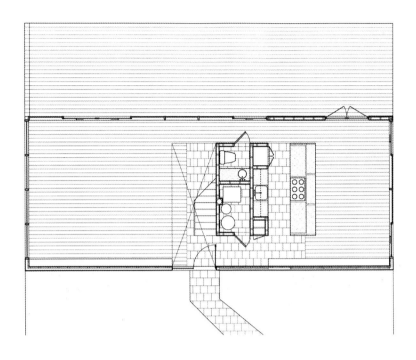

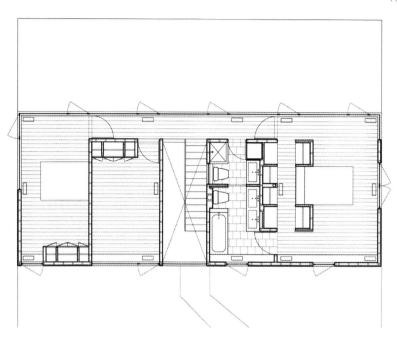

left: Living space. right: Floor plans_Wooden staircase_Living room_Kitchen and dining area.
links: Wohnrzimmer. rechts: Grundrisse  Hölzerne Treppe  Wohnzimmer  Küche und Esszimmer.
à gauche: Séjour. à droite: Plan des deux niveaux_Escalier en bois_Séjour_Cuisine/salle à manger.

# NEW YORK_NY **AVANT CHELSEA**

**ARCHITECTS:** 1100 ARCHITECT
**COMPLETION:** 2008_**TYPOLOGY:** LIVING
**PHOTOS:** EDUARD HUEBER

This twelve-story residential condominium comprises luxury units and a two story Community Facility Space. The top floors are penthouses, each with private outdoor space. This is achieved by an unconventional setback solution leading to the unusual appearance of the building; the main volume seems to be hollowed out and opening up to light with a gradation of terrace steps. The street façade floor-to-ceiling window wall system is proportioned to achieve a balance between the scale of the user and the building at large. The building is enclosed by a ribbon of panels that unfold as a mosaic of 2,500 panels in six different shades of indigo, contributing to the overall exterior identity.

Die zwölfgeschossige Eigentumsanlage umfasst Luxuswohnungen und einen zwei Stockwerke hohen Bereich mit Gemeinschaftseinrichtungen. In den obersten Etagen verfügen die Penthäuser über eigene Außenräume. Entstanden sind diese durch eine zurückgesetzte Fassade, die das ungewöhnliche Erscheinungsbild des Gebäudes ausmacht. Der ausgehöhlte Hauptbaukörper öffnet sich mit abgestuften Terrassenstufen zum Licht. Um zwischen dem menschlichen Maßstab und dem ganzen Gebäude ein Gleichgewicht herzustellen, ist das straßenseitige gebäudehohe Fenster-Wand-System aufgeteilt. Den Bau umgibt ein mosaikartiges, identitätsprägendes Band aus 2.500 Platten in sechs verschiedenen Indigotönen.

Deux des douze étages de cet immeuble résidentiel sont réservés à des services publics. Tous les logements disposent d'espaces de plein air grâce à des balcons et à la silhouette en gradins du bâtiment, qui prend ainsi un aspect inhabituel. Les terrasses aménagées sur les gradins assurent un bon éclairage naturel des appartements. Du côté rue, des murs entièrement vitrés du sol au plafond garantissent un équilibre entre la taille des logements et celle de l'immeuble dans son ensemble. La façade perpendiculaire à la rue se caractérise par une mosaïque composée de 2500 panneaux dans six teintes allant du blanc au gris en passant par le bleu indigo.

left: First floor plan_Exterior at night_Street side view. right: Façade.
links: Grundriss erstes Obergeschoss_Außenansicht bei Nacht_Straßenansicht. rechts: Fassade.
à gauche: Plan du rez-de-chaussée_L'immeuble au crépuscule_L'immeuble vu de la rue. à droite: Vue d'ensemble de la façade.

NEW YORK_NY **MUSEUM OF ARTS AND DESIGN (JEROME AND SIMONA CHAZEN BUILDING)**

**ARCHITECTS:** ALLIED WORKS ARCHITECTURE
**COMPLETION:** 2008_**TYPOLOGY:** CULTURE
**PHOTOS:** VICTORIA SAMBUNARIS (64), HELENE BINET, RICHARD BARNES (5 B. L.)

The 50,000-square-foot Museum of Arts and Design features reconfigured galleries, a restored auditorium and hands-on education spaces accessed by a new stair and elevator core. New public amenities at the ground floor orient visitors and enhance the surrounding streetscape. From the outside, a custom skin of glazed terracotta unifies the four façades while cuts through the shell of the building bring new light and energy to the building interior.

Das Museum of Arts and Design mit einer Fläche von 4.645 Quadratmetern enthält umgestaltete Galerien, einen instand gesetzten Vortragssaal sowie interaktive Schulungsräume, die von einer neuen Treppe und einem Aufzugskern erschlossen werden. Öffentliche Einrichtungen im Erdgeschoss dienen der Orientierung von Besuchern und werten die umliegende Straßenlandschaft auf. Außen werden die vier Fassaden von einer eigens gefertigten Haut aus glasiertem Terrakotta vereint. Durchbrüche in der Gebäudehülle bringen mehr Licht und Energie ins Innere.

Les collections de ce musée sont désormais présentées dans un bâtiment de plus de 4.645 mètres carrés abritant un auditorium, des salles d'exposition et des espaces éducatifs offrant la possibilité d'effectuer des exercices pratiques. L'aménagement du rez-de-chaussée a été conçu de manière à faciliter l'orientation des visiteurs et à valoriser l'environnement urbain. Les découpes réalisées sur l'enveloppe en carreaux de céramique vitrifiés fabriqués sur mesure dynamisent les façades et améliorent l'éclairage naturel de l'intérieur.

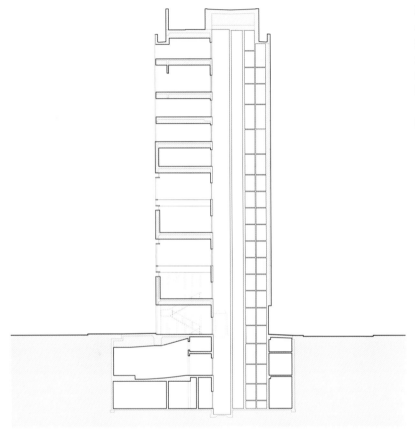

left: Section_View from the street_Aerial view. right: Façade.
links: Querschnitt_Straßenansicht_Luftbild. rechts: Fassade.
à gauche: Vue en coupe_Le rez-de-chaussée vu de la rue_Le bâtiment vu de haut. à droite: Vue d'ensemble.

left: Gallery. right: First and third floor plan_Interior_Façade.
links: Galerie. rechts: Grundriss erstes und drittes Obergeschoss_Innenansicht_Fassade.
à gauche: Espace d'exposition. à droite: Plan du rez-de-chaussée et du troisième niveau_Intérieur_
Vue d'ensemble.

# NEW YORK_NY **CRISTIANO CORA STUDIO**

**ARCHITECTS:** AVI OSTER
**COMPLETION:** 2008_**TYPOLOGY:** LEISURE
**PHOTOS:** MIKIKO KIKUYAMA PHOTOGRAPHY

The goal was to create a new essence of salon environment that captures the balance between modern architecture and the needs of the hair dressing industry. The fluid movement of the Cristiano salon truly captures the elements of simple modern design while the functionality of the design enables a smoother process of hair dressing. The aim was to create a space that would be distinctly appealing to women: curved, clean, and stylish, but at the same time comforting and transformational. The simplicity of the design encourages the client's focus to be on the inspiring experience of becoming transformed.

Der angestrebte neue Charakter des Salons sollte eine Balance halten zwischen moderner Architektur und den Erfordernissen des Friseurgewerbes. Die fließende Bewegung des Salons Cristiano fängt die Elemente eines schlichten modernen Entwurfs regelrecht ein, während seine funktionale Gestaltung zu glatteren Arbeitsabläufen beim Frisieren führt. Der Raum sollte in erster Linie Frauen gefallen, geschwungen, klar und modisch, doch gleichzeitig behaglich und wandelbar sein. Die schlichte Ausstattung unterstützt das Anliegen der Kunden, sich bei einem anregenden Erlebnis verwandeln zu lassen.

L'objectif consistait ici à créer un salon de coiffure d'un nouveau type, associant de manière harmonieuse l'architecture moderne et les impératifs de la profession. Les architectes y sont parvenus, puisque le salon Cristiano est à la fois d'une simplicité moderne et d'une fonctionnalité parfaite. Le cahier des charges stipulait également que l'aménagement intérieur devait être conçu afin de plaire aux femmes. C'est pourquoi il privilégie les formes courbes et se distingue par sa propreté, son élégance, son confort et son aspect transformationnel. La simplicité du design invite les clientes à se concentrer sur une expérience inspirante: se laisser transformer.

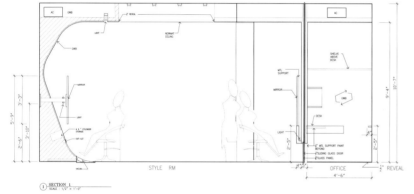

left: Section_Exterior_Embedded frame. right: Interior.
links: Querschnitt_Außenansicht_Integrierte Regale. rechts: Innenansicht.
à gauche: Vue en coupe_Le salon vu de l'extérieur_Vue de l'intérieur. à droite: Autre vue de l'intérieur.

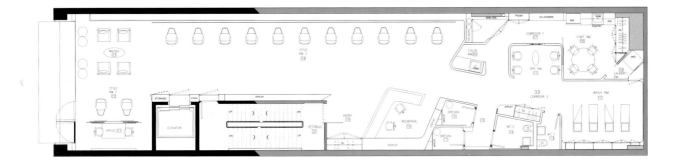

left: Hair washing area. right: Floor plan_Ceiling construction_Slanted mirrors.
links: Interieur. rechts: Grundriss_Deckenkonstruktion_Wandspiegel.
à gauche: Fauteuils avec lavabos. à droite: Plan_Mur et plafond_Miroirs inclinés.

NEW YORK_NY **CLIFF TREE HOUSE**

**ARCHITECTS:** BAUMRAUM / ANDREAS WENNING
**COMPLETION:** 2007_**TYPOLOGY:** LIVING
**PHOTOS:** MICHAEL DÖRING

The main body of the tree house projects over the cliff and is supported closest to the cliff edge by two short posts, and at the overhanging edge by a long, slanting fork. The weight of the terrace is borne by steel cables suspended from the Canadian maple. The lateral walls of the tree house have been constructed as framed supports. They have been clad on the interior with oak shuttering, mineral wool insulation and windproof foil sheeting, and on the outside with ventilated, horizontal panelling. Broad, rough-sawn larch boards, painted silver, were used for the exterior cladding. The interior furnishing of the tree house is sparse, comprising merely a reclining area and a wooden bench.

Der Baumhauskörper steht über der Klippe und wird nahe dem Felsen von zwei kurzen Stützen und an der weit überkragenden Seite von einer langen schrägen Gabelstütze getragen. Die Terrasse ist über Stahlseile von dem Ahorn abgehängt. Die Seitenwände des Baumhauses sind als Rahmentragwerk konstruiert. Innen sind sie mit Eichenholz, einer Dämmung aus Mineralwolle und windundurchlässiger Folie verschalt. Außen besteht ihre hinterlüftete Verkleidung aus breiten, sägerauen Lärchenbrettern, die silberfarben gestrichen wurden. Zu der spartanischen Inneneinrichtung gehören lediglich eine Liegefläche und eine Holzbank.

Cette maison construite dans un arbre surplombe un ravin situé près de la Hudson River. En porte-à-faux au-dessus du vide, elle repose sur deux piliers courts d'un côté et deux longs piliers en V de l'autre. La terrasse est quant à elle suspendue au grand érable du Canada par des câbles en acier. Les murs latéraux de la maison sont des cadres garnis à l'extérieur de larges planches en mélèze non rabotées et peintes couleur argent, et à l'intérieur d'un revêtement en chêne qui cache une isolation composée de laine minérale et d'un pare-vent. L'aménagement intérieur se limite à une couchette et une banquette en bois. Les quatre côtés s'ouvrent sur l'extérieur par des fenêtres garnies de moustiquaires de haute qualité. Le fenêtre zénithale aménagée dans le toit n'est pas sans rappeler une écoutille.

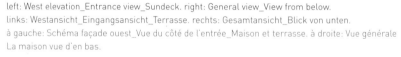

left: West elevation_Entrance view_Sundeck. right: General view_View from below.
links: Westansicht_Eingangsansicht_Terrasse. rechts: Gesamtansicht_Blick von unten.
à gauche: Schéma façade ouest_Vue du côté de l'entrée_Maison et terrasse. à droite: Vue générale
La maison vue d'en bas.

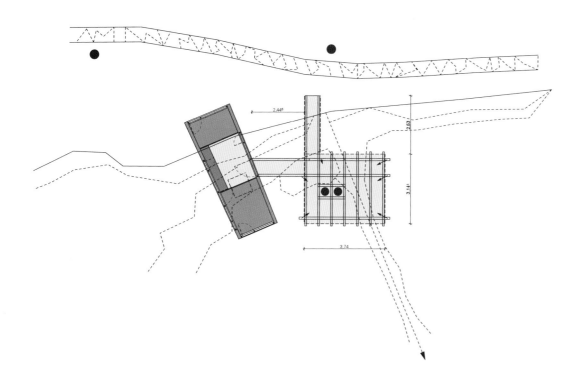

left: Steel construction. right: Floor plan_Rear view_Living space_View towards terrace.
links: Stahlkonstruktion. rechts: Grundriss_Rückansicht_Wohnraum_Blick auf die Terrasse.
à gauche: Double support en acier. à droite: Plan du rez-de-chausée_Vue de l'arrière_Séjour_Intérieur avec vue sur la terrasse.

# NEW YORK_NY **471 WASHINGTON STREET**

**ARCHITECTS:** BEN HANSEN ARCHITECT
**COMPLETION:** IN PROGRESS, 2010_**TYPOLOGY:** LIVING
**RENDERINGS:** BEN HANSEN ARCHITECT

The 471 Washington Street development project is nine-stories tall, with one apartment per floor, where irregular site geometries informed the overall building composition. The structure is poured in place concrete, with curtain walls of glass and perforated stainless steel, and large structural transfers give the building a muscular profile. Thinly profiled mullions and railings appear to stretch the glass skin taut over the concrete structure, while heating and cooling of the building employs three 1,500-foot deep geothermal wells. Extensive green walls and sedum terraces retain rainwater on site.

Das Projekt 471 Washington Street umfasst neun Geschosse mit jeweils einer Wohnung pro Etage, wobei das unregelmäßig geformte Grundstück den gesamten Gebäudeaufbau prägt. Der Ortbetonkonstruktion mit Vorhangwänden aus Glas und perforiertem Edelstahl sowie der konstruktive Spannbeton verleihen dem Gebäude ein kraftvolles Profil. Fein gegliederte Pfosten und Brüstungen scheinen die Glashaut straff über die Betonkonstruktion zu ziehen. Zum Heizen und Kühlen des Gebäudes dienen drei 457 Meter tiefe Erdwärmeschächte. Extensiv begrünte Mauern und mit Fetthenne bepflanzte Terrassen halten das Regenwasser auf dem Grundstück.

Les contours irréguliers du terrain ont déterminé la forme générale de cet immeuble résidentiel avec un appartement sur chacun de ses neuf étages. L'armature en béton coulé sur place se complète par des murs en verre et acier inox perforé. Des façades sur divers plans donnent à l'ensemble un profil musclé. De fines bandes verticales et horizontales structurent l'enveloppe en verre et l'armature en béton. Le chauffage et la climatisation sont assurés par trois puits géothermiques de 457 mètres de profondeur. De grands murs végétalisés et des terrasses couvertes d'orpins permettent de retenir l'eau de pluie sur place.

left: Floor plan_Open kitchen. right: Exterior view, concrete façade, glass, and steel_Bird´s eye view_Rooftop.
links: Grundriss_Offene Küche. rechts: Außenansicht, Fassade aus Beton, Glas und Stahl Luftbild_Dachterrasse.
à gauche: Plan du rez-de-chaussée_Cuisine ouverte. à droite: Le bâtiment en béton, verre et acier dans son contexte_Vue aérienne_Terrasses du toit.

# NEW YORK_NY **245 TENTH**

**ARCHITECTS:** DELLA VALLE BERNHEIMER
**COMPLETION:** 2008_**TYPOLOGY:** MIXED-USE
**PHOTOS:** FRANK OUDEMAN 2008©

This project looked to the natural context as inspiration for the design of this 11-story residential condominium located in Manhattan's West Chelsea gallery district. Its shape and surface is inspired by the beauty of the transient forms of clouds and in nostalgic reference to trains that once frequented the adjacent High Line. A unique cladding of expansive glass and stainless steel panels animates the building as it reflects the ever-changing play of light and vibrant surroundings. As light migrates across the building's skin, passers-byers may view a structure that appears to change in a display of mutable perspective.

Dieses Projekt nutzt den natürlichen Kontext als Inspirationsquelle für den Entwurf einer elfgeschossigen Wohnanlage in Manhattans Galerieviertel West Chelsea. Seine Gestalt und Oberfläche sind von der Schönheit vergänglicher Wolkenformen angeregt und verweisen nostalgisch auf die Züge, die einst die angrenzende High Line befuhren. Eine einzigartige Verkleidung aus Glas- und Edelstahlplatten belebt das Gebäude, indem sich das ständig verändernde Licht und die dynamische Umgebung in ihm widerspiegeln. Wenn das Licht über die Gebäudehaut streift, erleben Passanten eine Konstruktion mit scheinbar veränderlichen Perspektiven.

Cet immeuble résidentiel de onze étages se dresse à Manhattan, dans le quartier de West Chelsea où se trouvent de nombreuses galeries d'art. Sa forme et son revêtement de façade s'inspirent du caractère transitoire des nuages et rappellent les trains qui passaient autrefois sur la High Line toute proche. La façade en verre et acier inox, parfaitement exceptionnelle, anime le bâtiment en reflétant les effets de lumière toujours changeants de ce quartier de New York très vivant. Lorsque la lumière traverse l'enveloppe, on a l'impression d'être en face d'un immeuble qui offre une perspective en mutation.

left: Seventh floor plan_General view_Exterior. right: Detail façade_Glass façade.
links: Grundriss siebtes Obergeschoss_Gesamtansicht_Außenansicht. rechts: Fassadendetail Glasfassade.
à gauche: Plan du septième étage_Vue générale_Gros plan. à droite: La façade_Détail de la façade.

left: Night view. right: General view_Detail façade.
links: Nachtansicht. rechts: Gesamtansicht_Fassadendetail.
à gauche: La façade la nuit. à droite: Vue génerale_Détail de la facade.

NEW YORK_NY **HEARST HEADQUARTERS**

**ARCHITECTS:** FOSTER + PARTNERS
**COMPLETION:** 2006_**TYPOLOGY:** MIXED-USE
**PHOTOS:** COURTESY OF THE ARCHITECTS

The Hearst Tower's distinctive facetted silhouette rises dramatically above Joseph Urban's existing six-story Art Deco building, its main spatial event a vast internal plaza, occupying the entire shell of the historic base. Designed with sustainability in mind the tower consumes less energy, utilizing outside air ventilation up to 75% a year. It was the first building in New York city to achieve a LEED (Leadership in Energy and Environmental Design) gold rating. When constructed its triangulated structure used 20% less steel than a conventional office tower.

Die unverwechselbar facettierte Silhouette des Hearst Tower erhebt sich aufsehenerregend über dem bestehenden sechsgeschossigen Art-Deco-Gebäude von Joseph Urban. Sein Hauptaktionsraum ist ein weitläufiger innenliegender Platz, der den gesamten Gebäudekörper des historischen Sockels einnimmt. Das nachhaltig konzipierte Hochhaus verbraucht weniger Energie, da für die Belüftung bis zu 75% des Jahres die Außenluft genutzt wird. Der Hearst Tower ist das erste Hochhaus in New York City, das mit dem LEED (Leadership in Energy and Environmental Design)-Gold-Zertifikat ausgezeichnet wurde. Für die tragende Dreiecksstruktur wurde 20% weniger Stahl verwendet als bei einem herkömmlichen Bürohochhaus.

La tour Hearst, caractérisée par ses multiples facettes, forme un contraste saisissant avec le bâtiment art déco de six étages construit par Joseph Urban au-dessus duquel elle s'élève. Seule la façade de l'ancien immeuble a été conservée, de sorte que le rez-de-chaussée de la tour se présente sous la forme d'une vaste esplanade couverte. D'autre part, les architectes ont accordé une importance particulière au développement durable, de sorte que la consommation d'énergie est très basse car la tour utilise une ventilation naturelle neuf mois sur douze. C'est d'ailleurs le premier gratte-ciel new-yorkais à avoir bénéficié du label écologique LEED Gold. La structure triangulaire des facettes a de plus permis de réduire de vingt pour cent la quantité d'acier utilisée en comparaison avec une tour de bureaux conventionnelle.

left: Floor plan_North view_Detail façade_Street side view_Façade. right: Exterior.
links: Grundriss_Nordansicht_Detail der Fassade_Straßenansicht_Fassade. rechts: Außrnansicht.
à gauche: Plan du rez-de-chaussée_Le bâtiment vu du nord_L'ancien et le moderne_Le bâtiment vu de la rue_Détail de la façade.

NEW YORK_NY **ARMANI FIFTH AVENUE**

**ARCHITECTS:** MASSIMILIANO & DORIANA FUKSAS
**COMPLETION:** 2008_**TYPOLOGY:** RETAIL
**PHOTOS:** COURTESY OF THE ARCHITECTS

Situated in the center of New York, the project takes up the first three floors of two buildings localized between 5th Avenue and 56th Street. The showroom is developed on four different levels and is conceived of an only space, without clear distinctions, and a singing space connected with the power generated by the whirlwind of the staircase. The nucleus of the project, the staircase, is a structure wrought with the radiator grill of steel, highlighting the look of the sculpture. Every element of the internal design, from the exhibitors, rooms, and armchairs follow the movement concept generated by the staircase.

Im Zentrum von New York belegt das Projekt die ersten drei Geschosse zweier Bauten zwischen 5th Avenue und 56th Street. Der als Einraum ohne klare Unterscheidungen konzipierte Laden entwickelt sich auf vier unterschiedlichen Ebenen. Eine Wendeltreppe in Gestalt eines Wirbelwinds verbindet die einzelnen Geschosse miteinander. Als Herzstück des Projekts ist die Treppenkonstruktion mit einem Heizkörpergitter aus Stahl ausgeführt und betont das skulpturale Erscheinungsbild. Alle Elemente der Innenraumgestaltung wie Theken, Umkleiden und Sessel sind an der fließenden Bewegung der Treppe ausgerichtet.

Ce magasin occupe trois étages d'un immeuble situé au coin de la 5e Avenue et de la 56e Rue, c'est-à-dire au cœur de New York. L'espace de vente s'étend sur quatre niveaux interconnectés de manière fluide par un escalier en colimaçon aux formes chantantes et puissantes. Véritable centre du magasin, l'escalier est une structure à base d'acier qui se distingue par sa qualité parfaitement sculpturale. Tous les autres éléments de l'aménagement intérieur (rayons, fauteuils, comptoirs, etc.) suivent le mouvement généré par cette structure remarquable.

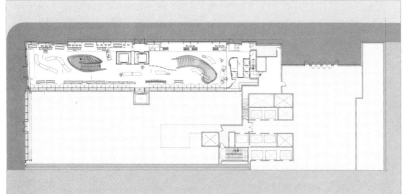

left: Ground floor plan_View from second floor_Stair construction. right: Street side view.
links: Grundriss Erdgeschoss_Blick vom zweiten Obergeschoss_Treppenkonstruktion. rechts: Straßenansicht.
à gauche: Plan du rez-de-chaussée_Vue du second étage_Escalier. à droite: Le magasin vu de la rue.

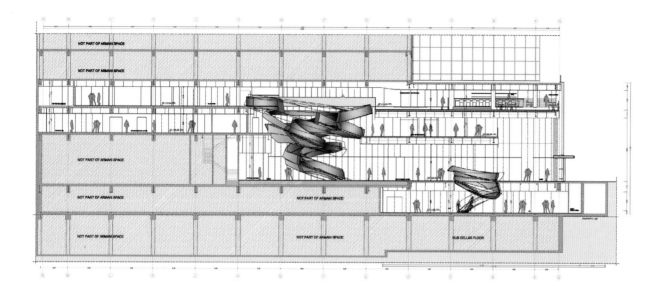

left: Curved stair. right: West section_Stair to second floor.
links: Geschwungene Treppe. rechts: Westschnitt_Treppe ins zweite Obergeschoss.
à gauche: Départ de l'escalier. à droite: Vue en coupe derrière la façade ouest_L'escalier menant au second étage.

NEW YORK_NY **NATIONAL SEPTEMBER 11TH MEMORIAL AT THE WORLD TRADE CENTER**

**ARCHITECTS:** MICHAEL ARAD, AIA / HANDEL ARCHITECTS, LL
**COMPLETION:** 2003_**TYPOLOGY:** PUBLIC
**RENDERINGS:** HANDEL ARCHITECTS

The project's elegant simplicity conceals an incredible complexity of architectural design and engineering. The fourteen-acre WTC site will contain, in addition to the memorial and the museum, a visitor center, a new train station, a subway station, an underground retail concourse, an underground road network with security screening areas, five new office towers, and an arts center. Most of these projects interlock physically and programmatically with the eight-acre Memorial site. The project presents creative design responses that are specific to the Memorial project yet address concerns ranging from sustainability to security.

Hinter der eleganten Einfachheit des Projekts verbirgt sich eine erstaunlich komplexe architektonische Gestaltung und Bautechnik. Auf dem 57.000 Quadratmeter großen Areal des World Trade Centers entstehen außer dem Mahnmal und Museum auch ein Besucherzentrum, ein neuer Bahnhof, eine U-Bahn-Station, eine unterirdische Halle mit Läden, ein unterirdisches Straßennetz mit Bereichen für Sicherheitskontrollen, fünf neue Bürotürme und ein Kunstzentrum. Die meisten dieser Projekte sind baulich-räumlich und programmatisch mit der 32.000 Quadratmeter großen Gedenkstätte verzahnt. Das Projekt präsentiert kreative, für das Mahnmal-Projekt spezifische gestalterische Antworten und spricht dennoch Anliegen an, die von Nachhaltigkeit bis Sicherheit reichen.

La simplicité élégante de ce projet qui couvre plus de cinq hectares — un mémorial aux victimes des attentats du 11-Septembre — cache un concept architectural et une ingénierie BTP d'une complexité surprenante. Le mémorial et son musée complétés physiquement et thématiquement par un centre d'accueil des visiteurs, une gare de train et de métro, un centre commercial souterrain, des voies d'accès également souterraines, cinq nouvelles tours de bureaux et un centre culturel, le tout couvrant une superficie de plus de trois hectares. Ce projet d'urbanisme prend en compte les exigences d'un mémorial, sans négliger celles relatives à la sécurité ni au développement durable.

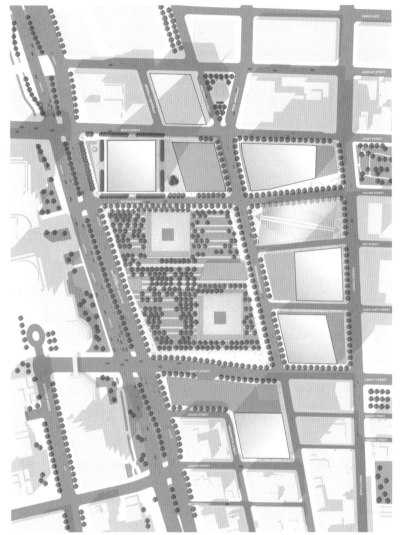

left: Site plan_Memorial plaza at night_Memorial plaque. right: Aerial view_Pools_South pool.
links: Lageplan_Memorial Plaza bei Nacht_Gedenktafel. rechts: Luftbild_Bassins_Bassin im Süden.
à gauche: Plan de situation_L'esplanade du mémorial la nuit_Plaque du mémorial. à droite: Trois vues aériennes des bassins.

NEW YORK_NY **JULIANA CURRAN TERIAN PRATT PAVILION**

**ARCHITECTS:** HMA: HANRAHANMEYERS ARCHITECTS
**COMPLETION:** 2006_**TYPOLOGY:** PUBLIC
**PHOTOS:** PAUL WARCHOL PHOTOGRAPHY

Showcasing work from the Institute's various arts programs, the project is a new focal point for the Pratt Institute campus in Brooklyn, New York. Clad with stainless steel and suspended between two existing industrial loft buildings, the project includes a glass entry area for the Pavilion and its neighbors, Steuben Hall and Pratt Studios. The overall new construction for the Pavilion and its auxiliary areas including the glass entrance and a new circulation bridge to the south, comprise of 10,000 square feet. Behind the Pavilion, a new courtyard makes an outdoor room for informal meetings and classes in warm weather.

Als Schaukasten für die verschiedenen Kunstprogramme des Instituts bildet das Projekt einen neuen Mittelpunkt auf dem Campus des Pratt Institutes in Brooklyn, New York. Das mit Edelstahl verkleidete, zwischen zwei bestehenden industriellen Speichergebäuden aufgehängte Projekt beinhaltet einen gläsernen Eingangsbereich für den Pavillon und seine Nachbarbauten, die Steuben Hall und die Pratt Studios. Insgesamt umfasst die Neubaumaßnahme für den Pavillon und seine Nebenflächen einschließlich einem Glaseingang und einer neuen Erschließungsbrücke im Süden 929 Quadratmeter. Hinter dem Pavillon schafft ein neuer Hof einen Außenraum für zwanglose Begegnungen und Unterricht bei warmer Witterung.

Un pavillon intégrant le travail de diverses équipes du Pratt Institute est devenu le nouveau point focal de cette célèbre école d'art de Brooklyn. Sa façade en verre et acier inox avec des éléments en porte-à-faux contraste avec celles des deux bâtiments voisins: le Steuben Hall et les Pratt Studios. Le pavillon et ses divers espaces annexes (notamment l'entrée vitrée et la passerelle construite au sud) couvrent plus de trois mille mètres carrés au total. La cour qui s'étend derrière le bâtiment permet aux étudiants de se réunir et peut être utilisée pour des cours en plein air lorsque le temps s'y prête.

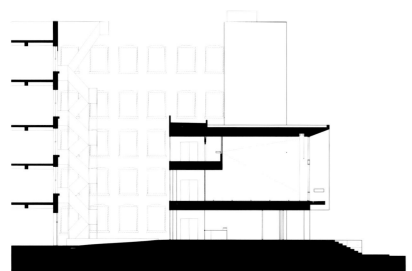

left: Section_Interior view, gallery_Detail stainless steal façade. right: Glass entry area_Exterior Stairs.
links: Schnitt_Innenansicht, Galerie_Detail der Edelstahlfassade. rechts: Eingangsbereich aus Glas_Außenansicht_Treppe.
à gauche: Vue en coupe_Galerie_Détail de la façade en acier inox. à droite: L'entrée du pavillon et l'immeuble voisin_Entrée en porte-à-faux_Escalier.

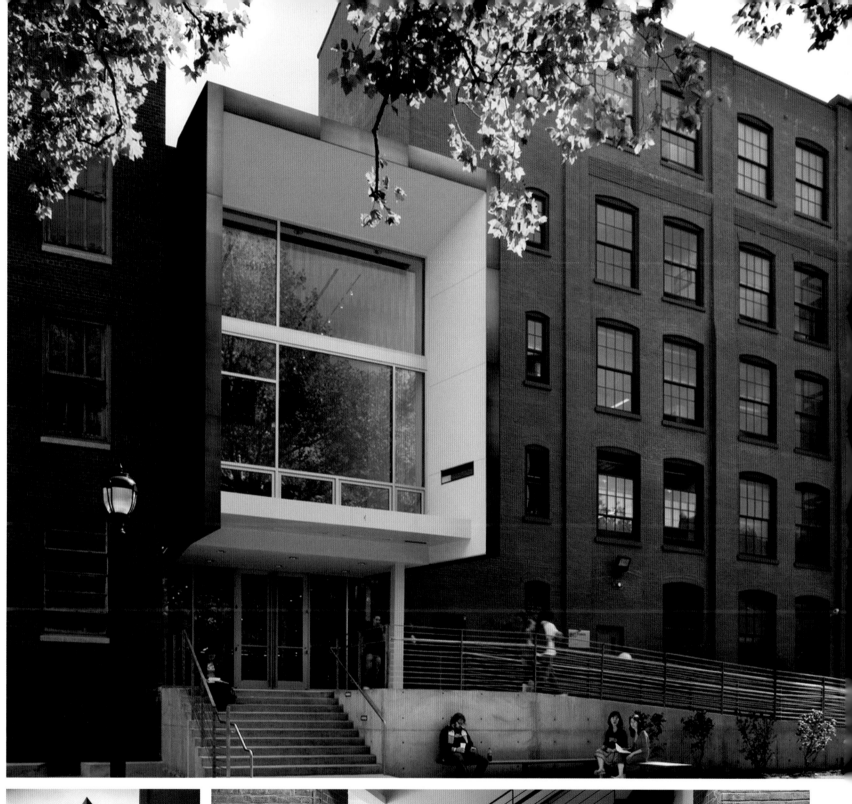

# NEW YORK_NY **WAVELINE**

**ARCHITECTS:** HMA: HANRAHANMEYERS ARCHITECTS
**COMPLETION:** 2007_**TYPOLOGY:** CULTURE
**PHOTOS:** MICHAEL MORAN PHOTOGRAPHY

Waveline is a 5,000-square-foot multi-purpose theater adjacent to an existing community center in Queens, New York. Within a 90-foot by 50-foot site footprint the structure is as large as possible to accommodate theatrical productions. The roof, the principal design feature of the new building, is a bent plane running east west and resting on columns. It was designed as a sculptural shape with standing seam stainless steel cladding. The roof shape is also a direct response to acoustic studies, developing optimal sound projections for theatrical productions in the space.

Waveline ist ein 465 Quadratmeter großes Mehrzwecktheater neben einem bestehenden Stadtteilzentrum in Queens, New York. Auf einer Grundfläche von 27 Meter mal 15 Meter wurde für die Unterbringung der Einrichtungen für die Theaterproduktion eine möglichst große Konstruktion entworfen. Das Dach, das wichtigste Gestaltungsmerkmal des Neubaus, bildet eine gekrümmte Ebene in Ost-West-Richtung und ruht auf Stützen. Es ist als plastische Form mit einer Stehfalzverkleidung aus Edelstahl konzipiert. Außerdem resultiert die Dachform aus Akustikuntersuchungen, in denen die optimalen Schallabstrahlungen für Theaterproduktionen in dem Raum erarbeitet wurden.

Cette salle de spectacle polyvalente de 464 mètres carrés, construite dans le Queens à New York, fait partie d'un centre culturel municipal situé à proximité. Le terrain disponible ne mesurant que vingt-sept mètres par quinze, les architectes ont dû utiliser la quasi-totalité de la surface disponible. Le bâtiment se caractérise par un toit orienté est-ouest qui repose sur des piliers. Revêtu d'acier inox, il prend une apparence sculpturale. Il a été conçu sur la base d'études acoustiques préalables afin d'offrir un environnement sonore optimal pour les spectacles devant avoir lieu ici.

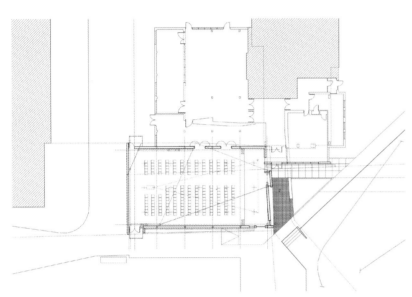

left: Main floor plan_Interior view_Ceiling construction. right: Entrance plaza_Exterior view of waveline with focus on stainless steel cladding.
links: Grundriss Hauptgeschoss_Innenansicht_Dachkonstruktion. rechts: Vorplatz_Außenansicht der gewellten Edelstahlfassade.
à gauche: Plan du niveau principal_Vue de l'intérieur_Charpente. à droite: Esplanade devant l'entrée_Façade avec bardage en acier inox.

# NEW YORK_NY **FLOWER HOUSE**

**ARCHITECTS:** LA-DESIGN, NEW YORK / LEONARDO ANNECA
**COMPLETION:** UNBUILT_**TYPOLOGY:** LIVING
**RENDERINGS:** LADESIGN NEW YORK

The Flower House is a design project brought to an architectural scale, challenging prefabrication and mobility. Playful in nature, it is an experimental design aimed at broadening our social conditioning of modern living. Although portable architecture is not new, the defining "new" element here is the way to look at it and the way to design it. Current architectural attempts at temporary living space reduce the idea of "mobility" to transportable boxes (containers turned into living spaces). The Flower House is about temporary living "outside of the box", enhancing the perception of the space inside and out.

Das Flower House ist ein zu architektonischem Maßstab entwickeltes Designprojekt, das den Fertigteilbau und die Mobilität herausfordert. Dieser spielerische, experimentelle Entwurf zielt auf eine Erweiterung unserer sozialen Konditionierung des modernen Lebensstils. Auch wenn ortsveränderliche Architektur nicht neu ist, besteht hier das bestimmende „neue" Element in ihrer Betrachtungs- und Entwurfsweise. Aktuelle architektonische Versuche zur Schaffung zeitgemäßen Lebensraums reduzieren die Vorstellung von „Mobilität" auf transportable Boxen (zu Wohnräumen umgebaute Container). Beim Flower House geht es um temporäres Wohnen „außerhalb der Box" und eine verstärkte Wahrnehmung des Innen- und Außenraums.

La Flower House est un projet de design élevé à la dimension architecturale en relevant les défis du préfabriqué et de la mobilité. Cette expérience de nature ludique vise à élargir notre conception du logement moderne. Certes, l'architecture « portable » n'est pas une nouveauté, mais la Flower House ambitionne de redéfinir le concept. Alors que la plupart des solutions pour logements temporaires réduisent la mobilité à des conteneurs et autres « boîtes à vivre » facilement transportables, cette nouvelle approche favorise le séjour hors du logement et met l'accent sur la perception tant de l'extérieur que de l'espace intérieur.

left: Section_Interior_Living room. right: Exterior_General view_Living space.
links: Schnitt_Innenansicht_Wohnzimmer. rechts: Außenansicht_Gesamtansicht_Wohnraum.
à gauche: Vue en coupe_Séjour_Autre vue du séjour. à droite: Extérieur_Vue générale_Intérieur.

NEW YORK_NY **MEMORY FOUNDATIONS /
WORLD TRADE CENTER DESIGN STUDY**

**ARCHITECTS:** STUDIO DANIEL LIBESKIND
**COMPLETION:** 2010_**TYPOLOGY:** CULTURE
**RENDERINGS:** SILVERSTEIN PROPERTIES

The design study was selected in February 2003 as the master site plan for the rebuilding of the World Trade Center Site. In addition to a towering spire of 1,776 feet, the plan proposed a complex program which called for the construction of a memorial with waterfalls, an underground museum, a visitor center, retail space, a special transit hub and four office towers spiraling to the height of the Freedom Tower. In addition to the the Freedom Tower, a world-class transportation hub designed by Santiago Calatrava, are four more towers and an awe-inspiring memorial currently under construction in Lower Manhattan.

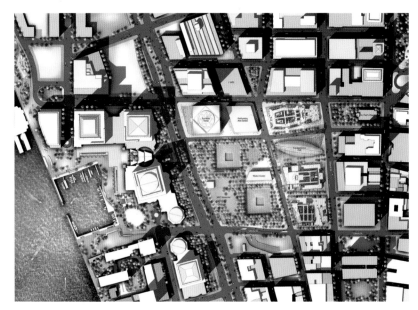

Die Entwurfsstudie wurde im Februar 2003 als Masterplan für den Wiederaufbau des Areals des World Trade Centers ausgewählt. Zusätzlich zu einem 541 Meter hochragenden schlanken Turm schlägt der Plan ein komplexes Programm vor, das ein Mahnmal mit Wasserfällen, ein unterirdisches Museum, ein Besucherzentrum, Ladenflächen, einen besonderen Verkehrsknotenpunkt und vier Bürotürme vorsieht, die bis zur Höhe des Freedom Towers in einer spiralförmigen Anordnung aufsteigen. Außer dem Freedom Tower und einem von Santiago Calatrava entworfenen Bahnhof entstehen derzeit in Lower Manhattan vier weitere Hochhäuser sowie eine eindrucksvolle Gedenkstätte.

En février 2003, ce schéma directeur a été retenu pour le plan d'urbanisme visant à la reconstruction du World Trade Center à Manhattan. Ses différents éléments sont les suivants: la Freedom Tower, gratte-ciel d'une hauteur de 541 mètres ; un mémorial aux victimes des attentats du 11-Septembre avec musée souterrain et centre d'accueil des visiteurs, le tout complété par des bassins et cascades ; un centre commercial et une gare souterraine de classe mondiale conçue par Santiago Calatrava ; et quatre tours de bureaux.

left: Site plan_Night skyline_Four office towers and the Freedom Tower_West elevation. right: Exterior view Freedom Tower.
links: Lageplan_Skyline am Abend_Vier Bürotürme und der Freedom Tower_Westansicht. rechts: Außenansicht des Freedom Towers.
à gauche: Plan de situation_Silhouette des gratte-ciel au crépuscule_Les quatre tours de bureaux et la Freedom Tower_La tour vue de l'ouest. à droite: La Freedom Tower dans son contexte urbain.

NEW YORK_NY

# NEW ACADEMIC BUILDING FOR THE COOPER UNION FOR THE ADVANCEMENT OF SCIENCE AND ART

**ARCHITECTS:** MORPHOSIS / THOM MAYNE
**COMPLETION:** 2008_**TYPOLOGY:** EDUCATION
**RENDERINGS:** MORPHOSIS

The facility is conceived as a stacked vertical piazza, contained within a semitransparent envelope, articulating the classroom and laboratory spaces. Organized around a central atrium, a connective volume, spanned by sky bridges, opens up view corridors across Third Avenue to the Foundation Building. Many of the public functions, including retail space and a lobby exhibition gallery, are located at ground level, while a second gallery and a 200-seat auditorium are easily accessible from the street. The interior space configuration encourages interconnection between the school's engineering, art, and architecture departments.

Das Universitätsgebäude ist als vertikaler, gestapelter Platz in einer halbtransparenten Hülle konzipiert, an der sich Seminarräume und Labors abbilden. Der Bau ist um ein zentrales Atrium organisiert, das von Brücken überspannt wird, die Sichtachsen zur Third Avenue und zum Hauptgebäude bieten. Viele der öffentlichen Funktionen, darunter Geschäfte und eine Ausstellungsgalerie in der Lobby, sind im Erdgeschoss untergebracht. Eine zweite Galerie und eine Aula mit 200 Sitzplätzen lassen sich bequem von der Straße aus erschließen. Die Anordnung der Innenräume unterstützt den Austausch zwischen den Ingenieur-, Kunst- und Architekturfakultäten.

Une enveloppe semi-transparente abritant des laboratoires et des salles de cours caractérise ce bâtiment conçu comme un empilement de plusieurs esplanades. Ce « campus vertical » s'organise autour d'un puits de lumière central traversé par des passerelles et ouvrant diverses perspectives, notamment sur la 3e Avenue et le bâtiment d'origine de la Cooper Union. On trouve au rez-de-chaussée plusieurs espaces ouverts au public tels que des boutiques et la salle d'exposition du hall d'entrée. Une autre salle d'exposition ainsi qu'un auditorium de deux cents places sont également accessibles de la rue. L'aménagement des espaces éducatifs a été conçu de manière à favoriser l'interconnexion des différents départements de l'école (Engineering, Art et Architecture).

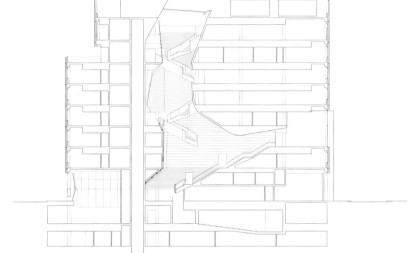

left: Section_Elevation_Street side view. right: Interior.
links: Schnitt_Ansicht_Straßenansicht. rechts: Interieur.
à gauche: Vue en coupe_Élévation_Le bâtiment vu de la rue. à droite: Intérieur.

# NEW YORK_NY **SWITCH BUILDING**

**ARCHITECTS:** NARCHITECTS
**COMPLETION:** 2007_**TYPOLOGY:** MIXED-USE
**PHOTOS:** FRANK OUDEMAN

Switch Building is a 7-story apartment and art gallery building in Manhattan's Lower East Side. The project's design emerges not only from a creative interpretation of some of the narrow constraints imposed by zoning, but also in regards to the developer's needs. While the apartment plans are identical, the `switching' of bay windows and balconies allow each unit to be unique in providing light qualities and views to the city. The gallery introduces a larger scale into the Lower East Side's burgeoning art scene, which has been primarily inserting cultural programs into former tenement buildings.

Das siebengeschossige Switch Building mit Wohnungen und Kunstgalerie liegt in Manhattans Lower East Side. Der Entwurf des Projekts basiert sowohl auf einer kreativen Interpretation einiger strenger Bebauungsvorschriften als auch auf dem Bedarf des Auftraggebers. Trotz identischer Wohnungsgrundrisse verfügt jede Einheit durch das „Umschalten" der Erkerfenster und Balkone über eine andere Lichtqualität und Aussicht auf die Stadt. Mit der Galerie erhält die aufstrebende Kunstszene in der Lower East Side größeres Gewicht, deren Kulturprogramme bislang hauptsächlich ehemalige Mehrfamilienhäuser aufnahmen.

Cet immeuble de sept étages situé à Manhattan, dans le Lower East Side, abrite des logements et une galerie d'art. Il a été construit en tenant compte à la fois des contraintes imposées par le zonage, et des besoins formulés par l'investisseur finançant le projet. Tous les appartements ont certes un plan identique, mais l'orientation différente des oriels et balcons dote chacun d'un éclairage naturel et de vues sur la ville qui lui sont propres. La galerie du rez-de-chaussée contribue à promouvoir la vie artistique du Lower East Side, qui est en pleine expansion et se développe principalement dans des immeubles locatifs reconvertis.

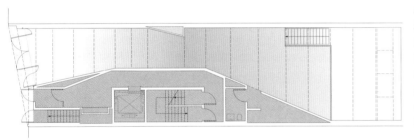

left: Floor plan_Lobby. right: View from the street.
links: Grundriss_Korridor. rechts: Straßenansicht.
à gauche: Plan_ Couloir. à droite: Façade côté rue.

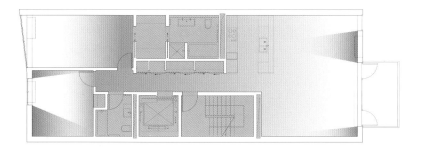

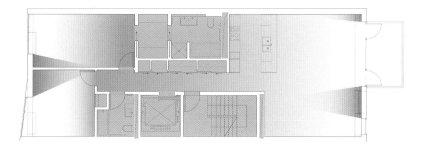

119

left: Detail bay windows. right: Floor plans_Interior view staircase.
links: Detail der Ausfluchtfenster. rechts: Grundrisse_Ansicht vom Treppenhaus.
à gauche: Oriels. à droite: Plans_Sommet de l'escalier.

# NEW YORK_NY **HL23**

**ARCHITECTS:** NEIL M. DENARI ARCHITECTS INC.
**COMPLETION:** 2009_**TYPOLOGY:** LIVING
**PHOTOS:** RENDERINGS BY HAYES DAVIDSON

HL23 will rise fourteen stories from a 40 foot-wide footprint, just steps from Tenth Avenue and half covered by the High Line, the historic elevated railway bed slated for transformation into one of the nation's most lyrical urban parks. Overcoming this through-block site's inherited restrictions Denari has conceived a building that will dramatically increase in size as it rises from its slender footing to cantilever gracefully over the rails. The reverse-tapering form will create cinematic views and unrivaled intimacy with the High Line for the residents.

HL23 wird von einer zwölf Meter breiten Grundfläche aus 14 Geschosse aufsteigen. In unmittelbarer Nähe der Tenth Avenue ist das Gebäude zur Hälfte von der High Line bedeckt, der historischen Hochbahntrasse, die zu einem der stimmungsvollsten Stadtparks der Nation umgewandelt werden soll. Denari meistert die sich aus dem durchgehenden Block ergebenden Restriktionen, indem er das Gebäude von seinem schmalen Unterbau nach oben hin dramatisch erweitert. Durch die nach unten verjüngte Form bieten sich den Bewohnern Aussichten wie im Film und eine unübertroffene Nähe zur High Line.

Cet immeuble de quatorze étages se dresse sur un terrain de seulement douze mètres de large situé entre la 10e Avenue et la High Line, ancienne ligne de chemin de fer sur viaduc devant être reconvertie pour devenir l'un des parcs urbains les plus remarquables des États-Unis. Afin de remédier aux limitations imposées par cette topographie, les architectes ont conçu un immeuble à la géométrie audacieuse, en porte-à-faux progressif au-dessus des anciennes voies de chemin de fer. Du fait de cette forme particulière, les occupants de la tour HL23 bénéficient de vues cinématiques et d'une proximité inégalée avec la High Line.

left: Site plan_View inside_Sundeck. right: Exterior view.
links: Lageplan_Blick in Wohnungen_Dachterrasse. rechts: Außenansicht.
à gauche: Plan de situation_L'intérieur vu de l'extérieur_Terrasse. à droite: Extérieur.

left: Façade. right: Bathroom_Street side view_Living room_Kitchen.
links: Fassade. rechts: Badezimmer_Straßenansicht_Wohnzimmer_Küche.
à gauche: Façade. à droite: Salle de bain_Le bâtiment vu de la rue_Séjour_Cuisine.

# NEW YORK_NY **TOUR DE VERRE**

**ARCHITECTS:** JEAN NOUVEL
**COMPLETION:** IN DESIGN_**TYPOLOGY:** MIXED-USE
**PHOTOS:** ATELIERS JEAN NOUVEL

Nouvel's bold design will rise 75 stories from the 17,000-square-foot-site between 53rd and 54th streets just west of MoMA. Currently, a mix of uses is contemplated for the building including: a 50,000-square-foot expansion of MoMA's galleries (levels two to five); a 100-room, seven-star hotel and 120 highest-end residential condominiums on the upper floors. The design maximizes the site while considering the city's zoning envelope. The proposed building's unique silhouette tapers as it rises to a distinctive spire. Its steel and glass façade reveals the diagrid structural design.

Nouvels kühner, 75 Stockwerke hoher Wolkenkratzer wird sich auf einem 1.580 Quadratmeter großen Grundstück zwischen der 53. und 54. Straße genau westlich vom MoMA erheben. Momentan ist für das Gebäude eine Mischnutzung geplant: eine 4.645 Quadratmeter Erweiterung der MoMA-Galerien (Ebenen zwei bis fünf); ein Sieben-Sterne-Hotel mit 100 Zimmern sowie 120 Luxuswohnungen in den Obergeschossen. Der Entwurf nutzt die Grundstücksfläche unter Beachtung der städtischen Geschossflächenzahl maximal aus. Die einzigartige Gebäudesilhouette verjüngt sich nach oben hin zu einer unverwechselbaren Turmspitze. An der Fassade aus Stahl und Glas lässt sich die diagonale Baukonstruktion ablesen.

Cette tour de soixante-quinze étages au design audacieux doit être construite sur un terrain de plus de 1.580 mètres carrés compris entre les 53e et 54e Rues, c'est-à-dire à proximité immédiate du Museum of Modern Art. Dans l'état actuel du projet, elle devrait abriter une annexe du MoMA couvrant environ quinze mille mètres carrés (niveaux deux à cinq), un hôtel sept étoiles d'une centaine de chambres, et cent-vingt appartements de très haut standing (étages supérieurs). Les architectes ont cherché à optimiser l'utilisation du terrain en tenant compte des contraintes imposées par le zonage. La tour se caractérise par sa silhouette exceptionnelle en forme de clocher. L'enveloppe en verre laisse transparaître le squelette en acier et ses éléments diagonaux.

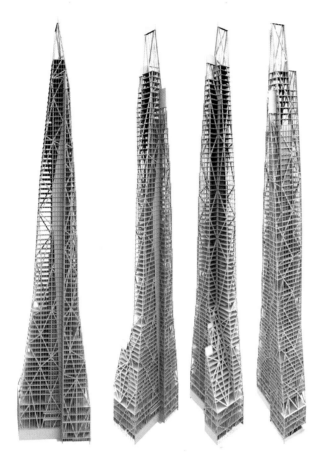

left: Drawing_Detail exterior_View from below. right: Restaurant.
links: Zeichnung_Detail der Außenansicht_Blick von unten. rechts: Restaurant.
gauche: Esquisse_Deux vues de la tour vers le ciel. à droite: Restaurant.

# NEW YORK_NY **23 EAST 22ND STREET**

**ARCHITECTS:** OMA
**COMPLETION:** 2010_**TYPOLOGY:** LIVING
**PHOTOS:** ARTEFACTORY, LUXIGON

The 355-foot-tall asymmetrical tower had to respond to a number of complex demands: in addition to the zoning law and neighbors, it had to avoid blocking the view of One Madison Park and its 60-story neighbor to the north. Using the complexity – even strangeness – of the site, unusual qualities were introduced to the apartments: irregular ceiling heights, views around the tower to the north, and overhangs with windows to the city below. Spanning ten floors of the 24-story building, the cantilever resembles an inverted staircase.

Bei der Errichtung des 108 Meter hohen asymmetrischen Turmhochhauses waren umfassende Vorgaben zu erfüllen. Zusätzlich zum Bau- und Nachbarrecht musste darauf geachtet werden, dass der Blick aus dem One Madison Park und seinem 60-geschossigen Nachbargebäude unverstellt blieb. Durch das Ausnutzen der komplexen – sogar seltsamen – Grundstückgegebenheiten erhielten die Apartments außergewöhnliche Eigenschaften: unregelmäßige Deckenhöhen, Aussichten um das Hochhaus in Richtung Norden und Auskragungen mit Fenstern auf die Stadt. Die sich über zehn Geschosse erstreckenden Vorsprünge des insgesamt 24 Stockwerke hohen Gebäudes erinnern an eine umgedrehte Treppe.

La conception de cette tour asymétrique de 108 mètres de haut n'a pas été simple, puisque les architectes ont dû tenir compte à la fois des contraintes du zonage et éviter de bloquer la vue sur One Madison Park, immeuble de soixante étages construit un peu plus au nord. La complexité — voire l'étrangeté — du site a conduit à l'élaboration de solutions originales. Citons notamment les différentes hauteurs de plafond à l'intérieur des appartements, les vues vers le nord et les surplombs avec des fenêtres donnant sur la ville en contrebas. Le porte-à-faux de dix étages sur vingt-quatre donne à la tour l'aspect d'un escalier à l'envers.

left: Living space_Lobby_Interior. right: General view_City view.
links: Wohnraum_Eingangshalle_Innenansicht. rechts: Gesamtansicht_Stadtansicht.
à gauche: Séjour_Hall d'entrée_Vue de l'intérieur. à droite: Deux vues d'ensemble du bâtiment dans son contexte urbain.

# NEW YORK_NY **TKTS BOOTH**

**ARCHITECTS:** PERKINS EASTMAN (DESIGN DEVELOPMENT & EXECUTIVE ARCHITECTS), CHOI ROPIHA (DESIGN CONCEPT)
**COMPLETION:** 2008_**TYPOLOGY:** PUBLIC
**PHOTOS:** PAÚL RIVERA / ARCHPHOTO

The new TKTS Booth responds to its location a top Father Duffy Square, a slender triangular-shaped public park in Times Square. The booth is a combination of structural integrity and innovative design made possible with the latest advances in glass technology and the collective knowledge of the world's leading industry experts. The TKTS Booth is the most complex and sophisticated glass structure ever created – a show-stopping urban sculpture of iconic proportions and forward-thinking ingenuity.

TKTS Booth reagiert auf seinen Standort auf dem Father Duffy Square, einem schmalen, dreieckigen, öffentlichen Park auf dem Times Square. Den Ticketverkaufsstand kennzeichnen eine konstruktive Geschlossenheit und innovative Gestaltung, die neueste Fortschritte in der Glastechnologie und das Wissen weltweit führender Industrieexperten ermöglichten. TKTS Booth ist die komplexeste und raffinierteste jemals geschaffene Glaskonstruktion – eine sensationelle Stadtskulptur mit ikonischen Proportionen und zukunftsweisenden Ideen.

Cette structure en gradins s'adapte à la forme triangulaire de Father Duffy Square, un espace public situé à Times Square. Son design novateur a été rendu possible par les dernières découvertes de l'industrie du verre et le savoir-faire collectif des plus grands experts mondiaux en la matière. Cet élément de mobilier urbain surprenant, appelé à devenir emblématique du quartier du fait de l'ingéniosité futuriste qu'il manifeste qu'il manifeste, constitue la structure en verre la plus complexe et la plus sophistiquée jamais réalisée.

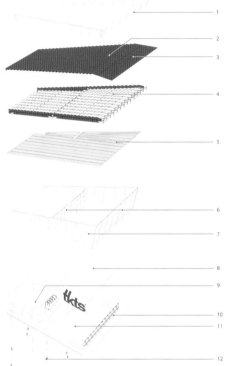

1. Glass Balustrades
2. Laminated Glass Treads (Ticket Slot Assembly Grouted into Position)
3. Glass Cantilevered Canopy
4. Glass Stringer Beams
5. Radiant Panels + Reflector Pans + LEDs
6. Load Bearing Glass Walls
7. Glass Sidewalls
8. Prefabricated Fiberglass Booth
9. Skid Mounted Mechanical Equipment
10. TKTS Counters
11. Raised Form Assembly
12. Geothermal Wells 450' deep

left: Exploded view_Glass façade of booth_Street side view. right: View towards stairs.
links: Auseinandergezogene Darstellung_Glasfassade des Verkaufsstands_Straßenansicht. rechts: Blick auf die Treppen.
à gauche: Vue en éclaté_Structure en verre_Le pavillon vu de la rue. à droite: Les gradins et les gratte-ciel voisins.

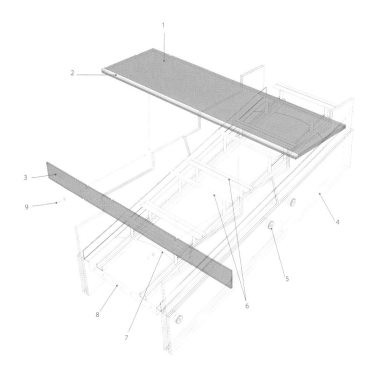

left: Stair detail. right: Sketch_Booth on a full night_Side view_View below stairs.
links: Detail der Treppe. rechts: Entwurf_Verkaufsstand am Abend_Seitenansicht_Ansicht von den Treppen.
à gauche: Gradins. à droite: Les différents éléments_Les gradins la nuit_Vue latérale_Vue du haut des gradins.

NEW YORK_NY **NEW MUSEUM OF CONTEMPORARY ART**

**ARCHITECTS:** KAZUYO SEJIMA + RYUE NISHIZAWA / S A N A A
**COMPLETION:** 2007_**TYPOLOGY:** CULTURE
**PHOTOS:** CHRISTIAN RICHTERS

The New Museum of Contemporary Art was designed as a stack of displaced boxes on seven levels, each one shifted off-centre from the level immediately below or above. This design decision served partly as a response to a tight zoning envelope. The site measures 71 feet across and 112 feet deep, and by shifting the boxes to the north, east, south, and west of the building's central axis, SANAA could fill more space without always extending the structure to the perimeter. The displacement also allows for skylights on every floor. Delicate, adjustable screens prevent the sunlight from bleaching the art or creating glare.

Beim New Museum of Contemporary Art stapelten die Architekten gegeneinander versetzte Boxen auf sieben Etagen. Diese Entwurfslösung ist teilweise durch die strengen Bebauungsvorschriften bedingt. Da das Grundstück nur 21 Meter breit und 34 Meter lang ist, drehten SANAA die Boxen von der Mittelachse des Gebäudes nach Norden, Osten, Süden und Westen und füllten mehr Raum aus, ohne die Konstruktion zu den Außenrändern auszudehnen. Durch die versetzte Anordnung entstanden in jedem Geschoss Oberlichter. Grazile, verstellbare Blenden verhindern die Exponate auszubleichen.

Le bâtiment qui abrite ce musée d'art moderne se présente comme sept boîtes empilées les unes sur les autres avec un certain décalage. Cet aspect inhabituel résulte partiellement des contraintes imposées par le zonage. Sur un terrain mesurant seulement vingt-deux mètres par trente-quatre, ne pas construire à la verticale mais décaler les différents volumes vers le nord, le sud, l'est et l'ouest a en effet permis d'optimiser l'utilisation de la surface au sol, tout en rendant possible l'éclairage zénithal à tous les étages. D'autre part, un système d'écrans réglables évite l'éblouissement des visiteurs et la détérioration des œuvres exposées sous l'effet de la lumière solaire.

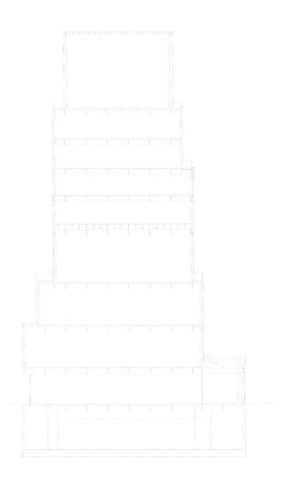

left: Section_General view_Street side view_Exhibition. right: Façade view.
links: Schnitt_Gesamtansicht_Straßenansicht_Ausstellung. rechts: Fassadenansicht.
à gauche: Vue en coupe_Vue d'ensemble_L'immeuble vu de la rue_Salle d'exposition. à droite: Façade.

# NEW YORK_NY **METAL SHUTTER HOUSES**

**ARCHITECTS:** SHIGERU BAN ARCHITECTS +
DEAN MALTZ ARCHITECT
**COMPLETION:** 2008_**TYPOLOGY:** LIVING
**PHOTOS:** DBOX

The Metal Shutter Houses is a dynamic building. The façade's motorized perforated metal shutters serve as light-modulating privacy screen at the outer edge of each residence's terrace adjacent to the double-height living rooms. This subtle "removable skin" echoes the neighboring gallery after-hours shutters, subtly contextualizing the building within its site. The building can literally close down, becoming a uniform minimal cube, or it can open completely. South of the terrace, twenty foot tall, upwardly pivoting glass windows open completely, thus blurring the boundary between the inside and outside – the double height living room and terrace become one.

Das Metal Shutter Houses ist ein dynamisches Gebäude. Vor seinen Terrassen und den angrenzenden Wohnzimmern dienen motorisierte, perforierte Rollläden aus Metall als Licht- und Sichtschutz. Diese subtile „bewegliche Haut" erinnert an die nach Geschäftsschluss heruntergefahrenen Rollläden der benachbarten Galerien und schafft einen subtilen Bezug zum Kontext. Das Gebäude lässt sich zu einem gleichförmigen minimalistischen Kubus schließen oder gänzlich öffnen. Südlich von der Terrasse können sechs Meter hohe Schwingflügelfenster komplett geöffnet werden, sodass die Grenzen zwischen Innen und Außen verschwimmen – der zweigeschossige Wohnraum und die Terrasse werden eins.

On peut qualifier cet immeuble de « dynamique » car ses façades sont pourvues de stores métalliques perforés à moteurs qui permettent, chacun des duplex, de moduler l'éclairage et le degré d'ouverture sur l'extérieur de la terrasse et du séjour. Cette « seconde peau » de la façade s'harmonise aux stores de l'immeuble commercial voisin et contribue ainsi à une intégration subtile du bâtiment dans son contexte urbain. Les stores métalliques permettent d'ouvrir ou fermer entièrement l'enveloppe, l'immeuble prenant dans ce dernier cas l'aspect d'un cube minimaliste. De plus, les panneaux vitrés qui ferment le séjour peuvent se rétracter vers le haut du côté de la terrasse large de six mètres, de sorte que les deux espaces n'en font plus qu'un et que la limite entre intérieur et extérieur s'estompe.

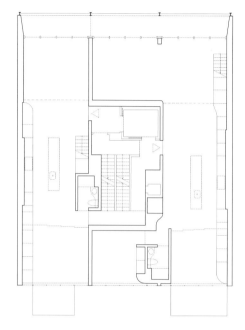

N

left: Lower level floor plan_Living room. right: Penthouse_Kitchen_Interior view from the exterior.
links: Grundriss unteres Geschoss_Wohnzimmer. rechts: Wohnraum mit Dachterrasse_Küche Blick nach Außen von Innen.
à gauche: Plan du rez-de-chaussée_Séjour. à droite: Appartement au dernier étage_Cuisine_Terrasse et intérieur.

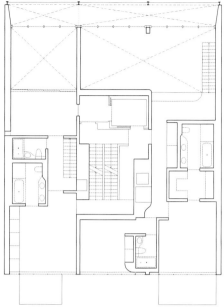

N

left: View at dusk. right: Typical floor plan_View with shutters closed_View during the day.
links: Ansicht bei Nacht. rechts: Regelgrundriss_Außenansicht mit geschlossenen Fensterläden
Ansicht bei Tag.
à gauche: L'immeuble le soir. à droite: Plan typique d'un appartement_Façade avec les stores
fermés_Façade avec les stores ouverts.

# NEW YORK_NY **BLUE**

**ARCHITECTS:** BERNARD TSCHUMI ARCHITECTS
**COMPLETION:** 2007_**TYPOLOGY:** LIVING
**PHOTOS:** BERNARD TSCHUMI ARCHITECTS

This residential mid-rise in New York's Lower East Side occupies a lot zoned for residential use and cantilevers over an existing building designated for commercial use. The slightly angled walls artfully negotiate the varying set-back rules, crossing the line between the commercial and residential zoning districts. The building consists of 32 residences ranging from one and two bedroom units, to full-floor units with large terraces, and finally crowned by a duplex penthouse. The apartments are fitted out with sustainable materials, including bamboo floors and wall panels, palm flooring, and river-pebble bathroom tiles.

Dieses mehrgeschossige Apartmenthaus auf einer Wohnparzelle in New Yorks Lower East Side kragt über einem bestehenden gewerblich genutzten Gebäude hervor. Seine leicht winkelförmig angeordneten Mauern reizen kunstvoll die örtlich zulässigen Baugrenzen aus, indem sie die Linie zwischen reinem Wohn- und Gewerbegebiet überschreiten. Das Gebäude enthält 32 Apartments, die von Wohneinheiten mit einem oder zwei Schlafzimmern über ganze Etagen mit großzügigen Terrassen bis zu einem krönenden Penthaus auf zwei Ebenen reichen. Ausgestattet sind die Wohnungen mit nachhaltigen Materialien, darunter Fußböden und Wandplatten aus Bambus, Kokosbelag und Badezimmerfliesen aus Flusskies.

D'une taille modeste dans le contexte new-yorkais, cet immeuble résidentiel du Lower East Side s'élève en porte-à-faux au-dessus d'un immeuble commercial préexistant. Ses façades non verticales jouent subtilement avec les lois de la pesanteur dans un quartier à la limite des zones résidentielles et industrielles. Le bâtiment abrite trente-deux logements de tailles diverses, allant du deux pièces au duplex en passant par de vastes appartements avec terrasse. Tous disposent d'aménagements intérieurs en matériaux naturels, notamment des revêtements de sol et de mur en bambou, des parquets en palmier et des galets de rivières dans les salles de bain.

left: Model_General view_View from the street. right: Detail of slightly angled walls.
links: Modell_Gesamtansicht_Straßenansicht. rechts: Detailansicht der leicht abgewinkelten Wände.
à gauche: Vue du volume reporté à plat_La tour dans son contexte_La tour vue de la rue. à droite: Gros plan sur les angles de la façade.

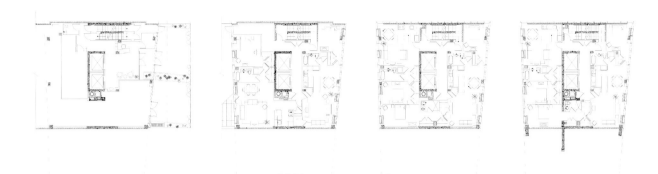

left: Fully glazed façade. right: Floor plans_Interior.
links: Verglaste Fassade. rechts: Grundrisse_Inneneinrichtung.
à gauche: Façade en verre. à droite: Plans de différents étages_Intérieur.

# NEW YORK_NY **FIVE FRANKLIN PLACE**

**ARCHITECTS:** UNSTUDIO
**COMPLETION:** 2009_**TYPOLOGY:** LIVING
**RENDERINGS:** ARCHPARTNERS 2008

Located in Tribeca's historic Cast Iron District in downtown Manhattan, Five Franklin will be the first major American building by internationally admired Dutch architect Ben van Berkel. The building is 20-stories high, offering impressive panoramic views of the Hudson River, East River and Manhattan Skyline. It will contain 55 homes, and will boast a dramatic, highly decorative exterior inspired by the applied metal façades of Tribeca's 19th century cast iron architecture. Gleaming black horizontal ribbons metal will wrap the façades, twisting into functional elements such as balconies, terraces, and sunshades.

In Tribecas historischem Cast Iron District in Downtown Manhattan wird Five Franklin Place das erste amerikanische Großprojekt des international gefeierten holländischen Architektens Ben van Berkel sein. Das 20-etagige Gebäude bietet beeindruckende Aussichten auf den Hudson River, den East River und Manhattans Skyline. Es beherbergt 55 Apartments und wartet mit einem dramatischen, sehr dekorativen Äußeren auf, das von den Metallfassaden der Gusseisenarchitektur Tribecas aus dem 19. Jahrhundert inspiriert ist. Funkelnde schwarze, horizontale Metallbänder werden die Fassaden umschlingen, die sich zu funktionalen Elementen wie Balkons, Terrassen und Sonnenblenden winden.

Situé dans le quartier à la mode de TriBeCa, sur l'île de Manhattan à New York, ce bâtiment est le premier projet d'importance réalisé aux États-Unis par le célèbre architecte néerlandais Ben van Berkel. Haut de vingt étages, il offre une vue remarquable sur l'Hudson River, l'East River et tout Manhattan. Il abrite cinquante-cinq appartements et présente une façade très décorative inspirée des immeubles à structure métalliques du XIXᵉ siècle qui caractérisent le quartier. Des bandes horizontales en métal noir brillant rythment la façade, où elles se transforment en divers éléments fonctionnels tels que les stores et les rambardes des balcons et terrasses.

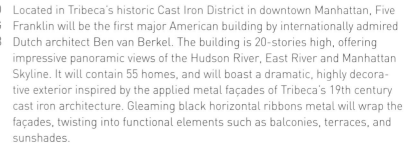

left: Diagram façade_Detail balconies_Rooftop. right: Street side view.
links: Diagramm der Fassade_Detail der Balkone_Dachterrasse. rechts: Straßenansicht.
à gauche: Schéma de la façade_Gros plan sur les balcons_Toit en terrasse. à droite: L'immeuble vu de la rue.

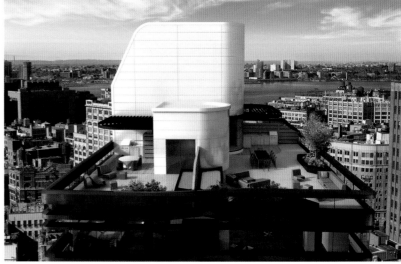

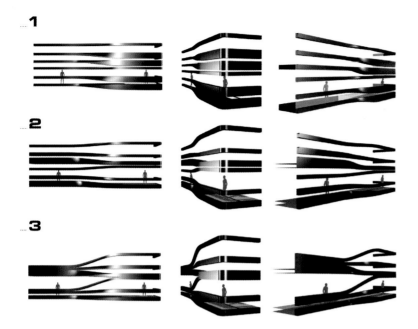

left: Living space. right: Diagrams façade_Bathroom_Kitchen_Bathroom.
links: Wohnraum. rechts: Digramme der Fassade_Badezimmer_Küche_Badezimmer.
à gauche: Séjour. à droite: Schémas de la façade_Salle de bain_Cuisine_Salle de bain au dernier étage.

# OLIVE BRANCH_NY **SCHOLAR'S LIBRARY**

**ARCHITECTS:** PETER L. GLUCK AND PARTNERS, ARCHITECTS
**COMPLETION:** 2003_**TYPOLOGY:** LIVING
**PHOTOS:** PAUL WARCHOL

In addition to the library, the family retreat features a restored farmhouse and a guest dormitory, which sleeps twenty-five. The library is a freestanding building containing a study space above and a 10,000-volume library below. The building is a cube with twenty-foot sides, with books stored in a window-less space on the first floor. The tightly packed stacks preserve the books and minimize the cost of heating them in the winter. The upper floor contains a workspace and has continuous glass on all four sides. The entire study can be turned into an open area by sliding open large glass panels.

Außer der Bibliothek gehören zum Rückzugsort für die Familie ein restau-riertes Bauernhaus und ein Gästeschlafsaal mit 25 Plätzen. Das freistehende Gebäude der Bibliothek enthält ein Arbeitszimmer über einem Raum mit einer 10.000 Bände umfassenden Büchersammlung. In dem kubusförmigen Bau mit einer Seitenlänge von 6,10 Metern werden die Bücher im fenster-losen Erdgeschoss aufbewahrt. Dicht gestellte Regale schützen die Bücher und minimieren die Kosten für ihre Beheizung im Winter. Das Arbeitszimmer im Obergeschoss ist an allen vier Seiten durchgehend verglast und lässt sich durch Öffnen großer Glasschiebeelemente in eine offene Fläche umwandeln.

Ce bâtiment isolé est la dépendance d'une ferme restaurée complétée par un dortoir de vingt-cinq places pour invités. Il s'agit d'un cube de six mètres de côté, qui abrite une bibliothèque d'environ dix mille volumes au rez-de-chaussée dépourvu de fenêtre, ainsi qu'un espace de lecture situé au niveau supérieur. Les livres, serrés les uns contre les autres sur les étagères, se conservent bien durant l'hiver sans qu'il soit nécessaire de chauffer la pièce. L'espace de lecture est entièrement vitré sur les quatre côtés, les vitres pou-vant coulisser pour ouvrir entièrement la pièce sur la forêt environnante.

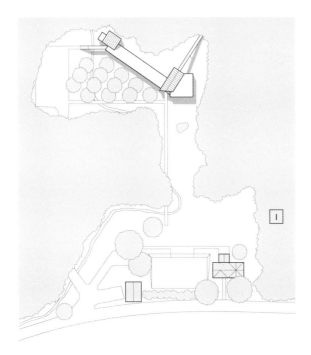

left: Site plan_Workspace with unobstructed views to forest_Exterior with light on. right: View from the forest.
links: Lageplan_Arbeitsplatz mit Blick in den Wald_Außenansicht mit Beleuchtung. rechts: Waldansicht.
à gauche: Plan de situation_Intérieur_Le cube au crépuscule. à droite: Le cube dans la forêt.

# ROCHESTER_NY **STRONG – NATIONAL MUSEUM OF PLAY**

**ARCHITECTS:** CHAINTREUIL | JENSEN | STARK ARCHITECTS LLP
**COMPLETION:** 2006_**TYPOLOGY:** CULTURE
**PHOTOS:** DON COCHRAN PHOTOGRAPHY

The Museum recast itself as the "Strong National Museum of Play" to increase the awareness and understanding of the role of play in learning and human development. The "Butterfly Garden" is a tensile fabric structure while the "Play Gallery," is an assembly of steel bents covered with colorful resin panels. The organically shaped "Eye Atrium" structure is an organizing element connecting galleries and floor levels. Providing shelter at the school entrance is a steel-clad space frame known as the "Blue Handkerchief". The "Red Wedge" houses the building's central mechanical equipment. The Museum's new presence in the community transforms it into the southeastern gateway to the city.

Das Museum möchte mit seiner Umgestaltung das Bewusstsein und das Verständnis für die Rolle des Spiels beim Lernen und bei der menschlichen Entwicklung erhöhen. Beim „Schmetterlingsgarten" handelt es sich um eine textile zugbeanspruchte Hängekonstruktion, bei der „Spielgalerie" um einen von farbenfrohen Kunstharzplatten bedeckten Stahlrahmenbau. Das organisch geformte „Augen-Atrium" vermittelt zwischen den Galerien und den Geschossebenen. Am Eingang zur Schule bietet ein als „Blaues Taschentuch" bekanntes stahlverkleidetes räumliches Tragwerk ein Schutzdach. Im „Roten Keil" ist die zentrale Haustechnik untergebracht. Das neue öffentliche Erscheinungsbild verwandelt das Museum zu einem Stadttor im Südwesten.

Le nom de ce musée entend souligner l'importance du jeu dans le processus d'apprentissage et le développement de la personnalité. Le Jardin des papillons est une structure en tissu tendu, la Galerie du jeu un assemblage de barres d'acier couvert de panneaux en résine colorée, et l'atrium un élément aux formes organiques qui relie les galeries et les différents niveaux du bâtiment. Citons encore le Mouchoir bleu, porche en acier s'étendant devant l'entrée, ainsi que le Coin rouge, qui abrite les locaux techniques. Du fait de sa position géographique, le nouveau musée est désormais la porte d'accès à la ville lorsqu'on arrive du sud-est.

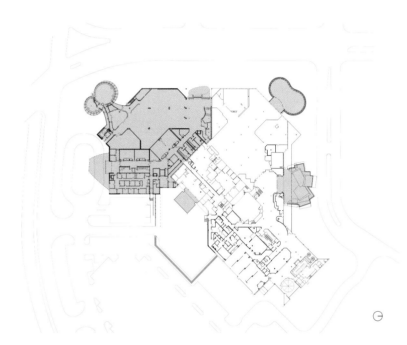

left: Site plan_Aerial view. right: Fully glazed construction_General view.
links: Lageplan_Luftbild. rechts: Verglaste Konstruktion_Gesamtansicht.
à gauche: Plan de situation_Vue aérienne. à droite: Structure entièrement vitrée_Vue générale.

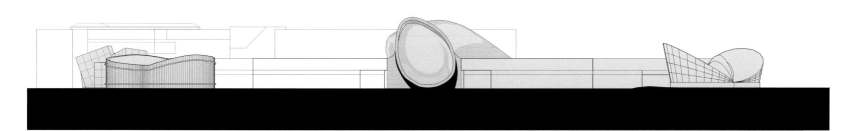

left: Detail exterior. right: Elevation_Roof construction.
links: Detail der Außenansicht. rechts: Ansicht_Dachkonstruktion.
à gauche: Un détail vu de l'extérieur. à droite: Vue en élévation_Structure métallique du porche.

HOPE_RI **SHEPHERD OF THE VALLEY CHAPEL IN HOPE**

**ARCHITECTS:** 3SIX0 ARCHITECTURE & DESIGN
**COMPLETION:** 2008_**TYPOLOGY:** ECCLESIASTICAL
**PHOTOS:** JOHN HORNER

The architects designed a freestanding addition with respect to the origin of the existing church and a need for "spirare" (spirit), "inspirare" (breath) and "spiral," (expanding and contracting space). The order of this chapel's design started with the narrowing trapezoidal plan and its supporting perimeter walls. The ceiling's geometry is square to each supporting wall and the lines of the geometry continue to spiral around like a string wrapping the space.

Die Architekten berücksichtigten bei dem freistehenden Anbau die Ausgangsform der vorhandenen Kirche und den Bedarf an „spirare" (Geist), „inspirare" (Atem) und „Spirale" (Raumausdehnung und -verengung). Beim Entwurf dieser Kapelle wurden zunächst der trapezförmige Grundriss und die tragenden Außenwände verjüngt. Die Geometrie der Decke ist an alle tragenden Wände angepasst. Ihre Linien winden sich spiralförmig um den Raum.

Les architectes ont conçu cette annexe d'une église selon trois axes qui s'imposaient du fait de la nature religieuse du bâtiment (l'esprit, le souffle et le mouvement de l'espace), prenant pour point de départ un plan trapézoïdal. Les lignes qui structurent le plafond sont perpendiculaires par rapport aux murs porteurs, sur lesquels elles redescendent à la verticale, pour se prolonger sur le plancher et enrober ainsi tout l'espace intérieur.

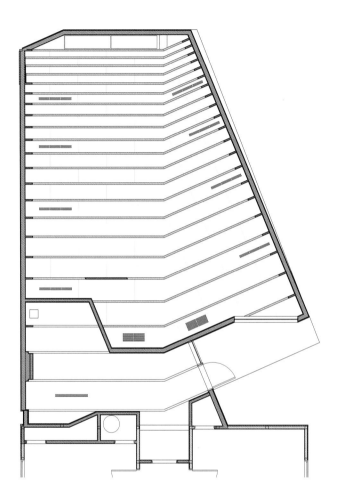

left: Ceiling plan_Exterior view of existing church with chapel extention_Chapel exterior. right: Wooden façade.
links: Deckenplan_Außenansicht der bestehenden Kirche mit erweiterter Kapelle_Außenansicht der Kapelle. rechts: Hölzerne Fassade.
à gauche: Plan du plafond_Vue de l'ensemble constitué par l'église et son annexe_Vue de l'extérieur. à droite: Façade en bois.

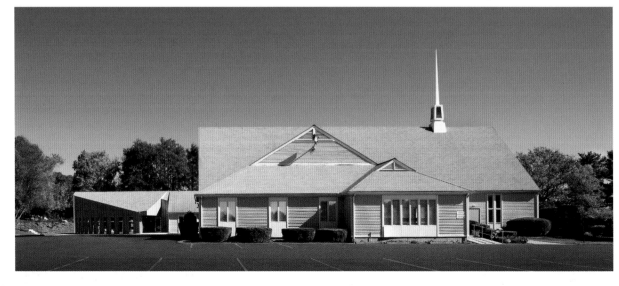

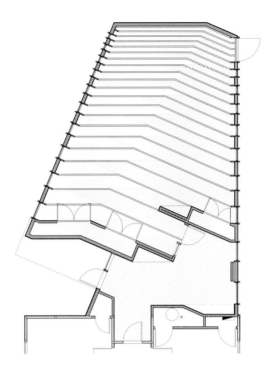

left: Chapel interior. right: Plan_Entrance view_Entry foyer interior_Chapel interior.
links: Blick in die Kapelle. rechts: Plan_Blick auf den Eingang_Eingangshalle_Interieur.
à gauche: Vue de l'intérieur. à droite: Esquisse_Vue de l'entrée_Intérieur du hall d'entrée_
Intérieur de l'annexe.

# FOLLY BEACH_SC **JETTY HOUSE**

**ARCHITECTS:** CUBE DESIGN + RESEARCH
**COMPLETION:** 2006_**TYPOLOGY:** LIVING
**PHOTOS:** RICHARD LEO JOHNSON / ATLANTIC ARCHIVES

The house turns a second-row beach lot into oceanfront property with an elongated structure pushed to one side of the lot that captures views between two houses across the street. Inspired by the beach jetties, the linear body is used like a camera lens to foreshorten the viewing distance. The design breaks with the neighborhood's ubiquitous built-on decks and pitched roofs by treating the roof as valuable real estate, and using negative space to carve out balconies shielding the interior from the summer sun. Selectively placed windows on the east and west walls reinforce telescopic views while providing complete privacy.

Das Haus macht aus einer Strandparzelle in der zweiten Reihe eine Liegenschaft am Meeresufer. Seine lang gestreckte, zu einer Seite des Grundstücks gerückte Konstruktion fängt die Aussichten zwischen zwei Bauten auf der gegenüberliegenden Straßenseite ein. Der lineare, von Strandmolen inspirierte Baukörper wird wie eine Kameralinse eingesetzt, um den Betrachtungsabstand zu verkürzen. Der Entwurf hält sich nicht an die aufgebauten Decks und Satteldächer der Nachbarschaft, sondern behandelt das Dach als wertvollen Grundbesitz, indem Balkons ausmodelliert werden, die das Gebäudeinnere vor der Sommersonne schützen. Gezielt platzierte Fenster verstärken die Fernsicht und sorgen gleichzeitig für völlige Privatsphäre.

Sans être construite sur le front de mer, cette maison offre néanmoins une vue panoramique sur l'océan grâce à sa position entre deux édifices situés de l'autre côté de la rue. Sa forme linaire toute en longueur évoque une jetée ou un téléobjectif qui réduirait les distances. Elle se distingue des bâtiments alentour, caractérisés par des toits à deux pentes, en ce qu'elle présente un toit en terrasse qui augmente la surface habitable, ainsi que par ses balcons en retrait qui protègent l'intérieur d'un réchauffement solaire excessif en été. Des fenêtres placées à des endroits judicieux sur les façades est et ouest offrent également des vues « télescopiques » tout en protégeant l'intérieur des regards indiscrets.

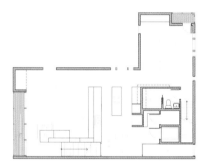

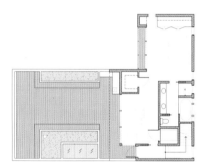

left: Floor plans_Wooden stairs_Staircase_Living space_Exterior view by night. right: East and West façade_View from roof deck to ocean front.
links: Grundrisse_Hölzerne Treppe_Treppenhaus_Wohnbereich_Außenansicht bei Nacht. rechts: Ost- und Westfassade_Blick von der Dachterrasse auf den Ozean.
à gauche: Plan des différents étages_Escaliers en bois_Cage d'escalier_Séjour_Façade au crépuscule. à droite: East and west façade.

GRAY_TN **EAST TENNESSEE STATE UNIVERSITY AND GENERAL SHALE BRICK NATURAL HISTORY MUSEUM AND VISITOR CENTER, GRAY FOSSIL SITE**

**ARCHITECTS:** HBG L HNEDAK BOBO GROUP (FORMERLY BULLOCK SMITH & PARTNERS), AND VAUGHAN & MELTON
**COMPLETION:** 2007_**TYPOLOGY:** CULTURE
**PHOTOS:** DENISE RETALLACK

Fittingly, one of man's oldest building materials, namely brick, has been used for the façade of one of the newest and most significant fossil museums in the United States. Part museum, part laboratory and part visitor center, the building, which sits on five acres of land in Gray, Tennessee, has been built directly at the site of one of the richest deposits of prehistoric animal fossils ever to be unearthed. Brick is used as the sole exterior cladding material along with transitional interior brick elements. At the entrance, an arrangement of three seemingly fragmented, irregular red brick elements evokes a dynamic geological "cave" metaphor and invites the visitor to enter through one of the gaps, which are spanned with dark glass.

Für die Fassade eines der neuesten und bedeutendsten Fossilienmuseen der Vereinigten Staaten kam passenderweise das uralte Material Ziegelstein zum Einsatz. Teils Museum, teils Labor und teils Besucherzentrum steht das Gebäude auf einem Grundstück mit einem der reichsten Vorkommen an prähistorischen Tierfossilien. Als alleiniges Material der Außenverkleidung wird Ziegelstein auch für überleitende Elemente im Innern verwendet. Am Eingang erinnern drei bruchstückhafte Ziegelsteinelemente an eine geologische „Höhlen"-Metapher und laden Besucher ein, durch eine der mit Sonnenschutzglas überspannten Öffnungen einzutreten.

Pour la façade de ce nouveau musée consacré aux fossiles, les architectes ont choisi le matériau le plus ancien utilisé par l'Humanité: la brique. Le bâtiment, qui abrite également un laboratoire et un centre d'accueil des visiteurs, se trouve à Gray, dans le Tennessee, sur un terrain de deux hectares situé à proximité immédiate de l'un des plus importants gisements de fossiles d'animaux jamais découverts. La brique, qui recouvre entièrement toutes les façades, est également présente à l'intérieur. L'entrée en verre teinté est positionnée entre trois volumes distincts de taille inégale qui évoquent une grotte des temps géologiques.

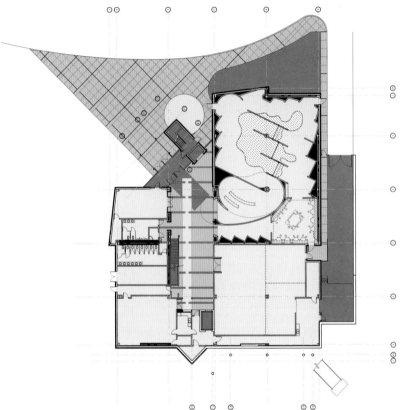

left: First floor plan_Exhibition_Lobby. right: Entrance view_Detail façade.
links: Grundriss erstes Obergeschoss_Ausstellung_Eingangshalle. rechts: Eingangsansicht_Fassadendetail.
à gauche: Plan du rez-de-chaussée_Salle d'exposition_Hall d'entrée. à droite: Vue de l'entrée_Bas-reliefs de la façade.

# CLARKE COUNTY_VA **BOXHEAD**

**ARCHITECTS:** CARTER + BURTON ARCHITECTURE
**COMPLETION:** 2007_**TYPOLOGY:** LIVING
**PHOTOS:** DANIEL AFZAL

This three-bedroom house has an open plan and a "boxes in boxes" design approach with an economy of scale strategy, in which each smaller box becomes more precious. The plastered insulated concrete block walls and the concrete floor provide thermal mass and a heat sink which works with the super insulation provided by the exposed structural insulated panels. These distinct materials blur the definition of inside and out. A reduction of new materials and waste is also achieved with concrete cut outs and are recycled from a dumpster into floor and wall tile, which were specifically used for the master bathroom.

Das Haus mit drei Schlafzimmern hat einen offenen Grundriss und setzt mit einer ökonomischen maßstabsgetreuen Strategie das „boxes in boxes" Design um. Mit abnehmender Größe wird jeder Kasten kostbarer. Die gedämmten verputzten Wände aus Betonblocksteinen und der Betonfußboden sorgen für eine thermisch wirksame Masse und ein Heizmedium, das mit dem Höchstwärmeschutz der exponierten Bauplatten zusammenwirkt. Diese spezifischen Materialien lassen die Grenzen zwischen Innen und Außen verschwimmen. Aussparungen im Beton verringern den Verbrauch an neuen Baustoffen und die Abfallmenge. Im Elternbad finden sich ein Fußbodenbelag und eine Wandverkleidungsplatte aus einem recycelten Container.

Cette maison avec trois chambres se caractérise par un plan ouvert et un concept gigogne qui vise à économiser l'espace, la valeur des pièces croissant de manière inversement proportionnelle à leur taille. Le sol et les murs en béton revêtus d'enduit créent une masse qui fonctionne comme un régulateur thermique en liaison avec les panneaux super-isolants de la façade. Ces différents matériaux contribuent à estomper la limite entre intérieur et extérieur. La découpe des ouvertures dans le béton et l'utilisation de produits recyclés (notamment les carrelages du sol et de la salle de bain principale) ont par ailleurs contribué à réduire les déchets et la consommation de matériaux.

left: Ground floor plan_Living space_View towards second floor. right: Exterior view by night_Kitchen.
links: Grundriss Erdgeschoss_Wohnraum_Blick ins zweite Obergeschoss. rechts: Außenansicht bei Nacht_Küche.
à gauche: Plan du rez-de-chaussée_Séjour_Séjour et mezzanine. à droite: La maison au crépuscule_Cuisine.

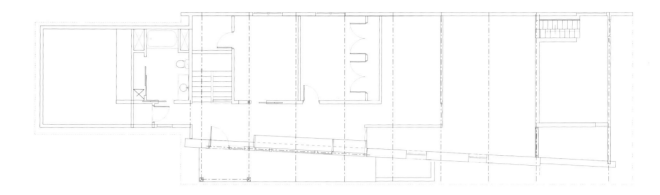

left: Exposed living space. right: Second floor plan_Bathroom.
links: Offener Wohnbereich. rechts: Grundriss zweites Obergeschoss_Badezimmer.
à gauche: Mezzanine au-dessus du séjour. à droite: Plan du niveau supérieur_Salle de bain.

MIDDLEBURY_VT **ATWATER COMMONS, MIDDLEBURY COLLEGE**

**ARCHITECTS:** KIERANTIMBERLAKE ASSOCIATES
**COMPLETION:** 2004_**TYPOLOGY:** EDUCATION
**PHOTOS:** HALKIN PHOTOGRAPHY LLC

Middlebury College is in the process of converting its 2,250-student campus into five residential commons of 450 students each. The Atwater project supplements existing housing with 154 new beds for seniors with single bedrooms in suite configurations and a new 225-seat dining hall. Two new stone-clad residential buildings frame distant views to the north and back to Le Chateau, an icon on campus. The dining hall is articulated as a glazed pavilion, nestled into the woods and providing tree-level views out to the town of Middlebury and the mountains beyond.

Middlebury College wird von einem Campus für 2.250 Studenten in fünf Wohnanlagen mit jeweils 450 Studenten umgebaut. Das Projekt Atwater ergänzt die vorhandenen Wohnbauten um 154 neue Betten für die Oberstufe mit aneinander gereihten Einzelzimmern und um einen neuen Speisesaal mit 225 Plätzen. Zwei mit Naturstein verkleidete Neubauten rahmen die Fernsicht nach Norden und auf die Rückfront von Le Chateau, einer Ikone auf dem Campus. Der Speisesaal liegt als verglaster Pavillon eingebettet in den Wäldern und bietet auf Baumebene Aussichten auf die Stadt Middlebury und die Berge dahinter.

Le Middlebury College est un institut universitaire pouvant accueillir 2.250 étudiants logés dans cinq bâtiments de 450 personnes chacun. Le projet Atwater, initié de manière à augmenter la capacité d'accueil, a porté sur la réalisation de logements pour 154 « seniors » supplémentaires, et sur la construction d'un restaurant de 225 places. Les deux nouveaux édifices de logements, dont les façades sont parées en pierres naturelles, déterminent une perspective sur le château emblématique du site. Le restaurant — un pavillon en verre entouré d'arbres qui s'élève sur trois niveaux — offre des vues sur la ville de Middlebury et les collines environnantes.

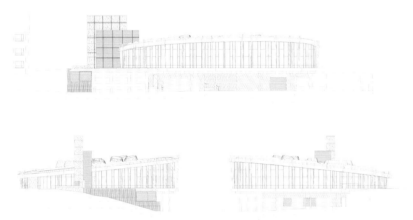

left: Elevations_Aeriel view_View from the common green to the stone-clad residential building.
right: Glass façade detail.
links: Ansichten_Luftbild_Blick von der Grünfläche auf die Häuser mit Steinummatelung. rechts: Detail der Glasfassade.
à gauche: Deux vues en élévation_Vue aérienne_Vue générale. à droite: Gros plan sur la façade en verre du restaurant.

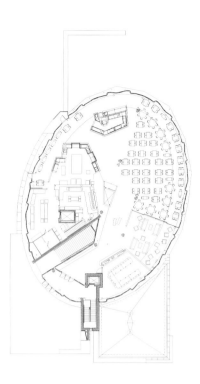

left: Cafeteria. right: Floor plans_Lounge.
links: Mensa. rechts: Grundrisse_Aufenthaltshalle.
à gauche. Cafétéria. à droite: Plans_Foyer.

# SMUGGLERS NOTCH_VT **VERTICAL HOUSE**

**ARCHITECTS:** AXIS MUNDI
**COMPLETION:** 2005_**TYPOLOGY:** LIVING
**PHOTOS:** REINHOLD & CO.

The vertical house offers urban living on a rural site. The concept of a town-house transposed to the country offers a unique solution to a difficult topology and affords spectacular views. A long and dramatic bridge provides entry to a viewing platform from which one ascends a staircase into the house. The kitchen and dining areas are located on the first level, the living area is on the second level, and the master bedroom is on the third level. An open-air garden is situated on the roof. The intention is that over time the house will be covered with vines descending from the roof, in effect making it into a modern ruin.

Das vertikale Haus bietet städtisches Wohnen auf einem Grundstück im ländlichen Raum. Der aufs Land übertragene Entwurf eines Stadthauses bietet eine einzigartige Lösung für eine schwierige Topologie und gewährt spektakuläre Aussichten. Eine lange Brücke dient als Eingang zu einer Aussichts-plattform, von der eine Treppe ins Haus hinaufführt. Im ersten Geschoss liegen die Küche und das Esszimmer, im zweiten der Wohnbereich und im dritten das Schlafzimmer. Auf dem Dach ist ein Freiluftgarten angelegt. Im Laufe der Zeit soll das Haus mit Kletterpflanzen bedeckt sein, die vom Dach hinabwachsen und es so in eine moderne Ruine verwandeln.

Cette maison toute en hauteur transpose à la campagne un concept architec-tural typiquement urbain: l'appartement sur plusieurs niveaux. Cette solu-tion inhabituelle rendue nécessaire par la configuration du terrain présente l'avantage d'offrir des vues remarquables sur les environs. Une longue pas-serelle permet d'accéder à une plate-forme panoramique et à l'escalier qui dessert l'intérieur. La cuisine et la salle à manger sont situées au premier étage, le séjour au-dessus et la chambre tout en haut. Le toit en terrasse est aménagé en jardin. La vigne prévue ici est appelée à couvrir l'ensemble des façades avec le temps, le bâtiment devant ainsi prendre l'aspect d'une ruine moderne.

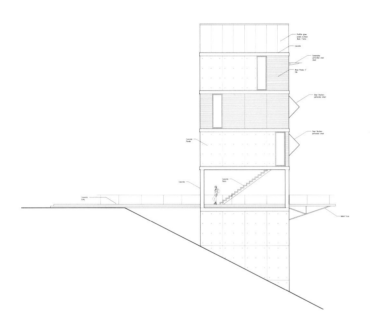

left: Section_Exterior view, hillside_Model_Model with alternative view. right: Entry bridge to viewing area.
links: Schnitt_Außenansicht, Hanglage_Modell_Alternative Modellansicht. rechts: Brückenaufgang zur Aussichtsplattform.
à gauche: Vues encoupe_La maison à flac de colline_Maquette_Autre vue de la maquette. à droite: Passerelle vers la plate-forme panoramique.

COLLECTION

# central

# DENVER_CO **MUSEUM OF CONTEMPORARY ART**

**ARCHITECTS:** ADJAYE ASSOCIATES
**COMPLETION:** 2007_**TYPOLOGY:** CULTURE
**PHOTOS:** LYNDON DOUGLAS

The new facility is an environmentally sustainable building, which has gained the distinction of Gold Leadership in Energy and Environment Design (LEED), and is the nation's first LEED certified contemporary art museum. LEED certification allows MCA/ Denver to take a leadership role in the reduction of energy consumption, greenhouse gas emissions and use of raw materials. With 20,000 square feet of exhibition, education and lecture spaces, bookshop and a roof garden for outdoor art, the new gallery is like a European 'kunsthalle', presenting new work from around the world.

Das nachhaltige Gebäude mit einem LEED- (Leadership in Energy and Environment Design-) Gold-Status ist das erste amerikanische Museum für zeitgenössische Kunst mit diesem Umweltsiegel. Die LEED-Zertifizierung macht MCA/ Denver zu einem Vorreiter bei der Senkung von Energie- und Rohstoffverbrauch sowie Treibhausgasemissionen. Auf einer Fläche von 1.860 Quadratmeter bietet das Museum Platz für Ausstellungen, Museumspädagogik und Vorträge, einen Buchladen und einen Dachgarten für Kunst im Freien. Wie eine europäische Kunsthalle präsentiert die neue Galerie Werke aus der ganzen Welt.

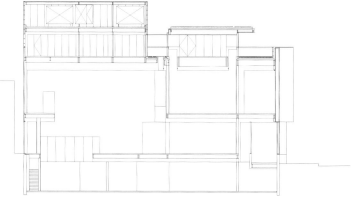

Le bâtiment qui abrite ce musée d'art contemporain se présente comme sept boîtes empilées les unes sur les autres avec un certain décalage. Cet aspect inhabituel résulte partiellement des contraintes imposées par le zonage. Sur un terrain mesurant seulement vingt-deux mètres par trente-quatre, ne pas construire à la verticale mais décaler les différents volumes vers le nord, le sud, l'est et l'ouest a en effet permis d'optimiser l'utilisation de la surface au sol, tout en rendant possible l'éclairage zénithal à tous les étages. D'autre part, un système d'écrans réglables évite l'éblouissement des visiteurs et la détérioration des œuvres exposées sous l'effet de la lumière solaire.

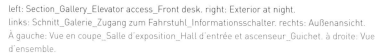

left: Section_Gallery_Elevator access_Front desk. right: Exterior at night.
links: Schnitt_Galerie_Zugang zum Fahrstuhl_Informationsschalter. rechts: Außenansicht.
À gauche: Vue en coupe_Salle d'exposition_Hall d'entrée et ascenseur_Guichet. à droite: Vue d'ensemble.

DENVER_CO **THE CHILDREN'S HOSPITAL**

**ARCHITECTS:** ZIMMER GUNSUL FRASCA ARCHITECTS
**COMPLETION:** 2007_**TYPOLOGY:** HEALTH
**PHOTOS:** COURTESY OF THE ARCHITECTS

When The Children's Hospital (TCH) set out to build its new $425 million facility, the mission was straightforward: create the most healing hospital for kids by embodying both the concept of family-centered care and utilizing the latest evidence-based design techniques. The result is a 1.44 million square-foot hospital (completed in October of 2007) that is bright, nurturing, calm and full of amenities – from a gelato bar, to a teen "hot spot" featuring a movie theater and pool table, to staff and patient lounges.

Bei der Planung einer neuen 425 Millionen Dollar teuren Einrichtung für The Children's Hospital waren die Vorgaben einfach: ein sehr effizientes Kinderkrankenhaus durch die Einbeziehung eines familienorientierten Behandlungskonzepts und die Verwendung modernster empirischer Entwurfs-methoden. Das Ergebnis ist eine Klinik mit einer Fläche von 133.780 Quadrat-metern. Sie zeichnet sich durch eine helle, fröhliche und ruhige Atmosphäre aus und besitzt viele Annehmlichkeiten – wie eine Gelato-Bar über einen Teenager-„Hotspot" mit Kino und Billardtisch bis zu den Sitzgelegenheiten für Mitarbeiter und Patienten.

L'objectif était clair lors du lancement de ce projet de 425 millions de dollars: optimiser les soins destinés aux enfants grâce à un concept reprenant les structures familiales et à l'utilisation des toutes dernières techniques archi-tecturales. Les travaux ont eu pour résultat un hôpital clair, calme, réconfor-tant et pourvu de divers agréments, notamment un café glacier, des salles de détente pour les patients et le personnel, ainsi qu'un espace pour les ados avec cinéma et billard.

left: First floor plan_Hallway_Patients' room. right: Street side view_General view.
links: Grundriss erstes Obergeschoss_Patientenzimmer. rechts: Straßenansicht_Gesamtansicht.
à gauche: Plan du rez-de-chaussée_Accueil et couloir_Vue d'une chambre. à droite: L'hôpital la nuit_L'hôpital le jour.

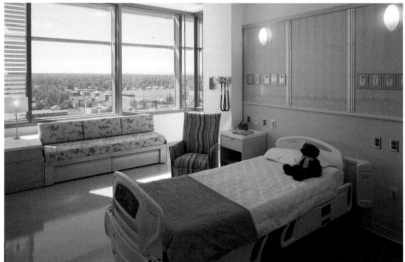

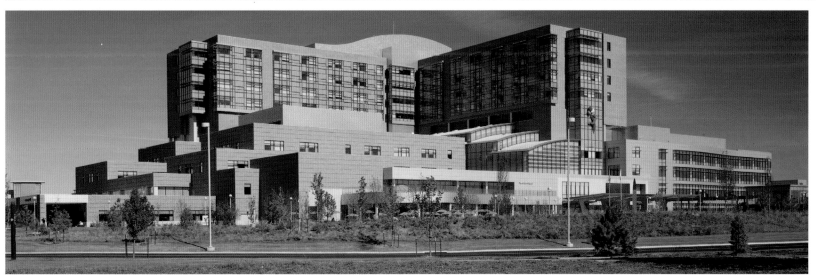

left: Detail of colorful floor design. right: Sixth floor plan_Inner courtyard_Waiting area.
links: Detail der Bodenbemalung. rechts: Grundriss sechstes Obergeschoss_Lichthof_Wartezimmer.
à gauche: Revêtement de sol multicolore. à droite: Plan du sixième étage_Vue du hall_Deux vues de la salle d'attente.

# DENVER_CO **DENVER ART MUSEUM RESIDENCES**

**ARCHITECTS:** STUDIO DANIEL LIBESKIND
**COMPLETION:** 2008_**TYPOLOGY:** MIXED-USE
**PHOTOS:** BITTER BREDT, RON POLLARD

The Museum Residences make an inspiring contribution to the cultural nexus of the city and complement the neighboring extension. The soft qualities of the translucent glass skin, combined with the metal-clad geometric forms, provide an elegant partner to the titanium-clad Museum. Six of the seven floors are residential, with space on the ground floor dedicated to retail. The building wraps around two sides of a 1000-car public parking garage. Its 56 luxury units range from 800 square feet studios to 5000 square feet penthouse suites.

Die Museum Residences tragen eindrucksvoll zur kulturellen Verknüpfung der Stadt bei und ergänzen den benachbarten Erweiterungsbau. Durch die zarte Beschaffenheit der lichtdurchlässigen Glashaut in Kombination mit den metallverkleideten geometrischen Formen erhält das mit Titan bedeckte Museum einen eleganten Partner. Sechs der sieben Geschosse sind für Wohnzwecke vorgesehen, wobei das Erdgeschoss für den Einzelhandel bestimmt ist. Das Gebäude umhüllt zwei Seiten einer öffentlichen Parkgarage für 1.000 Fahrzeuge. Seine 56 Luxuswohneinheiten reichen von 74 Quadratmeter großen Studios bis zu Penthaussuiten mit einer Fläche von 464 Quadratmeter.

Par son enveloppe en verre translucide et en plaques de métal aux formes géométriques, cet immeuble résidentiel constitue un élégant complément du musée revêtu de titanium qui compose le centre de la vie culturelle de Denver. Des boutiques sont installées au rez-de-chaussée, tandis que les six étages supérieurs abritent cinquante-six logements de standing d'une superficie allant de 243 à 1524 mètres carrés en duplex. Le complexe inclut également un parking public d'un millier de places.

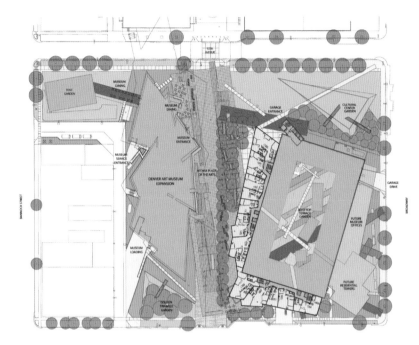

left: Site plan_Interior with view_Bathtub_View of museum expansion. right: Exterior_View from plaza_Detail of exterior.
links: Lageplan_Inneneinrichtung mit Ausblick_Badewanne_Blick auf die Museumserweiterung. rechts: Außenansicht_Vorplatz_Detail der Außenfassade.
à gauche: Plan de situation_Intérieur_Salle de bain_Vue sur l'annexe du musée. à droite: Extérieur_Le bâtiment et l'esplanade_Détail de l'extérieur.

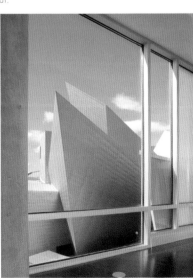

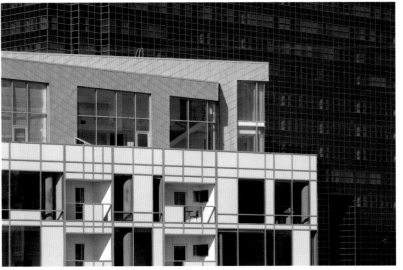

DENVER_CO **EXTENSION TO THE DENVER ART MUSEUM, FREDERIC C. HAMILTON BUILDING**

**ARCHITECTS:** STUDIO DANIEL LIBESKIND
**COMPLETION:** 2006_**TYPOLOGY:** CULTURE
**PHOTOS:** BITTER BREDT

The extension is an expansion of the existing museum, and is not designed as a stand-alone building, but as part of a composition of public spaces, monuments and gateways in this developing part of the city, contributing to the synergy amongst neighbors, large and intimate. The materials closely relate to the existing context (local stone) as well as innovative new materials (titanium), which together form spaces that connect local Denver tradition to the 21st century. The dialog between the boldness of construction and the romanticism of the landscape with its views of the sky and the Rocky Mountains creates a unique place.

Bei dem Anbau handelt es sich um die Erweiterung des bestehenden Museums. Er ist nicht als selbstständiges Gebäude konzipiert, sondern gehört zu einer Komposition aus öffentlichen Freiflächen, Denkmälern und Zugängen in diesem in der Entwicklung begriffenen Teil der Stadt. Das Gebäude trägt zum Zusammenhalt der Nachbarbauten bei. Seine Materialien korrespondieren sowohl mit dem vorhandenen Kontext (lokaler Naturstein) als auch mit innovativen neuen Baustoffen (Titan). Zusammen ergeben sie Räume, die Denvers örtliche Tradition mit dem 21. Jahrhundert verknüpfen. Der Dialog zwischen der kühnen Konstruktion und der romantischen Landschaft mit ihren Aussichten auf den Himmel und die Rocky Mountains schafft einen einzigartigen Ort.

Cette annexe du musée des beaux-arts de Denver fait partie d'un plan d'urbanisme qui inclut également des monuments et divers espaces publics, contribuant ainsi à générer une synergie au sein du quartier. Le bâtiment associe la pierre d'origine locale et le titanium de manière à jeter un pont entre le tissu urbain traditionnel et le XXIe siècle. L'originalité du site vient du contraste saisissant entre la hardiesse de l'architecture et l'aspect romantique des Montagnes Rocheuses qui se découpent à l'horizon.

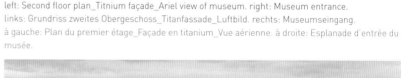

left: Second floor plan_Titnium façade_Ariel view of museum. right: Museum entrance.
links: Grundriss zweites Obergeschoss_Titanfassade_Luftbild. rechts: Museumseingang.
à gauche: Plan du premier étage_Façade en titanium_Vue aérienne. à droite: Esplanade d'entrée du musée.

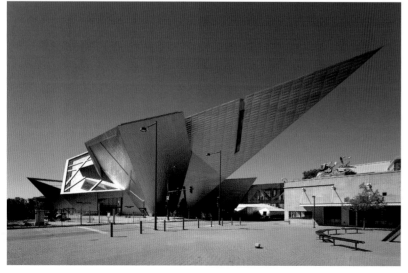

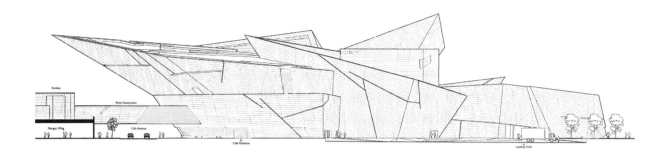

left: Atrium. right: Elevation_Atrium view from stairs_Gallery_Interior gallery.
links: Lichthof. rechts: Ansicht_Blick in den Lichthof_Galerie_Interieur.
à gauche: Plan du premier étage_Façade en titanium_Vue aérienne. à droite: Esplanade d'entrée du musée.

DES MOINES_IA **DES MOINES PUBLIC LIBRARY**

**ARCHITECTS:** DAVID CHIPPERFIELD ARCHITECTS
**COMPLETION:** 2006_**TYPOLOGY:** PUBLIC
**PHOTOS:** FARSHID ASSASSI

Located at the east end of the park, the new library acts as a link between downtown Des Moines and the park. The two-story concrete structure sits above an underground car park and is entirely wrapped in a composite energy efficient glass-metal skin. Laminated between two glass surfaces, a layer of expanded copper mesh reduces glare and solar gain, thus greatly reducing long-term energy costs. The mesh is the only sun-shading device necessary, ensuring that the view from the inside into the park is maintained at all times. Slight variations in the make up of the panels provide the library with a differentiated yet uniform skin, emphasizing the organic shape of the building.

Am östlichen Ende des Parks vermittelt die Bibliothek zwischen der Innenstadt von Des Moines und der Parkanlage. Die einer Tiefgarage aufgesetzte zweistöckige Betonkonstruktion wird von einer energieeffizienten Verbundfassade aus Glas und Metall umhüllt. Ein Kupfergewebe zwischen zwei Lagen Glas sorgt für Wärme- und Blendschutz, sodass die Energiekosten langfristig deutlich gesenkt werden. Als einzig erforderlicher Sonnenschutz gewährleistet das Gewebe jederzeit Ausblicke von innen in den Park. Leicht unterschiedlich aufgebaute Paneele verleihen der Fassade ein differenziertes, doch einheitliches Erscheinungsbild und unterstreichen so die organische Gebäudegestalt.

Cette nouvelle bibliothèque sert de lien entre le centre ville de Des Moines et le parc qui s'étend à l'ouest. Il s'agit d'un bâtiment en béton sur deux niveaux, construit au-dessus d'un parking souterrain et doté d'une enveloppe composite à haute efficacité thermique. L'enveloppe, formée par un filet en cuivre coulé entre deux plaques de verre, filtre les rayons du soleil et réduit considérablement les dépenses énergétiques sur le long terme. De plus, le filet de cuivre rend superflue l'installation de stores, de sorte que les utilisateurs bénéficient continuellement de vues sur le parc environnant. De légères variations dans la réalisation des panneaux de l'enveloppe introduisent certaines nuances dans l'apparente uniformité du bâtiment, tout en soulignant sa forme organique.

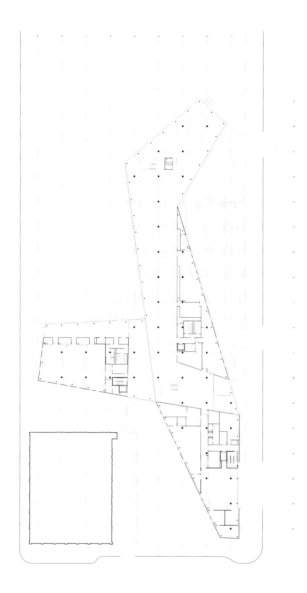

left: Floor plan_Bookcases and reading space_Reference desks. right: Façade detail_Exterior with city view_Entrance view.
links: Grundriss_Bücherregale und Leseplatz_Infromation. rechts: Fassadendetail_Außenansicht_ Eingangsansicht.
à gauche: Plan_Étagères dans la salle de lecture_Guichet d'information. à droite: Façade_La bibliothèque dans son contexte urbain_Vue de la façade et de l'entrée.

IOWA_IA **SCHOOL OF ART & ART HISTORY, UNIVERSITY OF IOWA**

**ARCHITECTS:** STEVEN HOLL ARCHITECTS, LOCAL ARCHITECT: HERBERT LEWIS KRUSE BLUNCK ARCHITECTURE
**COMPLETION:** 2006_**TYPOLOGY:** EDUCATION
**PHOTOS:** CHRISTIAN RICHTERS

The campus merges with the urban grid of Iowa City, which has the old State Capitol of 1842 as its symbolic center. Projected across the Iowa River, the grid becomes distorted as it meets the topography of ravines and hills descending to the river's west bank, where a series of buildings for the arts are aligned: theater, museum and the original 1936 School of Art building. Engaging the edges of the reclaimed pond, the building's fuzzy edges create new campus spaces and pathways. A double height reading room marks a new campus gateway, and bracketed between the elevated arms is a sunny desk suspended over the water forming a gathering space.

Der Campus verschmilzt mit dem städtischen Raster von Iowa City, deren symbolische Mitte das alte Regierungsgebäude von 1842 einnimmt. Das über den Fluss Iowa geplante Raster ist an der Stelle verformt, an der es auf die Schlucht- und Hügeltopographie trifft, die zum Westufer des Flusses hinuntersteigt. Hier reihen sich das Theater, das Museum und das Originalgebäude der Kunstschule von 1936 aneinander. Da die aufgelösten Gebäudekanten die Ränder eines sanierten Weihers einbeziehen, entstehen auf dem Campus weitere Bereiche und Wege. Ein zweigeschossiger Lesesaal markiert ein neues Tor zum Campus. Zwischen den erhöhten Querträgern „schwebt" eine sonnige Begegnungsstätte über dem Wasser.

l'autre côté de la rivière, les immeubles s'échelonnent sur les ravins et collines de la rive ouest. C'est ici que se trouvent divers édifices culturels, dont le théâtre, le musée et l'école des beaux-arts construite en 1936. Une annexe a été récemment construite, en partie au-dessus d'un étang. Elle se compose notamment d'une salle de lecture s'élevant sur deux étages qui marque désormais l'entrée du campus, et d'une plate-forme suspendue sur l'eau où les étudiants peuvent se réunir.

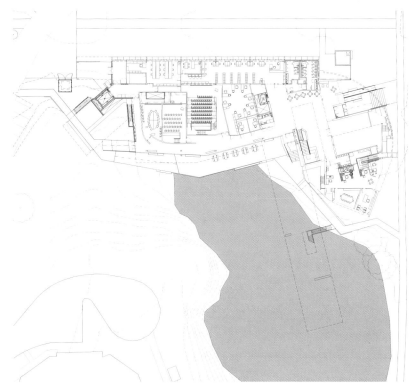

left: Site plan_General view_Façade. right: Entry view.
links: Lageplan_Gesamtansicht_Fassade. rechts: Eingangsansicht.
á gauche: Plan du situation_Vue générale_Façade. á droite: Vue de l'entrée.

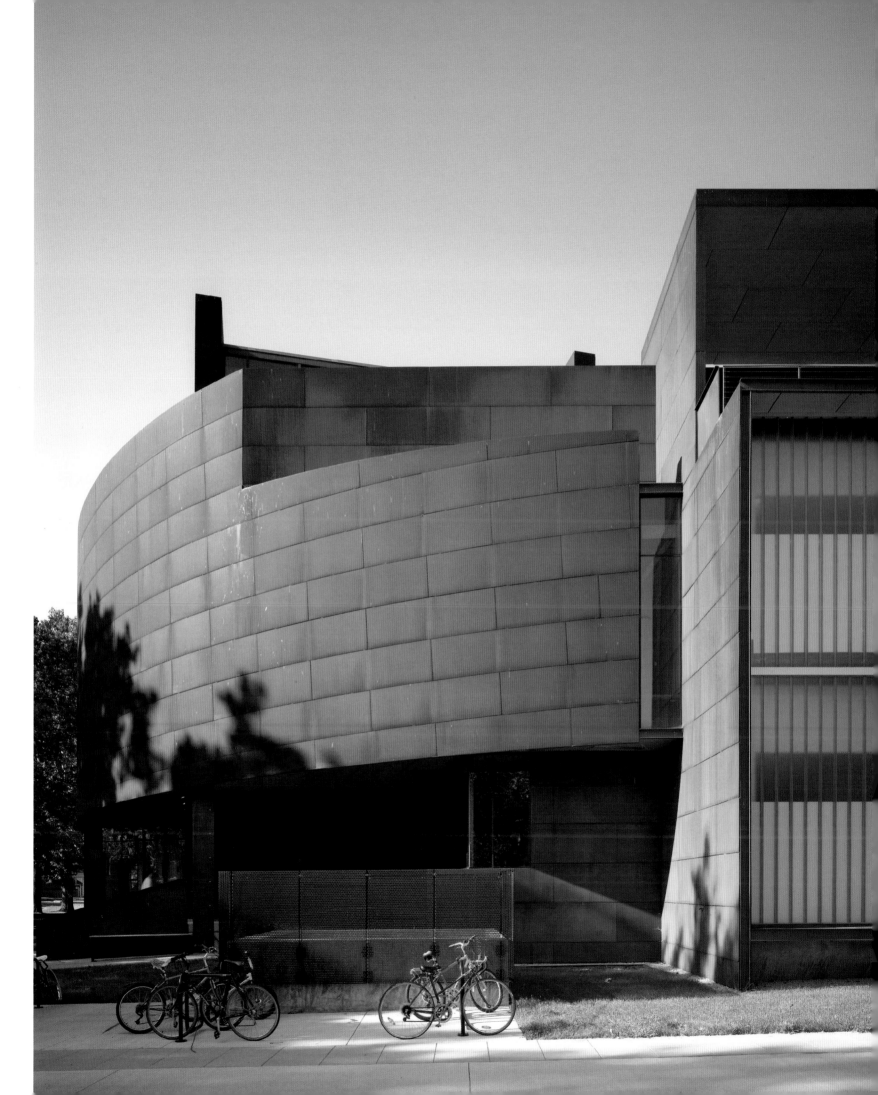

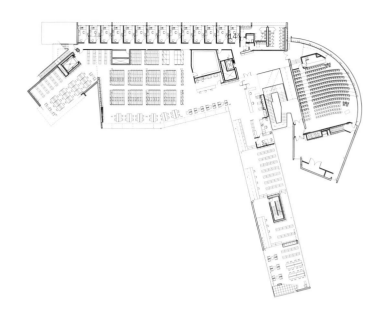

left: Interior. right: Floor plan_Entry.
links: Interieur. rechts: Grundriss_Eingang.
á gauche: Vue de l'intérieur. á droite: Plan_L'entrée.

CHICAGO_IL **GARY COMER YOUTH CENTER**

**ARCHITECTS:** JOHN RONAN ARCHITECTS
**COMPLETION:** 2006_**TYPOLOGY:** EDUCATION
**PHOTOS:** COURTESY OF THE ARCHITECTS

The award-winning Gary Comer Youth Center, a three-story, 75,000-square-foot facility was designed to specifically support the activities of The South Shore Drill Team and programs for children of the neighboring Paul Revere School. Educational and recreational spaces wrap the Drill Team's main practice and performance area, with major spaces exposed on the building exterior to promote the activity inside to the community, and invite participation.

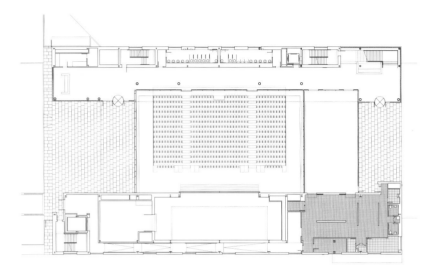

Das preisgekrönte Gary Comer Youth Center, eine dreigeschossige Einrichtung mit einer Fläche von 6.970 Quadratmetern, soll insbesondere die Aktivitäten des South Shore Drill Team und die Programme für Kinder der benachbarten Paul-Revere-Schule unterstützen. Um den Hauptübungs- und Vorführbereich des Drill Team reihen sich Unterrichts- und Pausenräume. Die größeren Räume weisen zur Außenfront, um mit Einblicken in das Geschehen im Gebäude bei der Gemeinde zu werben und zur Teilnahme aufzufordern.

Ce centre culturel de 6.970 mètres carrés sur trois niveaux qui a remporté un prix d'architecture a été construit spécialement pour la South Shore Drill Team, une association locale qui s'occupe des jeunes à problèmes scolarisés à la Paul Revere School voisine. On y trouve divers espaces récréatifs et éducatifs, notamment pour les répétitions et les spectacles. D'autre part, le centre culturel est largement ouvert sur l'extérieur de manière à accroître sa notoriété au niveau local et à inviter les jeunes à participer aux activités proposées.

left: Floor plan_Hallway_Auditorium. right: Street view at night_Exterior_Façade detail.
links: Grundriss_Korridor_Auditorium. rechts: Straßenansicht bei Nacht_Fassadendetail.
à gauche: Plan_Couloir_Auditorium. à droite: Le bâtiment vu de la rue la nuit_Vue générale_Détail de la façade.

# CHICAGO_IL **AQUA TOWER**

**ARCHITECTS:** STUDIO GANG ARCHITECTS
**ASSOCIATE ARCHITECTS:** LOEWENBERG ARCHITECTS
**COMPLETION:** 2009_**TYPOLOGY:** MIXED-USE
**PHOTOS:** STUDIO GANG ARCHITECTS

Aqua Tower is an 82-story mixed-use high-rise with apartments, condominiums, offices, parking and a hotel. Unlike a tower in an open field, new towers in urban environments must negotiate small view corridors between existing buildings. In response to this, a series of contours defined by outdoor terraces extends away from the face of Aqua to capture views between neighboring buildings. These terraces gradually undulate over the height of the building. Shaping of the terraces is further defined by criteria such as solar shading and dwelling type. The result is a high-rise tower particular to its site that allows residents to inhabit the façade of the building and the city simultaneously.

Aqua Tower ist ein 82 Stockwerke hoher Wolkenkratzer mit Apartments, Eigentumswohnungen, Büros, Parkhaus und Hotel. Im Gegensatz zu einem Turm in freier Landschaft sind neue Hochhäuser in städtischer Umwelt mit schmalen Blickschneisen zwischen bestehenden Bauten konfrontiert. Als Antwort darauf entfernen sich die Umrisslinien der Außenterrassen von der Gebäudefront, um zwischen den Nachbarbauten Ausblicke einzufangen. Diese Terrassen überziehen das Gebäude in einer sanften Wellenstruktur. Ihre Gestaltung bestimmen auch Aspekte wie Sonnenschutz und Wohnungstyp. Das Ergebnis ist ein vielgeschossiges, auf seinen Standort zugeschnittenes Gebäude, dessen Nutzer seine Fassade und die Stadt gleichzeitig bewohnen können.

Cette tour de quatre-vingt-deux étages abrite des appartements, un hôtel, des bureaux et un parking. À la différence des gratte-ciel construits en banlieue, les tours implantées dans un tissu urbain dense doivent être construites en prévoyant des vues en perspective. C'est pourquoi les architectes ont conçu ici une multitude de balcons aux contours ondulants qui permettent aux occupants d'apprécier des perspectives entre les bâtiments qui se dressent aux alentours. La forme générale des balcons sur l'ensemble de la façade a été déterminée en fonction du rayonnement solaire et des particularités de chacun des appartements. Avec pour résultat une tour à la silhouette caractéristique, qui permet aux occupants de sortir en plein air pour apprécier des vues sur la ville.

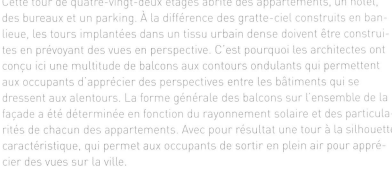

left: Typical floor plan_Aqua's terraces create wave-like forms_View of the terraces _Front façade. right: Perspective view.
links: Regelgrundriss_Aquas Terrassen erzeugen eine wellenartige Struktur_Blick auf die Terrassen_Vorderfassade. rechts: Perspektive.
à gauche: Plan typique_Balcons aux contours ondulants qui évoquent l'eau_Gros plan sur des balcons_Face avant. à droite: Vue en perspective.

CHICAGO_IL **SOS CHILDREN'S VILLAGES LAVEZZORIO COMMUNITY CENTER**

**ARCHITECTS:** STUDIO GANG ARCHITECTS
**COMPLETION:** 2007_**TYPOLOGY:** EDUCATION
**PHOTOS:** STEVE HALL © HEDRICH BLESSING

The 16,000-square-foot community center in Chicago enables the international nonprofit to fulfill its mission of training foster parents and reuniting siblings into foster care families. At the entry stands a stratified wall created by layering various concrete mixes. Wavy lines, articulating each pour, preserve the physics of concrete's once fluid nature. Inside, access to daylight is maximized through orientation around a courtyard. An extra-wide stair in the lobby doubles as seating and an impromptu stage for performances.

In dem 1.486 Quadratmeter großen Gemeinschaftszentrum in Chicago widmet sich die internationale gemeinnützige Organisation der Ausbildung von Pflegeeltern und der Zusammenführung von Geschwistern in Pflegefamilien. Am Eingang befindet sich eine aus verschiedenen Betonmischungen aufgeschichtete Wand. Wellenlinien artikulieren jede gegossene Schicht und bewahren die Eigenschaften des einst flüssigen Betons. Damit die Innenräume möglichst viel Tageslicht erhalten, sind sie um einen Hof angeordnet. In der Eingangshalle dient eine extra breite Treppe auch als Sitzgelegenheit und Bühne für spontane Vorführungen.

Ce bâtiment de 1.486 mètres carrés construit à Chicago abrite les locaux d'un organisme à but non lucratif dont la mission consiste à former des parents qui se proposent d'adopter des frères et sœurs séparés de leur famille. La façade d'entrée présente des bandes ondulantes de différentes teintes réalisées en utilisant plusieurs sortes de béton coulées l'une après l'autre de manière à rappeler que le matériau, aujourd'hui immuable, était à l'origine malléable. Sur l'autre façade, de grandes baies vitrées ouvrent largement l'intérieur sur une cour. L'escalier qui mène au premier étage se double de gradins sur lesquels on peut prendre place pour regarder un spectacle impromptu.

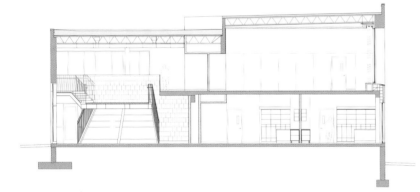

left: Section_Lobby_Children's play area. right: Exterior view_Concrete façade from courtyard.
links: Schnitt_Eingangshalle_Spielfläche für Kinder. rechts: Außenansicht_Betonfassade von Hofansicht.
à gauche: Vue en coupe_Hall d'entrée_Salle de jeux. à droite: Vue de l'extérieur_La façade en béton vue de la cour.

CHICAGO_IL **LITTLE VILLAGE HIGH SCHOOL**

**ARCHITECTS:** OWP/P
**COMPLETION:** 2005_**TYPOLOGY:** EDUCATION
**PHOTOS:** JAMES STEINKAMP

The Little Village was created with numerous community groups after a thorough planning process, in which OWP/P designed a new 1,400-student community high school that integrates four, small 350-student schools into one building. Highly visible from a nearby vehicular overpass, the school serves as a beacon to the urban Little Village community. In the central commons space, a solar calendar uses the reflection of the sun to display the date, while the details of this central space symbolically commemorate the community's successful 19-day hunger strike, which was driven by the goal of providing new local school facilities.

An der Entstehung von Little Village wirkten viele Gruppen der Schulgemeinschaft mit. Im Anschluss an einen sorgfältigen Planungsprozess entwarfen OWP/P eine neue Community High School für 1.400 Schüler. Diese vereint in einem Gebäude vier kleine Schulen für jeweils 350 Schüler. Die von einer nahe gelegenen Verkehrsüberführung deutlich sichtbare Einrichtung dient der städtischen Little Village-Gemeinschaft als Leitstern. In der Mitte der Anlage zeigt ein Sonnenkalender das Datum an. Details dieses zentralen Platzes erinnern symbolisch an den erfolgreichen 19-tägigen Hungerstreik, bei dem sich die Gemeinschaft für neue Schuleinrichtungen vor Ort einsetzte.

Ce lycée pour 1400 élèves a été construit en remplacement de quatre établissements de 350 élèves chacun dans le cadre d'un projet d'urbanisme. Distinctement visible depuis un pont routier qui passe à proximité, le bâtiment est désormais emblématique du quartier de Little Village, à Chicago. Dans le hall central, un calendrier solaire utilise la réflexion de la lumière naturelle pour afficher la date, tandis que divers détails rappellent qu'il a fallu une grève de la faim de dix-neuf jours pour convaincre les autorités municipales de la nécessité de construire ce nouvel établissement scolaire.

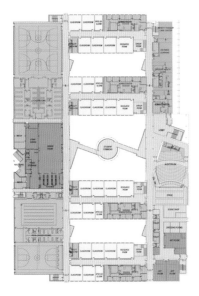
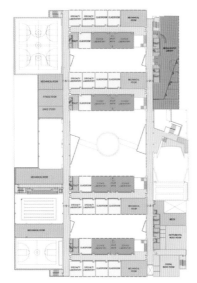

left: Floor plan_Total view by night. right: Inner courtyard, fully glazed façade.
links: Grundriss_Gesamtansicht bei Nacht. rechts: Innenhof, verglaste Fassade.
à gauche: Plan_Le bâtiment la nuit. à droite: Façade entièrement vitrée donnant sur la cour.

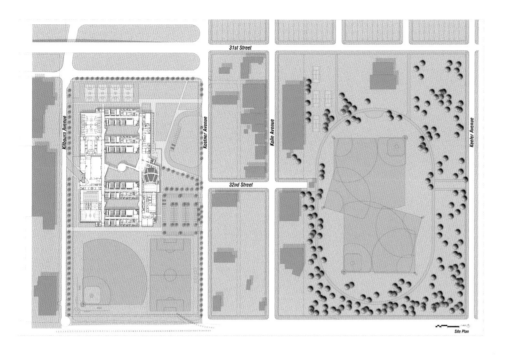

left: Solar calendar. right: Site plan_Entrance.
links: Sonnenuhr. rechts: Lageplan_Eingang.
à gauche: Calendrier solaire. à droite: Plan de situation_Le bâtiment avec l'entrée au premier plan.

# EFFINGHAM _IL **FIREFLY GRILL**

**ARCHITECTS:** CCS ARCHITECTURE
**COMPLETION:** 2005_**TYPOLOGY:** GASTRONOMY
**PHOTOS:** MARK BALLOGG PHOTOGRAPHY

The Firefly Grill is a modern "roadhouse" restaurant that is built with recycled barn wood siding and a corrugated metal roof, much like the beautiful old wooden barns that dot the Midwest. Large, sliding doors provide indoor-outdoor connections at all sides of the building, while a wrap-around porch is screened and heated along the lakeside. The kitchen counter, made from maple butcher block, is part of a large exhibition kitchen that anchors the interior and acts as a hearth. High ceilings are vaulted like the inside of a barn, while the dark-stained floors are wide-plank hardwood and will wear to a patina finish.

Die moderne Raststätte Firefly Grill erinnert mit der wiederverwendeten Ummantelung einer Scheune und dem Wellblechdach an die alten Holzscheunen, von denen der Mittlere Westen übersät ist. Große Schiebetüren bieten an allen Gebäudeseiten Verbindungen mach Außen, während eine Panoramaveranda zum See hin abgeschirmt und beheizt ist. Die Anrichte aus einem Metzgerblock in Walnussholz gehört zu einer weitläufigen offenen Küche, die dem Innenraum als Mittelpunkt dient. Hohe Decken sind wie die Innenseite einer Scheune gewölbt. Dunkel gebeizte Böden mit breiten Bohlen aus Hartholz werden sich zu einer Patina abnutzen.

Avec son bardage en planches recyclées et sa couverture en tôle ondulée, ce grill dans la tradition « roadhouse » rappelle les vieilles granges en bois qu'on trouve encore çà et là dans le Middle West. De grandes portes coulissantes ouvrent les quatre côtés sur l'extérieur, tandis qu'une terrasse couverte et vitrée s'étire le long d'un étang. L'intérieur est dominé par le grand comptoir, véritable « centre vital » du restaurant, réalisé en juxtaposant des blocs de boucher. Les plafonds, particulièrement hauts, retombent à la diagonale sur deux côtés comme dans les granges traditionnelles. Les planchers de couleur sombre ont été réalisés avec de larges planches et sont appelés à se patiner avec le temps.

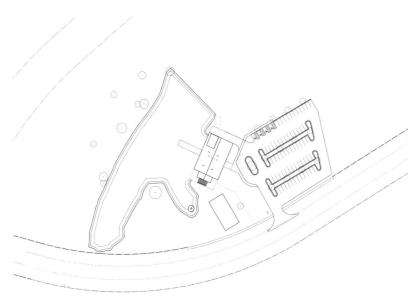

left: Site plan_Lakeside porch_Counter_Dining area. right: Metal roof_Wood siding_Wrap around porch.
links: Lageplan_Veranda an der Flußseite_Bar_Speiseraum. rechts: Metalldach_Holzverkleidung_ Umlaufende Veranda.
à gauche: Plan de situation_Bardage en bois et stock de bûches_Toit métallique. à droite: Terrasse.

# LAKE FOREST_IL **GLADE HOUSE**

**ARCHITECTS:** FREDERICK PHILLIPS AND ASSOCIATES
**COMPLETION:** 2005_**TYPOLOGY:** LIVING
**PHOTOS:** BARBARA KARANT

In a community where large, traditional houses prevail, this house is a refreshing and uplifting return to the more modest wood frame structures typical of the area before it became suburbanized. Two distinct gable structures recall, loosely, a farmhouse T-plan. Tall awning windows are proportioned and spaced with classical regularity, while a continuous band of clerestory windows separates volumes and adds light and dimension to certain interior spaces. Five species of lightwood, teak, cedar, Douglas fir, maple, and white oak provide a quiet but rich palette of interior and exterior materials.

In einer Gemeinde mit vorwiegend großen traditionellen Bauten ist dieses Haus eine erfrischende Rückkehr zu den eher bescheidenen Holzrahmenk onstruktionen, wie sie für dieses Gebiet vor seiner Eingemeindung typisch waren. Zwei unterschiedliche Giebelkonstruktionen geben in etwa den T-Grundriss eines Bauernhauses wieder. Hohe Klappflügelfenster sind mit klassischer Regelmäßigkeit dimensioniert und in Abständen angeordnet. Ein durchgehendes Oberlichtband trennt die Baukörper voneinander ab und sorgt in einigen Innenräumen für zusätzliches Licht. Fünf Nadelholzarten, Teak,. Zeder, Douglasie, Fichte, Ahorn und Weißeiche führen zu einer ruhigen, aber reichhaltigen Palette an Innen- und Außenmaterialien.

Située dans une zone où l'on trouve principalement des édifices traditionnels de taille imposante, cette petite maison a quelque chose de rafraîchissant qui rappelle les modestes structures en bois qui caractérisaient l'endroit avant qu'il devienne une banlieue. La maison se compose de deux volumes perpendiculaires couverts de toits à deux pentes. L'intérieur est éclairé par de hautes ouvertures positionnées avec une régularité classique, ainsi que par un clair-étage qui sépare deux volumes verticaux et assurent un bon éclairage naturel. Tant pour le revêtement de façade que pour les aménagements intérieurs, les architectes ont privilégié le bois et sélectionné cinq essences qui offrent une gamme de couleurs riche et harmonieuse: teck, cèdre, érable, pin Douglas et chêne blanc.

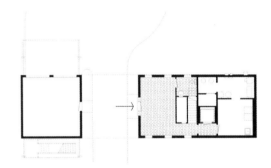

left: Site plan_Tall awning windows_Lightwood exterior. right: Side view.
links: Lageplan_Große Fenster mit Sonnenschutz_Verkleidung aus Leichtholz. rechts: Seitenansicht.
à gauche: Plan de situation_Grande fenêtre avec protection contre le soleil_Façade avec bardage en bois. à droite: Vue générale.

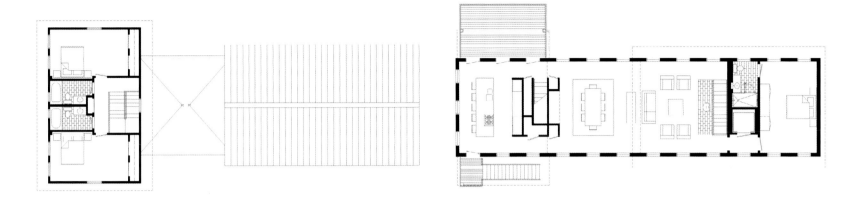

left: Interior with clerestory windows. right: Floor plan_Kitchen.
links: Inneneinrichtung mit Oberlicht. rechts: Grundriss_Küche.
à gauche: Intérieur avec clair-étage. à droite: Plan des différents niveaux_Cuisine.

# KANSAS CITY_KS **MODULAR 4 PROJECT**

**ARCHITECTS:** ROCKHILL+ASSOCIATES/STUDIO 804
**COMPLETION:** 2007_**TYPOLOGY:** LIVING
**PHOTOS:** DAN ROCKHILL

Prefabricated modular housing by nature focuses on the lifecycle of a building. By completing a majority of the construction in a warehouse, the integrity of materials are preserved, and scraps are reused which promotes less construction waste. Modular 4 features a 1,500 square foot floor plan with a remarkably flexible design anchored by a core of service spaces. The project continues Studio 804's commitment towards developing responsible architecture through the means of prefabrication, materiality, and sustainability. The site consists of a once vacant Brownfield lot in the heart of Kansas City.

Fertigteilbauweisen zielen naturgemäß auf die Nutzungsdauer eines Gebäudes ab. Indem ein Großteil der Konstruktion in einem Lager fertiggestellt wird, bleiben die Materialien intakt, Reste werden wiederverwendet und Bauabfälle vermieden. Der bemerkenswert flexible, 139 Quadratmeter große Geschossgrundriss von Modular 4 wird von einem Versorgungskern verankert. Wie Studio 804 setzt sich das Projekt mit den Mitteln der Vorfertigung, Materialauswahl und Nachhaltigkeit für eine verantwortungsbewusste Architektur ein. Sein Grundstück ist eine ehemalige Industriebrache im Herzen von Kansas City.

Les bâtiments modulaires en matériaux préfabriqués ont un grand potentiel écologique. La fabrication des éléments en usine permet de préserver l'intégrité des matériaux, de réutiliser certains déchets sur place et de limiter ainsi la production de déchets sur le chantier. La maison Modular 4, d'une superficie de 139 mètres carrés, est construite sur une ancienne friche urbaine au centre de Kansas City. Concentrant tous les équipements ménagers et sanitaires au même endroit, elle offre un plan remarquablement flexible. Elle reflète par ailleurs les efforts des architectes en matière de développement durable, notamment par l'utilisation du préfabriqué et l'attention accordée à la sélection des matériaux.

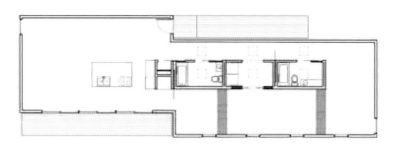

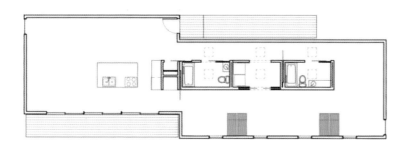

left: Floor plan_Oblique deck_Living room. right: Ramp elevation_Full view from East.
links: Grundriss_Abgestufte Terrasse_Wohnzimmer. rechts: Ansicht der Zufahrtsrampe_Östliche Gesamtansicht.
à gauche: Plans_Façade et plate-forme_Séjour. à droite: Façade et rampe_La maison vue de l'est.

LAFAYETTE_LA **PAUL AND LULU HILLIARD UNIVERSITY ART MUSEUM**

**ARCHITECTS:** ESKEW+DUMEZ+RIPPLE
**COMPLETION:** 2003_**TYPOLOGY:** CULTURE
**PHOTOS:** TIMOTHY HURSLEY

This 25,850-square-foot museum serves as a backdrop to the original 1967 University Art Museum a replica of an antebellum plantation designed by noted Louisiana architect A. Hays Town. Conceived as a tightly wrapped solid, the construction module of the new museum responds to the rhythm of the original building developing a strong site organization. Its glass façade hovers above entering visitors, reflecting in its surface the existing Hays Town building and surrounding live oaks. Depending upon position and time of day, the façade oscillates between opaque and transparent and at night is rendered a deep blue using cold cathode tubes, contrasting the new museum with its older neighbor.

Dieses Museum mit einer Fläche von 2.400 Quadratmetern bildet den Hintergrund des University Art Museum von 1967 ein nachgebildetes Plantagenhaus des bekannten Architekten A. Hays Town aus Louisiana. Das Konstruktionsraster des dicht umhüllten neuen Baukörpers greift den Rhythmus des Originalgebäudes auf und bildet ein streng organisiertes Grundstück. In der über den Besuchern schwebenden Glasfassade spiegeln sich das Hays-Town-Gebäude und die umgebenden Lebenseichen. Je nach Lage und Tageszeit schimmert die Fassade zwischen opak und transparent. Am Abend verwandeln Kaltkathodenröhren sie in ein dunkles Blau, das den Museumsneubau von seinem älteren Nachbarn abhebt.

Ce bâtiment d'environ 2.400 mètres carrés est une annexe de l'University Art Museum construit en 1967 sur des plans d'A. Hays Town en tant que copie d'une maison de maître de Louisiane érigée avant la guerre de Sécession. Les deux bâtiments établissent un dialogue entre l'ancien et le moderne par l'intermédiaire du rythme strict des colonnes, auquel répond une enveloppe compacte. Le bâtiment d'origine et les chênes qui l'entourent se reflètent dans la façade en porte-à-faux de l'annexe. Cette surface en verre est tantôt opaque, tantôt transparente en fonction de la position de l'observateur et du moment de la journée. Elle se colore en bleu à la nuit tombée grâce à des tubes cathodiques, contrastant ainsi avec la façade blanche du bâtiment voisin.

left: Floor plan_Second floor, atrium gallery / small gallery_Interior view of atrium gallery. right: Night view from entrance plaza_Exterior view from street.
links: Grundriss_Zweite Etage, Galerie im Atrium / kleine Galerie_Innenansicht der Galerie im Atrium. rechts: Nachtansicht Vorplatz_Außenansicht von der Straße.
à gauche: Plan_Galerie et salle d'exposition du second étage_Vue du rez-de-chaussée et de la galerie. à droite: Les deux bâtiments et l'esplanade d'entrée la nuit_Les deux bâtiments vus de la rue.

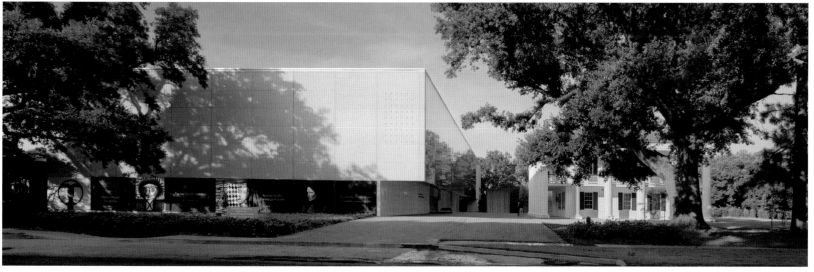

NEW ORLEANS_LA **REPAIRS AND RENOVATIONS TO THE LOUISIANA SUPERDOME**

**ARCHITECTS:** BILLES ARCHITECTURE
**COMPLETION:** IN PROGRESS_**TYPOLOGY:** LEISURE
**PHOTOS:** BILLES ARCHITECTURE

When the iconic Louisiana Superdome was devastated in the aftermath of Hurricane Katrina, Billes Architecture, LLC was successfully teamed with Trahan Architects and Sizeler Thompson Brown Architects to design and manage the $125 million repair project and the additional $41 million renovation. Though the project required a fast-track delivery, it was essential that extensive documentation of damage, assessment, design and coordination with numerous oversight agencies including the State of Louisiana, FEMA, insurance underwriters, and consultants around the United States occur. The firm's stunning new additions include a 100-foot band of windows that allow for greater transparency and a more direct connection to the city.

Nach dem verheerenden Wirbelsturm Katrina schlossen sich Billes Architecture mit Trahan Architects und Sizeler Thompson Brown Architects für ein Projekt zusammen, das die Instandsetzung und eine ergänzende Neugestaltung des ikonischen Louisiana Superdome vorsah. Obwohl das Projekt eine zügige Umsetzung erforderte, waren eine umfassende Schadensaufnahme, Bewertung, Konzeption und Koordination mit Aufsichtsbehörden – darunter der Staat Louisiana und die Katastrophenschutzbehörde –, Versicherungsgebern und Beratern aus allen Teilen der USA unabdingbar. Zu den sensationellen Ergänzungen des Büros gehört ein 30 Meter langes Fensterband, das für mehr Transparenz und eine direktere Verbindung zur Stadt sorgt.

Le « Superdome », palais des sports emblématique de la Louisiane, a été sévèrement endommagé par l'ouragan Katrina en 2005. Une équipe composée de Billes Architecture/LLC, Trahan Architects et Sizeler Thompson Brown Architects a été chargée de le réparer (125 millions de dollars) et de le moderniser (41 millions). Bien que le projet eût été considéré comme particulièrement urgent, il a été nécessaire d'établir une liste détaillée des dommages, d'estimer les nouveaux besoins et d'élaborer des plans en coordination avec tout un ensemble de partenaires, notamment le gouvernement de Louisiane, la FEMA (Agence fédérale pour l'aide d'urgence), les compagnies d'assurance et divers consultants répartis dans tous les États-Unis. La plus remarquable des innovations apportées est une bande de fenêtres de trente mètres de long qui améliore l'éclairage naturel de l'intérieur et établit un lien visuel avec la ville.

left: Perspective_View of the roof_Exterior view. right: Hallway_Bar_Seating area.
links: Perspektive_Blick auf das Dach_Außenansicht. rechts: Gang_Bar_Sitzmöglichkeiten.
à gauche: Perspective_Dôme_Extérieur. à droite: Couloir_Bar_Salle du bar.

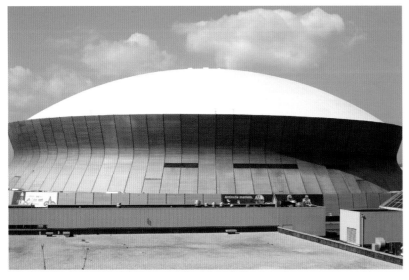

ANN ARBOR_MI **UNIVERSITY OF MICHIGAN MUSEUM OF ART**

**ARCHITECTS:** ALLIED WORKS ARCHITECTURE
**ASSOCIATE ARCHITECTS:** I.D.S.
**COMPLETION:** 2009_**TYPOLOGY:** EDUCATION
**PHOTOS:** JEREMY BITTERMANN

The new University of Michigan Museum of Art completely renovates and modernizes the existing 49,000 square foot space in a dramatic new wing. The expansion takes the form of a modified T-shape, with one arm extending to engage the existing structure, one defining the street wall on the western edge of the original 40-acre campus, and one reaching towards the 'Diag', the central identity space at the Universitiy.

Im Rahmen des Umbaus und der Renovierung des Michigan Museum of Art auf dem Campus der Universität entsteht aus der vorhandenen 4.550 Quadratmeter großen Fläche ein spannungsvoller neuer Flügelbau. Bei dem Erweiterungsbau in einer modifizierten T-Form wird ein Kragarm die vorhandene Konstruktion berühren, ein Zweiter die Straßenmauer am westlichen Rand des ursprünglich 16 Hektar großen Campus definieren und ein Dritter zum „Diag" reichen, dem zentralen Identifikationsraum an der Universität.

La nouvelle annexe du musée des Beaux-arts de l'université du Michigan vient s'ajouter aux 4.550 mille mètres carrés du bâtiment d'origine. Elle prend la forme d'un T, la première branche reliant le nouveau volume au vieux musée, la seconde marquant la limite ouest du campus qui s'étend sur seize hectares, la troisième étant orientée vers le « Diag », c'est-à-dire l'espace central de l'université.

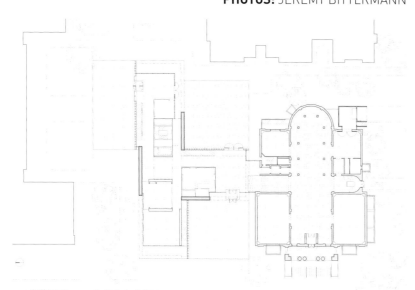

left: Floor plan_Street side view. right: New expansion.
links: Grundriss_Straßenansicht. rechts: Erweiterungsbau.
à gauche: Plan_Musée vu de la rue. à droite: Vue de l'annexe.

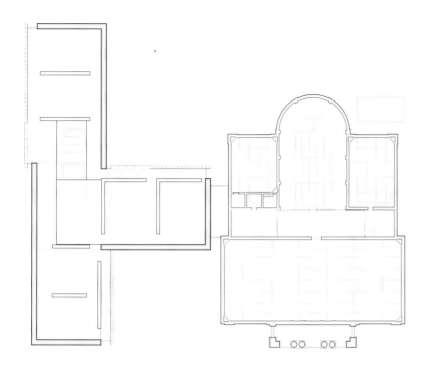

left: New space for exhibition. right: Third floor plan_Façade of new building_Staircase.
links: Neue Ausstellungsfläche. rechts: Grundriss drittes Obergeschoss_Treppenhaus.
à gauche: Nouvel espace d'exposition. à droite: Plan du troisième étage_Façade de l'annexe. Escalier.

GRAND RAPIDS_MI **GRAND RAPIDS ART MUSEUM**

**ARCHITECTS:** WHY ARCHITECTURE
**COMPLETION:** 2007_**TYPOLOGY:** CULTURE
**PHOTOS:** GRAND RAPIDS ART MUSEUM,
WHY ARCHITECTURE

The Grand Rapids Art Museum in Michigan is home to one of the oldest museums in the Midwest. The new museum is designed through the integration of the arts and technology, with a mission in obtaining a high-level certification from the Leadership in Energy and Environmental Design (LEED), thus making it one of the first art museums with such recognition. The Grand Rapids Art Museum features a unique design that compliments its prominent location, in the heart of downtown, with a grand urban gesture while offering an intimate atmosphere to enjoy the arts.

Das Grand Rapids Art Museum in Michigan ist eines der ältesten Kunstmuseen im Mittleren Westen der USA. Sein Neubau integriert Kunst und Technologie, um ein LEED (Leadership in Energy and Environmental Design)- Zertifikat mit einer hohen Punktzahl zu erreichen, und so zu einem der ersten Kunstmuseen mit einer solchen Auszeichnung zu werden. Mit einer großartigen urbanen Geste erweist das einzigartig gestaltete Grand Rapids Art Museum seinem berühmten Standort alle Ehre und bietet gleichzeitig eine intime Atmosphäre für den Kunstgenuss.

Ce musée nouvellement construit abrite l'une des plus anciennes collections artistiques du Middle West. Les architectes ont cherché à réaliser une synthèse entre l'art et la technologie, tout en construisant le premier musée des beaux-arts des États-Unis disposant du label écologique LEED (Leadership in Energy and Environmental Design). D'un style grandiose adapté à une situation privilégiée au cœur de la ville, le Grand Rapids Art Museum offre l'atmosphère feutrée qu'apprécient les amateurs de peinture et sculpture.

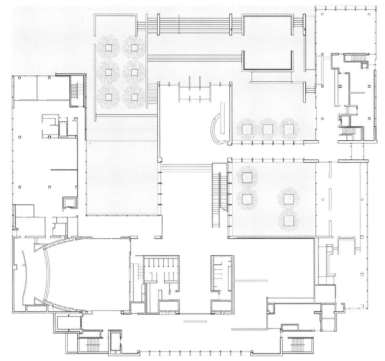

left: First floor plan_Front façade with courtyard_Aerial view. right: Entrance at night_Pocket park_Entrance.
links: Grundriss erstes Obergeschoss_Vorderseite mit Park_Luftbild. rechts: Eingang bei Nacht Pocketpark_Eingang.
à gauche: Plan du rez-de-chaussée_Esplanade et façade principale_Vue aérienne. à droite: Le porche la nuit_Miniparc_Entrée.

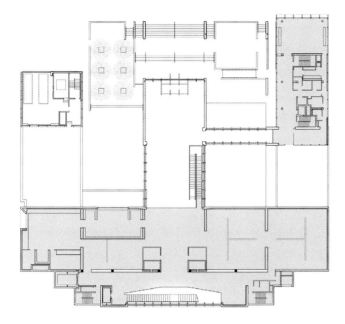

left: Stairs to upper floor. right: Second floor plan_Gallery_Upper lobby with Warhol_Modern art gallery.
links: Treppenaufgang zum Obergeschoss. rechts: Grundriss zweites Obergeschoss_Galerie_Obere Ausstellung mit Warhol Bildern_Galerie für zeitgenössische Kunst.
à gauche: Intérieur. à droite: Plan du second étage_Galerie_Hall supérieur avec des œuvres d'Andy Warhol_Salle d'exposition d'art moderne.

# EAST LANSING_MI **ELI & EDYTHE BROAD ART MUSEUM**

**ARCHITECTS:** ZAHA HADID ARCHITECTS, ZAHA HADID WITH
PATRIK SCHUMACHER (DESIGN)
**COMPLETION:** 2010 / ON SITE_**TYPOLOGY:** CULTURE
**PHOTOS:** ZAHA HADID ARCHITECTS

The sculptural folds of the Eli and Edythe Broad Art Museum's design and enigmatic qualities of its steel and glass surface follow a coherent formal logic, offering a sense of unlimited possibilities. The 41,000-square-foot building will comprise three levels, including a basement. It will be constructed of steel and concrete with an aluminium and glass exterior and be adjoined by an expansive outdoor sculpture garden to the east.

Der skulptural gefaltete Entwurf des Eli and Edythe Broad Art Museum mit seiner rätselhaften Stahl- und Glasfläche folgt einer in sich geschlossenen Logik und erweckt den Eindruck unbegrenzter Möglichkeiten. Das 3.810 Quadratmeter große Museum wird drei Ebenen einschließlich Untergeschoss umfassen. Der Stahlbetonbau soll eine Fassade aus Aluminium und Glas erhalten. Ergänzt wird das Gebäude im Osten um einen großen Skulpturengarten.

L'apparence sculpturale et les qualités énigmatiques de ce bâtiment qui allie le verre, l'acier, l'aluminium et le béton répondent à une logique formelle cohérente et suggèrent des possibilités infinies. Le musée offre une superficie de 12 500 mètres carrés sur trois niveaux, y compris le sous-sol. L'armature en béton et acier porte une enveloppe en verre et aluminium, qui se complète à l'est par un grand jardin où sont exposées des sculptures.

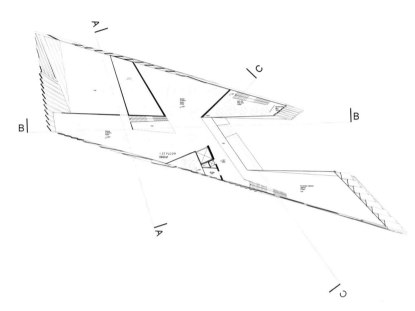

left: First floor plan_Façade. right: Entrance area_Aerial view.
links: Grundriss erstes Obergeschoss_Fassade. rechts: Luftbild.
à gauche: Plan du rez-de-chaussée_Façade. à droite: Esplanade d'entrée_Vue aérienne.

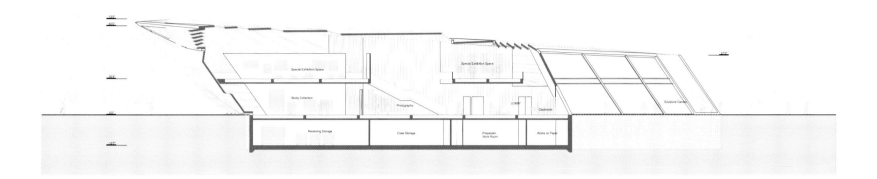

left: Exterior, glazed façade. right: Section_Interior with skylight_Exhibition_Exhibiton, staircase_
Lounge.
links: Außenansicht, verglaste Fassade. rechts: Schnitt_Interieur mit Oberlicht_Ausstellungsraum
Ausstelungsraum, Treppenaufgang_Lounge.
à gauche: Façade vitrée. à droite: Vue en coupe_Intérieur avec lumière zénithale_Salle d'exposi-
tion_Salle d'exposition et escalier_Hall d'entrée.

KANSAS CITY_MO **NELSON-ATKINS MUSEUM OF ART**

**ARCHITECTS:** STEVEN HOLL ARCHITECTS
**COMPLETION:** 2007_**TYPOLOGY:** CULTURE
**PHOTOS:** ANDY RYAN PHOTOGRAPHY

The Bloch Building addition to the Nelson-Atkins Museum of Art fuses architecture with landscape to create a dynamic experience for visitors as they enter. Engaging the existing sculpture garden, the addition transforms the entire site and is distinguished by five glass lenses that traverse the existing building through the Sculpture Park to form new spaces and angles of vision. The innovative merging of landscape, architecture and art was executed through close collaboration with museum curators and artists to achieve a dynamic and supportive relationship between art and architecture.

Beim Betreten des Bloch Building, dem Erweiterungsbau des Nelson-Atkins Kunstmuseums, verschmelzen Architektur und Landschaft zu einem dynamischen Erlebnis für die Besucher. Indem der Anbau den vorhandenen Skulpturengarten einbezieht, gestaltet er das gesamte Gelände um. Der Erweiterungsbau zeichnet sich durch fünf längliche gläserne Körper aus, die den Bestandsbau durch den Skulpturenpark queren und so neue Räume und Betrachtungswinkel schaffen. Das innovative Verschmelzen von Landschaft, Architektur und Kunst erfolgte in enger Zusammenarbeit mit Museumskuratoren und Künstlern, sodass eine spannungsvolle und hilfreiche Beziehung zwischen Kunst und Architektur entstand.

L'immeuble Bloch, annexe du Nelson-Atkins Museum of Art, crée une symbiose dynamique entre l'architecture et le paysage. Il se compose de cinq pavillons en verre reliés entre eux qui créent de nouveaux espaces et de nouvelles perspectives dans le « parc des sculptures », changeant ainsi radicalement l'apparence de tout le site. Cette synthèse novatrice entre le paysage, l'architecture et les beaux-arts, rendue possible grâce à une collaboration étroite entre les différents artistes et directeurs de collections, a pour résultat une relation dynamique et vivifiante entre l'art et l'architecture.

left: Ground floor plan_Entry_Glass lenses with double-glass cavities. right: Transparent and opaque façade.
links: Grundriss_Eingang_Glaswürfel mit Doppelverglasung. rechts: Transparente und lichtdurchlässige Fassade.
à gauche: Plan du rez-de-chaussée_Entrée de l'annexe_ Façade en verre double épaisseur. à droite: Intérieur avec surface transparente et translucide.

ST. LOUIS_MO **SAM FOX SCHOOL OF DESIGN AND VISUAL ARTS**

**ARCHITECTS:** MAKI & ASSOCIATES
**COMPLETION:** 2006_**TYPOLOGY:** EDUCATION
**PHOTOS:** ROBERT PETTUS

The Sam Fox School of Design & Arts consolidates and enhances all facilities and programs related to the study of the visual arts and architecture. Together with the three existing buildings, an ensemble is created to form a "mini-campus", cloistering a series of open outdoor spaces in the tradition of campus planning at Washington University. The Mildred Lane Kemper Art Museum and Earl E. and Myrtle E. Walker Hall are largely designed to reinforce the horizontal composition of the former three buildings, not to mimic them, but to be harmonious with the existing context. The ensemble of traditional and new materials creates a harmonious dialogue with the existing architectural and historic context while belonging to its own time.

Die Schule vereinigt alle mit dem Studium der bildenden Künste und Architektur verbundenen Einrichtungen und Programme. Zusammen mit drei Bestandsbauten ergibt das Gebäudeensemble einen „Mini-Campus" mit mehreren Freianlagen in der Tradition der Campusgelände an der Washington University. Das Mildred Lane Kemper Art Museum und die Earl E. and Myrtle E. Walker Hall sollen in erster Linie die horizontale Komposition der früheren Bauten hervorheben, aber nicht kopieren, sondern mit dem vorhandenen Kontext in Einklang stehen. Traditionelle und neue Materialien stellen einen harmonischen Dialog mit dem architektonischen und historischen Umfeld her und sind dennoch zeitgemäß.

Les architectes ont été chargés de concevoir un complexe regroupant toutes les activités en rapport avec l'étude de l'architecture et des beaux-arts. Il est venu s'ajouter à trois bâtiments préexistants afin de créer un « minicampus » intégrant des espaces de plein air dans la tradition de l'université Washington de Saint Louis. Deux nouveaux édifices (Mildred Lane Kemper Art Museum et Earl E. and Myrtle E. Walker Hall) viennent renforcer la composition horizontale des anciens bâtiments, se démarquant par rapport aux structures antérieures tout en s'y intégrant de manière harmonieuse. L'ensemble ainsi formé se caractérise par un dialogue entre l'ancien et le moderne, tant au niveau des matériaux que du style architectural.

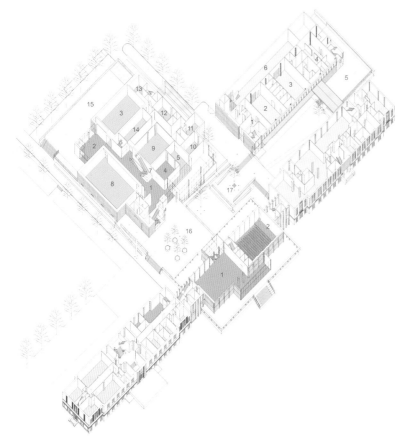

left: Floor plan_Street side view_Façade. right: Front entrance_Aerial view.
links: Grundriss_Straßenansicht_Fassade. rechts: Entrance view_Luftbild.
à gauche: Axonométrie_Façade côté rue_Détail de la façade. à droite: Entrée principale_Vue aérienne.

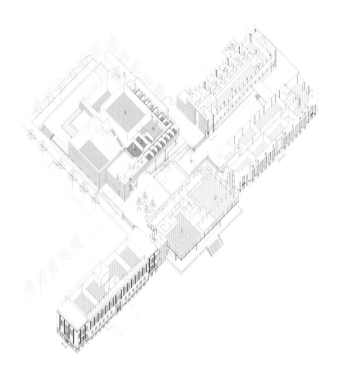

left: Exhibition. right: Floor plan_Gallery displaying student work__Gallery_Detail of glass walls.
links: Ausstellung. rechts: Grundriss_Ausstellung von Studentenarbeiten_Galerie_Detail der Glasfassade.
à gauche: Salle d'exposition. à droite: Axonométrie_Exposition des œuvres des étudiants_Salle d'exposition_Salle avec murs vitrés.

# GALISTEO BASIN PRESERVE, SANTA FE_NM **WEST BASIN HOUSE**

**ARCHITECTS:** SIGNER HARRIS ARCHITECTS
**COMPLETION:** 2007_**TYPOLOGY:** LIVING
**PHOTOS:** KIRK GITTINGS PHOTOGRAPHY

West Basin House is nestled into 125 acres of the Galisteo Basin Preserve, a low-impact and resource-efficient community 15 miles south of Santa Fe, New Mexico. The design reinterprets the traditional 'courtyard house' typology. The architects looked to traditional methods, like Rammed Earth construction, as well as modern Aerated Autoclaved Concrete (AAC) to craft an energy efficient building envelope. 36 solar electric panels, situated in the landscape on the south side of the house, and 11 solar thermal panels, fixed to the roof of the nearby horse barn, resolve nearly all of the house's heat and electricity needs.

Das West Basin House liegt eingebettet in einem 50 Hektar großen Areal des Galisteo Basin Preserve, einer umweltschonenden und ressourceneffizienten Gemeinde 24 Kilometer südlich von Santa Fe in New Mexico entfernt. Der Entwurf interpretiert den traditionellen Gebäudetyp des Hofhauses neu. Für die energieeffiziente Gebäudehülle verwendeten die Architekten sowohl herkömmlichen Stampflehm als auch modernen dampfgehärteten Gasbeton. 36 solarelektrische Paneele in der Landschaft auf der Südseite des Hauses und 11 solarthermische Paneele auf dem Dach einer nahe gelegenen Pferdescheune decken nahezu den gesamten Wärme- und Elektrizitätsbedarf des Hauses.

Cet ensemble architectural est construit sur une propriété de cinquante hectares dans le parc naturel de Galisteo Basin, à environ vingt-cinq kilomètres au sud de Santa Fe, au Nouveau-Mexique. Son style rappelle les constructions traditionnelles de la région. Afin de réaliser un bâtiment à faible consommation d'énergie, les architectes se sont inspirés à la fois des méthodes traditionnelles comme le pisé, et de la technologie moderne, notamment le béton AAC (Aerated Autoclaved Concrete). Les besoins énergétiques sont presque entièrement couverts par trente-six panneaux photovoltaïques situés au sud des bâtiments, et par onze panneaux de chauffage solaire installés sur le toit de l'écurie.

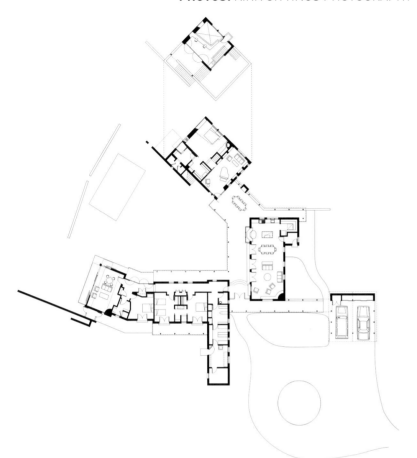

left: Floor plan_View from pool_Exterior façade. right: Front façade_View of Galisteo Basin Reserve.
links: Grundriss_Blick auf den Pool_Fassade. rechts: Frontfassade_Blick auf das Galisteo Basin Reserve.
à gauche: Plan_Piscine_Extérieur. à droite: Vue partielle de la façade_Vue d'ensemble avec les collines du parc naturel de Galisteo Basin.

# HOUSTON_TX **ONETWO TOWNHOUSE**

**ARCHITECTS:** FDM:ARCH FRONCOIS DE MENIL
**COMPLETION:** 2007_**TYPOLOGY:** LIVING
**PHOTOS:** PAUL WARCHOL PHOTOGRAPHY

This project's tectonic expression results from the needs of the program; two independent 2,500-square-foot town houses and the constraints of a small triangular lot in Houston's Montrose District. The study of turning radiuses evoked the Andy Warhol painting, "Dance Diagrams" as a planametric inspiration. Each house "steps" around the other maintaining its individuality yet at the same time is part of the greater whole within the constrained lot. The structural system is drilled concrete piers supporting grade beams with reinforced concrete masonry units, steel columns, beams and composite deck up to the height of the first floor.

Der tektonische Ausdruck dieses Projekts resultiert aus den programmatischen Anforderungen. Zu realisieren waren zwei unabhängige Stadthäuser mit einer Fläche von 232 Quadrtatmetern auf einer kleinen rechteckigen Parzelle im Montrose District von Houston. Die Untersuchung der Kurvenradien erinnert an Andy Warhols Gemälde „Tanzdiagramme" als planimetrische Inspiration. Jedes Haus „schreitet" um das andere, wobei es seine Eigenständigkeit bewahrt und dennoch zum größeren Ganzen innerhalb des knappen Grundstücks gehört. Das Tragwerk besteht aus Betonbohrpfeilern, denen Gründungsbalken aus Stahlbetonelementen aufliegen, sowie Stahlstützen, Trägern und Verbundplatten bis zum ersten Obergeschoss.

L'aspect de ce bâtiment est le résultat direct des contraintes imposées par le projet: construire deux maisons indépendantes de 232 mètres carrés chacune sur un petit terrain triangulaire du Montrose District, à Houston. La structure rayonnante de la planimétrie évoque le tableau Dance Diagrams d'Andy Warhol. Chacune des deux maisons « empiète » sur l'autre tout en gardant son individualité de manière à constituer un ensemble uni sur ce terrain de dimensions limitées. L'ossature des bâtiments se compose de longrines qui répartissent sur des piliers en béton la masse des colonnes en acier et des plaques en béton armé des étages supérieurs.

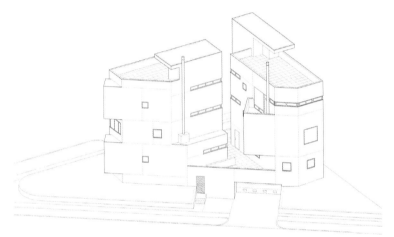

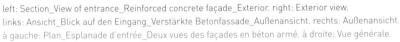

left: Section_View of entrance_Reinforced concrete façade_Exterior. right: Exterior view.
links: Ansicht_Blick auf den Eingang_Verstärkte Betonfassade_Außenansicht. rechts: Außenansicht.
à gauche: Plan_Esplanade d'entrée_Deux vues des façades en béton armé. à droite: Vue générale.

# SPRING PRAIRIE_WI **FERROUS HOUSE**

**ARCHITECTS:** JOHNSEN SCHMALING ARCHITECTS
**COMPLETION:** 2007_**TYPOLOGY:** LIVING
**PHOTOS:** DOUG EDMUNDS STUDIOS

Sitting on top an existing foundation, the rectangular volume of the house is wrapped on three sides with a suspended curtain of weathering steel panels, protecting the inside of the house from the scrutiny of suspicious neighbors and the elements, and it extends beyond the building's back where it shelters the sides of a linear south-facing terrace. Linear storage boxes penetrate the steel curtain and cantilever over the edge of the building. The long northern clerestory radiates its warm light into the night, echoing the iconic glow of the dairy barns that once dotted the area.

Der einem bestehenden Fundament aufgesetzte rechtwinklige Baukörper des Hauses wird an drei Seiten von einer vorgehängten Wand aus witterungsbeständigen Stahlplatten umhüllt. Als Schutz vor Einblicken und Naturgewalten erstreckt sich die Wand bis hinter die Gebäuderückseite, an der sie eine Südterrasse abschirmt. Lineare Schrankwände durchdringen die stählerne Vorhangwand, wobei sie über den Gebäuderand vorkragen. Das lange Oberlichtfenster im Norden strahlt sein warmes Licht in die Nacht und greift so das zeichenhafte Leuchten der einst in diesem Gebiet verstreuten Molkereien auf.

Ce parallélépipède posé sur des fondations préexistantes présente sur trois faces des plaques en acier Corten qui protègent l'intérieur des intempéries et des regards indiscrets. On retrouve ce matériau au sud, où il est utilisé pour délimiter latéralement une terrasse linéaire. Des caisses utilisées comme lieux de stockage sont en protubérance sur le plan vertical des façades. Le clair-étage qui s'étire juste sous le toit tout au long de la façade nord irradie une lumière chaleureuse qui rappelle celle des laiteries qui se trouvaient jadis sur ce terrain anciennement agricole.

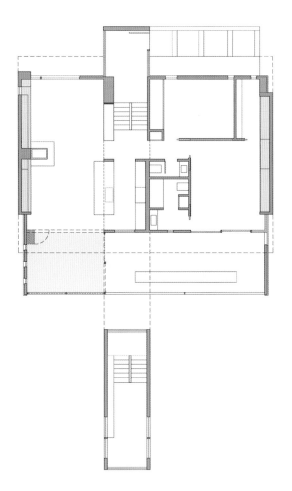

left: Floor plan_Detail steel façade and storage box. right: Exterior view_Alternate exterior view with skylight.
links: Grundriss_Detail der Stahlfassade und der Ablage. rechts: Außenansicht_Außenansicht mit Oberlicht.
à gauche: Plan de la maison_Gros plan sur la façade en acier et sur une caisse. à droite: Deux vues de la maison éclairée.

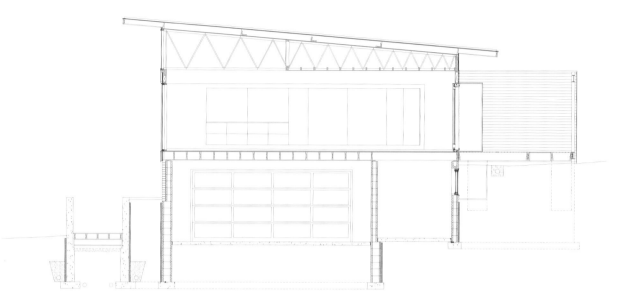

left: View from stairway to upper level. right: Section_Living room with fireplace.
links: Blick aus dem Treppenhaus in die obere Etage. rechts: Schnitt_Wohnzimmer mit Kamin.
à gauche: Niveau supérieur vu de l'escalier. à droite: Vue en coupe_Séjour avec cheminée.

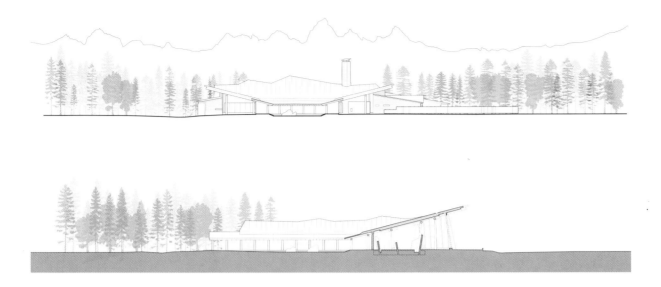

left: Detail interior. right: Sections_Lobby_Courtyard_Exhibition.
links: Detail des Interieurs. rechts: Schnitte_Eingangshalle_Hofausstellung.
à gauche: Détail de l'intérieur. à droite: Vues en coupe_Hall d'entrée_Colonnade dans la cour_Salle d'exposition.

# JACKSON_WY **WINE SILO**

**ARCHITECTS:** CARNEY ARCHITECTS
**COMPLETION:** 2006_**TYPOLOGY:** LEISURE
**PHOTOS:** PAUL WARCHOL PHOTOGRAPHY

The project, a 300-square-foot wine silo, is designed to house the owner's private wine collection, and is connected to an existing "entertainment" building. The structure lies in the Snake River flood plain, therefore, a traditional wine cellar was out of the question. Borrowing from agrarian structures, the pure silo form is clad in oxidized steel plates to weather and blend with the existing buildings and landscape. Reclaimed fir woodwork and a spiral staircase, which accesses carefully the displayed wine bottles organized around the perimeter, characterize the interior, inspired by a wine cask.

Das an eine vorhandene Gaststätte angeschlossene Projekt, ein 28 Quadratmeter großes Weinsilo, soll die private Weinsammlung des Eigentümers aufnehmen. Da es im Überflutungsgebiet des Flusses Snake liegt, kam ein traditioneller Weinkeller nicht infrage. Die landwirtschaftlichen Gebäuden entlehnte Siloform ist mit oxidierten Stahlplatten verkleidet, damit sie im Laufe der Zeit verwittert und mit den bestehenden Häusern und der Landschaft verschmilzt. Tischlerarbeiten aus wiederverwertetem Fichtenholz und eine Wendeltreppe zu den sorgfältig am Außenrand platzierten Weinflaschen prägen das von einem Weinfass inspirierte Innere.

Ce silo d'une surface totale de quatre-vingt-onze mètres carrés abrite une collection de bouteilles de vin. Relié à un « bâtiment de spectacle », il fait partie d'une résidence privée construite dans une plaine inondable près de la Snake River, ce qui explique pourquoi une cave traditionnelle était hors de question. Le silo proprement dit, dont la forme s'inspire directement d'un bâtiment agricole, est revêtu de plaques d'acier oxydées, ce qui lui permet d'être en harmonie avec les édifices voisins et de se fondre dans le paysage. L'intérieur, qui évoque un tonneau, se caractérise par un escalier en spirale qui permet d'accéder aux casiers à bouteilles en pin recyclé.

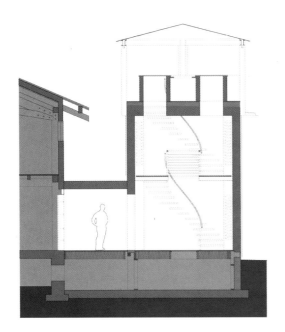

left: Section_General view_Stairs. right: View from the South.
links: Schnitt_Gesamtansicht_Treppe. rechts: Südansicht.
à gauche: Vue en coupe_Vue générale_Escalier. à droite: Le bâtiment vu du sud.

# JACKSON_WY **W- HOUSE**

**ARCHITECTS:** E/YE DESIGN
**COMPLETION:** 2006_**TYPOLOGY:** LIVING
**PHOTOS:** COURTESY OF ELLINGER /
YEHIA DESIGN LLC (E/YE DESIGN)

Nestled in a u-shaped, sloped terrain, the W-House's position on its site maximizes the views of the Teton Range, while at the same time utilizes the natural east-west flow of the landscape as an opportunistic moment for exchange. As the house cascades into the gully, each surface acts as a moving datum, interacting to create a new internal landscape that challenges the relationship between the geometry of the site and the surface of the building. Traditionally discernable boundaries become eroded and new spatial identities are configured. The result is one where building becomes landscape and landscape becomes space.

Eingebettet in ein U-förmiges Gefälle nutzt die Ausrichtung des W-Houses die Aussichten auf die Bergkette Teton Range maximal aus. Gleichzeitig ermöglicht die von Osten nach Westen verlaufende natürliche Landschaft einen Lagewechsel. Da sich das Haus kaskadenartig in die Schlucht erstreckt, fungiert jede Fläche als bewegliche Richtgröße. Die einzelnen Flächen wirken aufeinander ein, um eine neue innere Landschaft zu schaffen, welche die Beziehung zwischen der Geometrie des Grundstücks und der Oberfläche des Gebäudes infrage stellt. Traditionell erkennbare Grenzen werden aufgelöst, neue räumliche Identitäten erzeugt. Auf diese Weise entwickelt sich aus dem Haus eine Landschaft und aus der Landschaft ein Raum.

Cette maison a été construite sur un terrain en pente de manière à optimiser les vues sur les montagnes environnantes, tout en tirant profit de l'orientation est/ouest du paysage pour créer des opportunités d'échange entre le bâtiment et la nature. Ses différents niveaux à flanc de colline lui confèrent un dynamisme, tandis que son paysage intérieur redéfinit la relation entre la géométrie du site et la surface du bâtiment, érodant ainsi les limites traditionnelles et configurant de nouvelles identités spatiales. Avec pour résultat un immeuble devenu paysage—et un paysage devenu espace architectural.

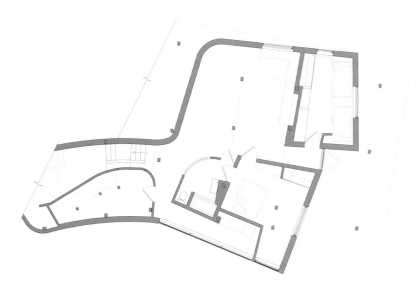

left: Ground floor plan_North view of exterior. right: East view_South view.
links: Grundriss Erdgeschoss_Außenansicht von Norden. rechts: Ostansicht_Südansicht.
à gauche: Plan du rez-de-chaussée_Le bâtiment vu du nord. à droite: Façade est_Façade sud.

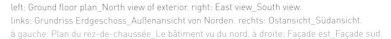

left: Stair. right: Site plan_Living area_Kitchen_Living room with fireplace.
links: Treppe. rechts: Lageplan_Wohnbereich_Küche_Wohnzimmer mit Kamin.
à gauche: Escalier. à droite: Plan de situation_Salon_Cuisine_Salon avec cheminée.

COLLECTION

# west

ERT BROOM PUBLIC LIBRARY CAVE CREEK_AZ_THE COMMONS GILBERT
BANNER GATEWAY MEDICAL CENTER GILBERT_AZ_SUNRISE MOUNTAIN LI
RY PEORIA_AZ_THE PRAYER CHAPEL PHOENIX_AZ_HOOVER HOUSE PHOE
AZ_DUPLEX RESIDENCE PHOENIX_AZ_TEMPE CENTER FOR THE ART
PE_AZ_LANDSOURCE TEMPE TEMPE_AZ_MEINEL OPTICAL SCIENCE
DING - UNIVERSITY OF ARIZONA TUCSON_AZ_THE UNIVERSITY OF ARI
A_CHEMICAL SCIENCES BUILDING TUCSON_AZ_PETER AND PAULA FAS
CANCER CLINIC AT UNIVERSITY MEDICAL CENTER TUSCON_AZ_DOWNIN
DENCE TUCSON_AZ_JACKSON FAMILY RETREAT_ BIG SUR_CA_TIGERTAIL
NTWOOD_CA_WOODBURY UNIVERSITY NEW STUDIO BUILDING_ BURBANK
FALCON HOUSE_ CARMEL VALLEY_CA_RESIDENCE FOR A BRIARD_ CUL
CITY_CA_MODAA BUILDING_ CULVER CITY_CA_JACKSON HOUSE IN CULVE
CULVERCITY_CA_HERCULES PUBLIC LIBRARY_ HERCULES_CA_SURF
SE HERMOSA BEACH CA STRAND RESIDENCE HERMOSA BEACH C

# CAVE CREEK_AZ **DESERT BROOM PUBLIC LIBRARY**

**ARCHITECTS:** RICHARD+BAUER
**COMPLETION:** 2005_**TYPOLOGY:** PUBLIC
**PHOTOS:** BILL TIMMERMAN PHOTOGRAPHY

Borrowing from the symbiotic relationship of a young saguaro cacti and its nurse tree along the arroyos edge, the expansive roof of the Desert Broom Public Library, a branch library, creates a shaded microclimate, providing filtered daylight, shelter, and a nurturing environment for intellectual growth and development. This project's strength is in the integration of the exterior with the interior of the building. The roof form extends above an adjoining arroyo 60 feet out into the natural desert, creating indoor and outdoor transitional spaces, which provides a seamless transition into the desert.

Von der symbiotischen Beziehung zwischen einem jungen Saguaro-Kaktus und seinem Ammenbaum am Bachrand inspiriert, schafft das ausladende Dach der Zweigbibliothek Desert Broom Public Library ein geschütztes Mikroklima. Dieses bietet gefiltertes Tageslicht, Sonnenschutz und ein der geistigen Entfaltung und Entwicklung förderliches Umfeld. Die Stärke dieses Projekts liegt in der Einbindung der äußeren Umgebung in das Gebäudeinnere. Da sich das Dach über einem angrenzenden Bach 18 Meter in die Wüstenlandschaft ausdehnt, entstehen überleitende Innen- und Außenräume für einen nahtlosen Übergang in die Wüste.

Le grand toit en surplomb de cette bibliothèque, inspiré par la relation symbiotique qui existe entre les jeunes cactus saguaro et les arbres sur lesquels ils se développent près des ruisseaux asséchés du désert de l'Arizona, filtre la lumière solaire et crée ainsi un microclimat favorable au travail intellectuel. La ligne de force du bâtiment est d'ailleurs l'interpénétration des espaces intérieurs et extérieurs. Le toit couvre en fait un ruisseau asséché, assurant ainsi une transition progressive non seulement entre l'intérieur et l'extérieur, mais aussi entre la ville et le désert tout proche.

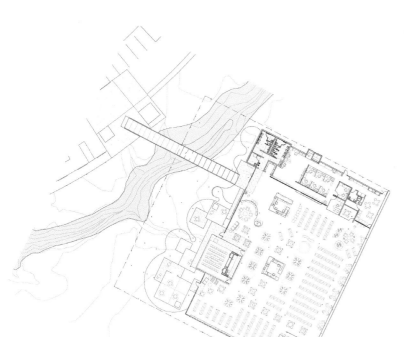

N

left: Floor plan_Seating area_Reading space. right: Extended roof into desert_Exterior view by night_Interior space.
links: Grundriss_Sitzecke_Leseplatz. rechts: Erweitertes Dach_Außenansicht bei Nacht_Innenansicht.
à gauche: Plan_Espace de repos_Espace de lecture. à droite: Grand toit en surplomb avec le désert à l'arrière plan_Extérieur la nuit_Intérieur.

# GILBERT_AZ **THE COMMONS**

**ARCHITECTS:** DEBARTOLO ARCHITECTS
**COMPLETION:** 2007_**TYPOLOGY:** EDUCATION
**PHOTOS:** BILL TIMMERMAN PHOTOGRAPHY

A large regional church in Arizona challenged the visionary architects to design a strategic building to facilitate the new core of the campus and serve as the social center for all activities. As the first building of a new master plan, the bookstore and coffee shop have positively changed and transformed the campus by becoming an inside-out building that literally opens on all sides. The transparency of the building, opened up in times of temperate weather, allows the material clarity and the overextending roof to combine and work together to successfully become the epicenter of the campus.

Eine große regionale Kirche in Arizona beauftragte die visionären Architekten mit dem Entwurf eines strategisch platzierten Gebäudes, das den neuen Kern des Campus entlasten und als Gemeinschaftszentrum für alle Aktivitäten dienen sollte. Als erster Bau eines neuen Masterplans hat das Gebäude mit dem Buchladen und Café den Campus zweifellos verändert und umgestaltet. Sein nach außen gekehrtes Inneres ist zu allen Seiten hin buchstäblich offen. Die Transparenz des bei mildem Wetter geöffneten Gebäudes, die Klarheit der Materialien und das weit ausladende Dach machen es zu einem gelungenen Mittelpunkt auf dem Campus.

Une importante congrégation de l'Arizona a demandé à des architectes visionnaires de concevoir un ensemble de bâtiments « stratégiques », intégrés à un campus et qui puissent servir à toute une gamme d'activités. Le premier de ces bâtiments, la bibliothèque/cafétéria, a radicalement changé l'aspect du campus par son caractère résolument ouvert sur l'extérieur. Il s'agit d'un immeuble transparent, aux façades en partie escamotables lorsque le temps le permet. Par ses lignes claires et son toit aux formes volontaires, la bibliothèque/cafétéria s'est d'emblée imposée comme le nouveau centre du campus.

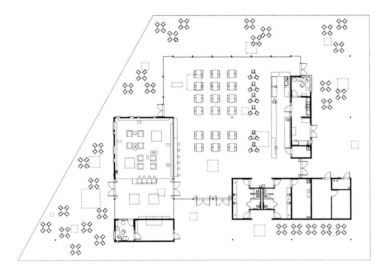

left: Ground floor plan_Building elevation. right: Exterior seating area_General view.
links: Grundriss Erdgeschoss_Gebäudeansicht. rechts: Terrasse_Gesamtansicht.
à gauche: Plan du rez-de-chaussée_Vue générale. à droite: Terrasse_Vue générale.

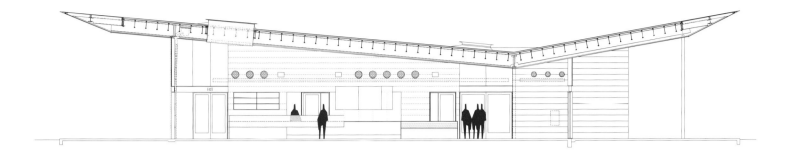

left: Coffee shop. right: Section_Canteen_Exterior view_Seating.
links: Caféteria. rechts: Schnitt_Mensa_Außenansicht_Sitzgelegenheiten.
à gauche: Cafétéria. à droite: Vue en coupe_Autre vue de la cafétéria_Extérieur_Tables et chaises sur la terrasse.

GILBERT_AZ **BANNER GATEWAY MEDICAL CENTER**

**ARCHITECTS:** NBBJ
**COMPLETION:** 2008_**TYPOLOGY:** HEALTH
**PHOTOS:** FRANK OOMS

Gateway Medical Center is the first of Banner Health's "Franchise Model" hospitals following the award-winning prototype, Banner Estrella. At the heart of the concept is a building that enables flexibility and growth over time, allowing efficient reconfiguration while preserving innovation, safety, and clinical excellence standards. The facility combines 165 private patient rooms with obstetrics, pediatrics, general surgery, and emergency services. A regional connection to the community, along with beautifully crafted interiors and a patient-and-staff centered environment, is also incorporated.

Nach dem preisgekrönten Prototyp Banner Estrella ist das Gateway Medical Center das erste der „Franchise-Modell"-Krankenhäuser von Banner Health. Wesentlich für das Konzept ist ein flexibles und erweiterbares Gebäude, das sich unter Beibehaltung von Innovationen, Sicherheit und klinischen Qualitätsstandards effizient umgestalten lässt. Zur Einrichtung gehören 165 Einbettzimmer sowie eine Abteilung für Geburtshilfe, Kinderheilkunde, allgemeine Chirurgie und eine Notfallaufnahme. Neben einem regionalen Bezug zur Gemeinde werden schön gestaltete Innenräume und eine patienten- und mitarbeiterorientierte Umgebung geboten.

Ce centre médical est le premier d'une chaîne de frânchisés dont le prototype, Banner Estrella, a été lauréat d'un concours. Au cœur du concept se trouve un bâtiment flexible et compatible avec des agrandissement ultérieurs, qui peut être reconfiguré de manière efficace en conservant de hauts standards en matière d'innovation, de sécurité et d'excellence médicale. Le centre se compose de 165 chambres pour des malades suivis par les services d'obstétrique, de pédiatrie et de chirurgie générale, ainsi que pour ceux admis en urgence. Bien intégré à son environnement urbain, le centre médical se caractérise encore par la beauté de ses aménagements intérieurs et sa conception axée sur les besoins des malades et du personnel soignant.

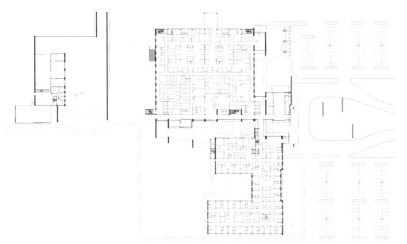

left: First floor plan_Exterior_General view. right: Front façade.
links: Grundriss Erdgeschoss_Außenansicht_Gesamtansicht. rechts: Vorderfassade.
à gauche: Plan du rez-de-chaussée_Extérieur_Autre vue de l'extérieur. à droite: Façade principale.

# PEORIA_AZ **SUNRISE MOUNTAIN LIBRARY**

**ARCHITECTS:** RICHARD+BAUER
**COMPLETION:** 2007_**TYPOLOGY:** PUBLIC
**PHOTOS:** BILL TIMMERMAN PHOTOGRAPHY

This 22,000-square-foot library houses a collection of approximately 75,000 items in three light filled galleries: The children's collection, adult and teen fiction gallery and the third gallery offers a spacious community room. The library features an extensive use of glass and open spacious indoor and outdoor areas. Its distinctive swooping roofline is symbolic of the waves of the nearby Lake Pleasant water marina.

Diese 7.000 Quadratmeter große Bibliothek umfasst ein Sammlung mit etwa 75.000 Medien in drei lichtdurchfluteten Galerien: Die Büchersammlung für Kinder, die Galerie für Erwachsene und Jugendliche und die dritte Zone mit einem großzügigen Gemeinschaftsraum. Die Bibliothek zeichnet sich durch ausgedehnte Glasflächen und offene, weitläufige Innen- und Außenbereiche aus. Ihre charakteristische, schwungvolle Dachsilhouette symbolisiert die Wellen im Segelboothafen des nahe gelegenen Lake Pleasants.

Les 75.000 volumes qui composent le fonds de cette bibliothèque couvrant près de sept mille mètres carrés sont disponibles dans trois grands espaces baignés de lumière. La salle des livres pour enfants, celle des romans pour adultes et ados, ainsi que la troisième grande salle sont interconnectées par un vaste espace commun. La bibliothèque, abondamment vitrée, dispose également de grands espaces de plein air. Son toit caractéristique, aux formes ondulantes, rappelle de manière symbolique les vagues à la surface du Lake Pleasant qui se trouve à proximité.

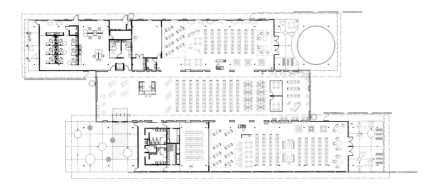

left: Floor plan_Entry view_East entry. right: Children's court at night_North elevation.
links: Grundriss_Eingangsansicht_Östlicher Eingang. rechts: Kinderspielplatz bei Nacht_Nordansicht.
à gauche: Plan_Vue de la zone d'entrée_Entrée est. à droite: La cour des enfants la nuit_Façade nord.

left: Lounge. right: General view_Glazed reading room_Children's reading room_Entry.
links: Aufenthaltsraum. rechts: Gesamtansicht_Verglaster Leseraum_Lesesaal für Kinder_Eingang.
à gauche: Foyer. à droite: Vue d'ensemble_Salle de lecture vitrée_Salle de lecture des enfants_Accueil.

PHOENIX_AZ **THE PRAYER CHAPEL**

**ARCHITECTS:** DEBARTOLO ARCHITECTS
**COMPLETION:** 2007_**TYPOLOGY:** ECCLESIASTICAL
**PHOTOS:** BILL TIMMERMANN PHOTOGRAPHY

The Prayer Pavilion of Light is part of a large church campus in Phoenix, Arizona. Sited along the edge of a desert preserve, a series of inclined planes are incised by a long processional walk, revealing the orthogonal chapel as one gradually ascends the 28-foot vertical between the chapel mount and garden entrance. Arrival upon the exposed-aggregate plaza, one is met with an orderly, yet inviting bosque of desert trees and a black reflection pool. Emerging from the water, a flame burns adjacent to a 50 foot-high steel cross.

Der Pavillon ist Teil eines weitläufigen Kirchengeländes am Rande eines Wüstenschutzgebietes. Mehrere schräge Ebenen werden durch einen langen Prozessionsweg eingeschnitten. Dieser führt zu der rechtwinklig angelegten Kapelle – nach einem achteinhalb Meter hohen Anstieg zwischen dem Kapellhügel und dem Garteneingang. Oben auf einem Platz findet sich der Besucher in einem gepflegten Wüstenwäldchen mit einem schwarzen Becken wieder. Aus diesem ragt eine brennende Flamme neben dem 15 Meter hohen Kreuz aus Stahl.

Cette église de Phoenix se dresse en bordure d'une réserve naturelle du désert de l'Arizona. Une allée servant lors des processions traverse plusieurs plans inclinés qui, avec une dénivellation de 8,50 mètres, mènent de l'entrée du jardin au bâtiment orthogonal construit sur un monticule. Il est entouré d'une esplanade couverte de graviers où poussent des arbustes du désert et où se trouve un bassin aux reflets noirs. Une flamme brûle au milieu de l'eau au pied d'une croix en acier de quinze mètres de haut.

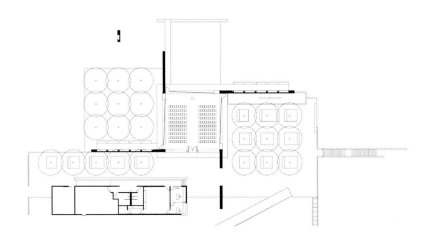

left: Floor plan_General view_Side view. right: Illuminated volume_General view by night.
links: Grundriss_Gesamtansicht_Seitenansicht. rechts: Beleuchteter Baukörper_Gesamtansicht bei Nacht.
à gauche: Plan_ Vue générale_ Vue latérale. à droite: Volume éclairé la nuit_ Vue générale de l'église la nuit.

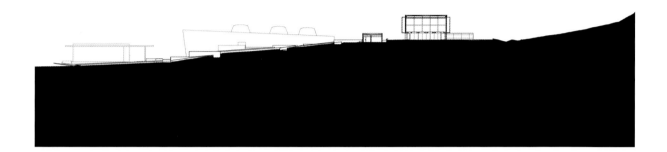

left: View into chapel. right: Chapel section_Interior view_Entrance view_View outside.
links: Blick in die Kapelle. rechts: Schnitt_Innenansicht_Eingang_Blick nach draußen.
à gauche: L'église la nuit. à droite: Vue en coupe_ Intérieur la nuit_ L'entrée_Deux vues intérieur/extérieur.

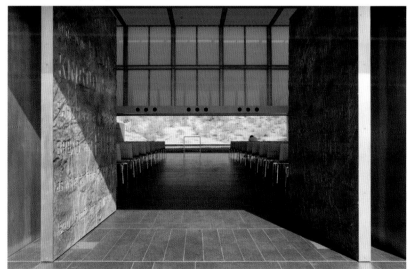

# PHOENIX_AZ **HOOVER HOUSE**

**ARCHITECTS:** [MERZ]PROJECT
**COMPLETION:** 2007_**TYPOLOGY:** LIVING
**PHOTOS:** MATT WINQUIST

This urban-infill project located in the Ashland Historic District near downtown Phoenix is an addition and remodel of an existing bungalow originally constructed in 1924. The cellular character of the original floor plan was dissolved in the old house, opening it up to large multi-use indoor/outdoor rooms, including a graphic design studio, a retail store, and a top-floor private residence/roof garden. While the urban personality and street connectivity is straightforward, the interior of the building has an organizational complexity that blurs many traditional boundaries between living and working at all three levels.

Bei dieser Nachverdichtung im Ashland Historic District unweit der Stadtmitte von Phoenix wurden ein 1924 errichteter Bungalow erweitert und umgestaltet. Der zellenförmige Geschossgrundriss im Altbau wird zu großzügigen, vielseitig verwendbaren Innen-Außen-Räumen aufgelöst. Dadurch entstehen unter anderem ein Studio für Grafikdesign, ein Einzelhandelsgeschäft und eine Privatwohnung mit Dachgarten im obersten Geschoss. Während sich das Haus zur Stadt und zur Straße hin unkompliziert gibt, verfügt sein Inneres über eine organisatorische Komplexität, die auf allen drei Ebenen viele traditionelle Grenzen zwischen Wohnen und Arbeiten verschwimmen lässt.

La tâche des architectes consistait ici à remodeler et agrandir un bungalow construit en 1924 dans le vieux quartier d'Ashland, près du centre ville de Phoenix. Le plan d'origine a été fondamentalement modifié de manière à créer de grands espaces intérieurs/extérieurs polyvalents, notamment un studio d'arts graphiques, une boutique et des pièces privées situées à l'étage et complétées par un jardin suspendu. Tandis que la façade sur rue et l'extérieur en général sont d'un style assez strict, l'intérieur sur trois niveaux présente toute une complexité qui tend à estomper les limites traditionnelles entre espaces de séjour et zones de travail.

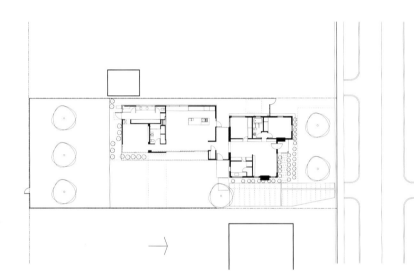

left: Ground floor plan_View from master bedroom to living room. right: Fully glazed façade_Exterior view.
links: Grundriss Erdgeschoss_Blick vom Schlafzimmer in den Wohnbereich. rechts: Verglaste Fassade_Außenansicht.
à gauche: Plan du rez-de-chaussée_Vue de la chambre en direction du séjour. à droite: Façade entièrement vitrée_Extérieur.

left: Interior. right: Elevation and section_Kitchen.
links: Innenansicht. rechts: Ansicht und Schnitt_Küche.
à gauche: Intérieur. à droite: Vues en élévation et en coupe_Cuisine.

# PHOENIX_AZ **DUPLEX RESIDENCE**

**ARCHITECTS:** PLUS MINUS STUDIO + C U P
**COMPLETION:** 2006_**TYPOLOGY:** LIVING
**PHOTOS:** TERRY SURJAN

The Duplex Residence is a project that combines two units being built on a single city lot, and is intended for a couple and their best friend. An important feature that made this possible was a spatial joint, which was developed in the overlap of entrances and the roof access. The L-shaped complex is a double bar scheme that is divided into served and service areas. This division allows all functions including cooking, bathing, washing, etc., to be built-in as furniture, for example an inhabitable loaded core wall. The house also provides relief from the desert sun with a lap pool for all residences.

Das Projekt Duplex Residence vereint auf einer einzigen Stadtparzelle zwei Wohneinheiten für ein Paar und deren besten Freund. Möglich machte dies eine räumliche Fuge, die in der Überschneidung der Eingänge und im Dachzugang entwickelt wurde. Der L-förmige Komplex aus zwei Riegelbauten ist in öffentliche und private Bereiche unterteilt. Dadurch lassen sich alle Funktionen – darunter Kochen, Baden, Waschen usw. – als Möbel einbauen, beispielsweise in einer unbewohnbaren tragenden Kernwand. Ein Schwimmbecken macht allen Bewohnern die Wüstensonne erträglicher.

Cette villa urbaine se compose de deux logements destinés à un couple et son meilleur ami, les deux unités étant séparées par un espace couvert audessus de leur entrée respective. Le bâtiment a un plan en forme de L, chacune des barres étant divisée en plusieurs espaces de séjour et de service. Tous les équipements ménagers (notamment la cuisinière, la baignoire et les lavabos) sont intégrés aux aménagements intérieurs. Une piscine mise à la disposition de tous les occupants leur permet de trouver la fraîcheur nécessaire lorsque le soleil du désert se fait trop insistant.

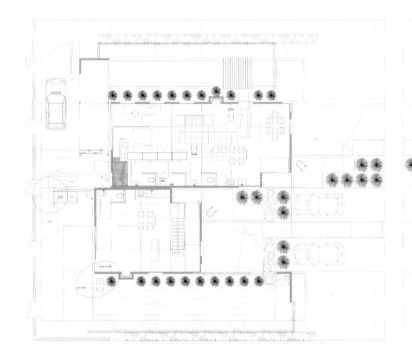

left: Ground floor plan_Exterior_Courtyard. right: Detail overlap entrances_General view.
links: Grundriss Erdgeschoss_Hof. rechts: Überdachter Eingangsbereich_Gesamtansicht.
à gauche: Plan du rez-de-chaussée_Cour_Extérieur. à droite: Pergola devant l'entrée_Vue d'ensemble.

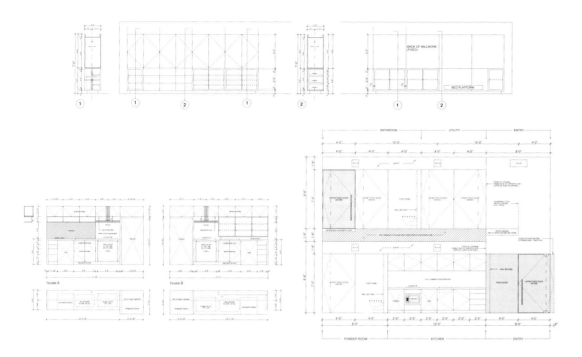

left: Exterior view. right: Elevations_Façade and pool_Living space.
links: Außenansicht. rechts: Schnitte_Ansicht von Fassade und Pool_Wohnbereich.
à gauche: Extérieur. à droite: Vues en élévation_Bâtiment et piscine_Séjour.

# TEMPE_AZ **TEMPE CENTER FOR THE ARTS**

**ARCHITECTS:** BARTON MYERS ASSOCIATES, INC. + ARCHITEKTON
**COMPLETION:** 2007_**TYPOLOGY:** CULTURE
**PHOTOS:** JOHN EDWARD LINDEN (264 L., 265, 266),
PETER ROBERTSON (267 L., 267 B. R.),
MICHAEL MASENGARB (267 A. R.), RICHARD KRULL (264 R.)

The Tempe Center for the Arts is a vibrant gathering place integrating performing arts and park activities on the developing riverfront. The Center's design draws upon significant historic, climatic, and contextual traditions for inspiration, specifically the organizing concepts of two indigenous desert builders, the Chocoan and Hohokam peoples. A unifying, exterior curved wall made of poured in place concrete serves to enclose the main building and shields extreme desert temperatures. The Center is sheltered by an extensive and sculptural shed roof, which serves as a memorable icon when viewed from the river area, passing aircraft, and the city.

Das Tempe Center for the Arts am sich entwickelnden Flussufer ist ein dynamischer Treff- und Begegnungsort für darstellende Künste und Aktivitäten im Park. Sein Entwurf ist von wichtigen historischen, klimatischen und kontextspezifischen Traditionen inspiriert. Eingeflossen sind vor allem die Organisationskonzepte der beiden einheimischen Wüstenvölker Chocoan und Hohokam. Eine vereinheitlichende, gebogene Außenwand aus Ortbeton dient als Umfassung des Hauptgebäudes und schützt vor den extremen Temperaturen in der Wüste. Das ausgedehnte, plastisch ausgebildete Sheddach des Centers wirkt vom Flussufer, aus der Luft und von der Stadt aus betrachtet als einprägsame Ikone.

Le style architectural de ce centre culturel construit dans un parc au bord d'un plan d'eau a été dicté par le climat désertique et inspiré par l'histoire et les tradition locales, notamment celles de deux tribus indiennes de l'Arizona: les Chocoans et les Hohakams. Un grand mur en béton coulé sur place, de forme presque circulaire, protège l'intérieur des températures extrêmes qui règnent dans le désert. La qualité sculpturale du grand toit qui unifie le bâtiment caractérise le centre culturel et permet de le reconnaître lorsqu'on l'observe de la rivière, du centre ville ou lorsqu'on le survole en avion.

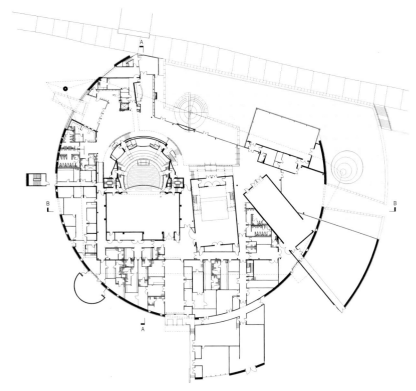

left: Ground floor plan_Front façade_Shed roof detail for rain collection. right: Fireplace and infinity pool_Exterior view by night.
links: Grundriss Erdgeschoss_Vorderfassade_Detail des Regenspeichers. rechts: Feuerstelle, Wasserbecken_Außenansicht bei Nacht.
à gauche: Plan du rez-de-chaussée_Façade principale_Noue pour récupération de l'eau de pluie. à droite: Espace avec brasero au bord du plan d'eau_Le centre culturel la nuit.

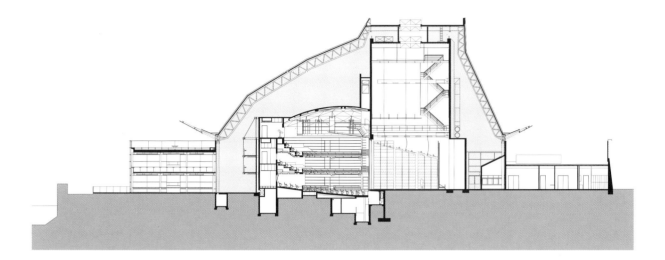

left: Lobby. right: Section_Tiered lobby balconies outside the main theater_600-seat main theater_Art gallery.
links: Eingangshalle. rechts: Schnitt_Abgestufte Eingangshalle mit äußeren Balkonen des Theaters_Theater mit 600 Sitzen_Kunstgalerie.
à gauche: Hall d'entrée. à droite: Vue en coupe_Galeries autour du grand auditorium_Auditorium de six cents places_Galerie d'art.

# TEMPE_AZ **LANDSOURCE TEMPE**

**ARCHITECTS:** CIRCLE WEST
**COMPLETION:** UNBUILT_**TYPOLOGY:** LIVING
**RENDERINGS:** CIRCLE WEST

The design was to develop a vertically integrated neighborhood, with an emphasis on identity, connectivity to neighbors, and gathering spaces. Located in a neglected area of Tempe, Arizona, the project will serve as a strong visual "filter". A prominent, articulated entry at ground level highlights the transparency and activity of the first three floors, while live workspaces reinforce the vertically integrated neighborhood. The parking structure roof is utilized as an amenities deck, providing a community gathering space that includes appropriate desert landscaping, shade, and a swimming pool.

Der Entwurf sollte eine vertikal integrierte Nachbarschaft mit einem Schwerpunkt auf Identität, Verbindungen zu Nachbarn und Treffpunkten entwickeln. In einem verwahrlosten Gebiet von Tempe in Arizona wird das Projekt als starker visueller „Filter" dienen. Eine vorspringende, aufgegliederte Vorhalle unterstreicht auf Straßenebene die Transparenz und Aktivität der ersten drei Geschosse, während sich darüber die Wohn- und Arbeitsbereiche stapeln. Die Dachterrasse des Parkhauses dient als gemeinschaftlicher Aufenthaltsraum, zu dem eine auf das Wüstenklima abgestimmte Bepflanzung, Schattenplätze und ein Swimmingpool gehören.

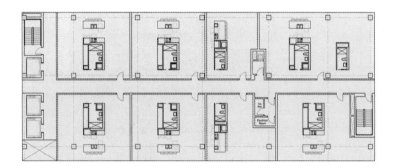

L'objectif du projet est de créer un complexe vertical à forte personnalité qui favorise les rapports de voisinage grâce à divers espaces de rencontre. Devant être construit dans une zone jusqu'à présent négligée de Tempe, en Arizona, le nouveau complexe doit également servir de « filtre visuel ». La zone d'entrée s'articule au rez-de-chaussée et met en évidence la transparence et l'activité des trois premiers niveaux, tandis que des espaces de travail vivants renforcent l'intégration verticale des éléments de voisinage. Le toit du parking accueille divers équipements de loisirs, notamment un espace de rencontre ombragé qui rappelle le désert environnant, mais où se trouve néanmoins une piscine.

left: Floor plan_Community space with swimming pool_General view by night. right: Detail of living unit_Lobby.
links: Grundriss_Gemeinschaftsfläche mit swimmingpool_Gesamtansicht bei Nacht. rechts: Detailansicht des Wohnraums_Eingangshalle.
à gauche: Plan_Immeuble et piscine_L'immeuble la nuit. à droite: Gros plan sur les logements la nuit_Hall d'entrée.

TUCSON_AZ **MEINEL OPTICAL SCIENCES BUILDING – UNIVERSITY OF ARIZONA**

**ARCHITECTS:** RICHARD+BAUER
**COMPLETION:** 2007_**TYPOLOGY:** EDUCATION
**PHOTOS:** BILL TIMMERMAN PHOTOGRAPHY

The Meinel Building is a study of light, where it's form is conceived from the Camera Obscura. The design demonstrates the power that light possesses in illuminating the experience inside of the building. Within the simple volume, daylight is introduced through a series of apertures, interacting and modulating the spaces within. Three vertical light shafts penetrate the building and terminate in a series of two-story interaction spaces. Each shaft features a specific optical effect rendered in a white veneer plaster, allowing natural daylight to actively integrate into the daily activities of the building.

Das Meinel Optical Forschungsgebäude ist eine Lichtstudie, deren Form von einer Camera Obscura abgeleitet ist. Sein Entwurf verdeutlicht, in welchem Maße Licht das Raumerlebnis beeinflussen kann. Durch eine Reihe von Öffnungen fällt Tageslicht in den einfachen Baukörper, setzt die Innenräume in Beziehung und moduliert sie. Drei vertikale Lichtschächte durchdringen das Gebäude und schließen mit mehreren zweigeschossigen Interaktionsräumen ab. Jeder Schacht hat eine spezifische optische Wirkung und ist mit einem weißen Überzug verputzt, sodass natürliches Licht in die täglichen Aktivitäten im Gebäude einbezogen ist.

Les architectes ont conçu le bâtiment en s'inspirant des chambres noires d'antan afin de démontrer le pouvoir de la lumière lorsqu'il s'agit de mettre un intérieur en valeur. Diverses ouvertures permettent aux rayons du soleil de s'introduire dans un volume simple et d'en modeler l'intérieur. Citons notamment les trois puits de lumière qui éclairent des espaces interactifs sur deux niveaux. Chacun des puits génère un effet spécial sur les murs blancs, la lumière naturelle influant ainsi directement sur les activités ayant lieu à l'intérieur du bâtiment.

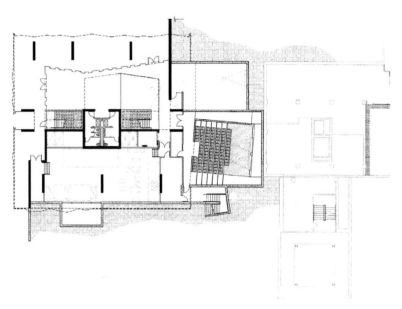

left: Floor plan_Atrium_View of ceiling and stairs. right: Façade.
links: Grundriss_Lichthof_Blick von unten in das Treppenhaus. rechts: Fassade.
à gauche: Plan_Hall en dessous d'un puits de lumière_Vue de l'escalier et d'un puits de lumière. à droite: Extérieur du bâtiment.

left: Fully glazed façade. right: Sections_Exterior_Copper façade_Auditorium.
links: Verglaste Fassade. rechts: Schnitte_Außenansicht_Fassade aus Kupfer_Versammlungsraum.
à gauche: Façade entièrement vitrée. à droite: Vues en coupe_Extérieur_Façade avec revêtement en cuivre_Auditorium.

TUCSON_AZ **THE UNIVERSITY OF ARIZONA, CHEMICAL SCIENCES BUILDING**

**ARCHITECTS:** ZIMMER GUNSUL FRASCA ARCHITECTS
**COMPLETION:** 2006_**TYPOLOGY:** EDUCATION
**PHOTOS:** ROBERT CANFIELD

ZGF programmed and designed a new 85,661-square-foot laboratory building to house the Department of Chemistry. Program areas include organic, inorganic, analytical and physical chemistry research laboratories and support spaces, a Class 1000 clean room, instrument laboratories, faculty and student offices, and administrative support spaces. Brick, a campus tradition, was the primary building material, updated with glass and copper. Conference rooms and corridor windows are covered by a copper skin, which is perforated at these locations to provide sun protection while allowing natural daylight into the spaces.

ZGF planten und entwarfen ein neues 7.960 Quadratmeter großes Laborgebäude für den Fachbereich Chemie. Zu den Programmbereichen zählen Forschungslabors für organische, anorganische, analytische und physikalische Chemie sowie Serviceflächen, ein Reinraum der Klasse ISO 6, Gerätelabors, Dozenten- und Studentenbüros sowie Verwaltungseinrichtungen. Neben dem auf dem Campus traditionell verwendeten Backstein kamen hauptsächlich Glas und Kupfer als neue Materialien hinzu. Besprechungsräume und Korridorfenster sind mit einer perforierten Kupferhaut bedeckt, die für Sonnenschutz und natürliches Tageslicht sorgt.

Les architectes ont été chargés de concevoir un immeuble de 7.960 mètres carrés devant abriter la faculté de chimie de l'université d'Arizona. Parmi les divers espaces du bâtiment, citons les laboratoires de chimie organique, inorganique, analytique et physique, une salle de haute propreté de classe 1000, des laboratoires d'instruments, les espaces de travail des étudiants et de leurs professeurs, ainsi que tous les bureaux administratifs. Les architectes ont choisi la brique — matériau déjà utilisé pour les autres immeubles du campus — et l'ont complétée avec du verre et du cuivre, notamment dans les salles de conférence et les couloirs, où des plaques en métal perforé protègent du rayonnement solaire toute en assurant un bon éclairage naturel de l'intérieur.

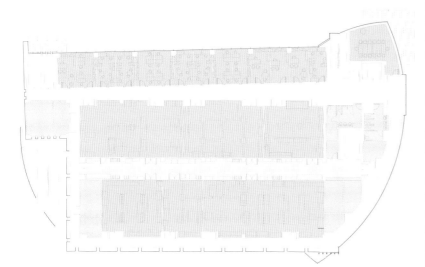

left: Second floor plan_Courtyard_Conference room. right: Garden.
links: Grundriss zweites Obergeschoss_Innenhof_Konferenzraum. rechts: Garten.
à gauche: Plan du second étage_Vue de la cour_Salle de conférence. à droite: Vue du jardin.

TUSCON_AZ **PETER AND PAULA FASSEAS CANCER CLINIC AT UNIVERSITY MEDICAL CENTER**

**ARCHITECTS:** CO ARCHITECTS
**COMPLETION:** 2007_**TYPOLOGY:** HEALTH
**PHOTOS:** ROBERT CANFIELD

The architecture and nature are closely integrated through use of elements such as abundant daylight, trellised terraces, and vistas to beautiful mountain ranges beyond. All elements of the building's design are intended to relate to the natural landscape. A sense of beauty and calm is provided by a healing garden that is an integral part of the design. Arizona sandstone, plaster, and metal panels are used on the exterior. Trellises and covered entries provide shade from the sun. Interior finishes include natural materials or those made from natural products, such as stone flooring and wood paneling.

Architektur und Natur gehen durch reichlich Tageslicht, Terrassen mit Gitterwerk und Ausblicke auf die schöne Bergkette eine enge Verbindung ein. Alle Gestaltungselemente sollen sich auf die natürliche Landschaft beziehen. Ein Garten mit Heilpflanzen vermittelt einen Eindruck von Schönheit und Ruhe. An den Außenwänden finden sich Arizona-Sandstein, Putz und Metalltafeln. Pergolen und überdachte Eingänge schützen vor der Sonne. Die Innenausstattung besteht aus natürlichen Materialien oder solchen, die aus Naturprodukten hergestellt wurden, wie Steinböden und Holzvertäfelungen.

Cet hôpital intègre la nature environnante grâce à des terrasses agrémentées de treillis et à de grands espaces vitrés qui assurent un bon éclairage naturel et offrent des vues magnifiques sur les montagnes voisines. De fait, tous les éléments architecturaux visent ici à établir des liens avec la nature. C'est le cas notamment du jardin, qui contribue au processus de guérison par le calme et la beauté qui s'en dégagent. Les façades se composent de grès de l'Arizona, de panneaux métalliques et de surfaces enduites de plâtre. Des treillis protègent du soleil, notamment au niveau des entrées. Les aménagements intérieurs utilisent des matériaux naturels, en particulier le bois qu'on trouve sur le plancher et les murs.

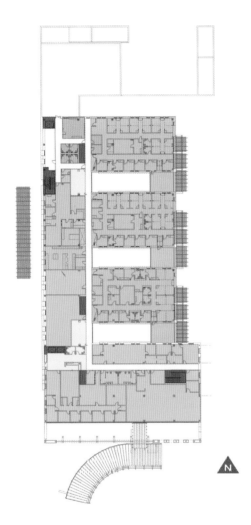

left: Floor plan_Roofed entrance area_Fountain in courtyard. right: General view_Entrance view_Exterior view.
links: Grundriss_Überdachter Eingangsbereich_Springbrunnen im Hof. rechts: Gesamtansicht_Eingangsbereich_Außenansicht.
à gauche: Plan_Pergola de la zone d'entrée_Fontaine dans la cour. à droite: Vue générale_Vue de l'entrée_Extérieur.

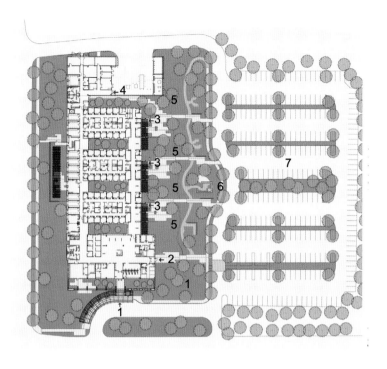

left: Planted courtyard. right: Site plan_Space between volumes_Terrace_Lobby, information desk.
links: Bepflanzter Innenhof. rechts: Lageplan_Raum zwischen den Gebäuden_Terrasse_Aufent-
haltsraum, Information.
à gauche: Cour végétalisée. à droite: Plan de situation_Espace entre deux volumes_Terrasse_Hall
d'accueil.

# TUCSON_AZ **DOWNING RESIDENCE**

**ARCHITECTS:** IBARRA ROSANO DESIGN ARCHITECTS
**COMPLETION:** 2003_**TYPOLOGY:** LIVING
**PHOTOS:** BILL TIMMERMAN

The Downing Residence is a carefully nested desert dwelling on a hillside west of Tucson organized between existing saguaros. The 3,500 square foot design splits the floor plan into three smaller pavilion-like footprints in order to rest more gently between areas of dense vegetation. From a distance, the Downing Residence is barely discernable from its east-facing mountainside backdrop. The structure blends with the surrounding rock outcroppings as each of its three volumes sit reverently within a grove of saguaro that dot the hillside.

Downing Residence liegt sorgfältig eingefügt auf einem Hang westlich von Tucson. Zwei Riesenkakteen bestimmen die Anordnung des Hauses in der Wüstenlandschaft. Der 325 Quadratmeter große Grundriss ist in drei kleinere pavillonähnliche Flächen aufgeteilt, um das Haus behutsam zwischen Bereichen mit dichter Vegetation zu integrieren. Von Weitem ist der Bau von seiner dem Osten zugewandten Bergkulisse kaum zu unterscheiden. Er verschmilzt mit den umgebenden, zutage tretenden Felsen, da sich jeder seiner drei Baukörper zwischen den am Hang verstreuten Kakteen duckt.

Cette villa a été construite parmi des cactus du type saguaro, sur une colline désertique située à l'ouest de Tucson. D'une superficie totale de 325 mètres carrés, elle s'organise selon trois volumes distincts afin de minimiser l'impact sur la végétation du désert de l'Arizona. À tel point qu'on distingue à peine la villa lorsqu'on s'éloigne à quelque distance dans les collines qui lui servent d'écrin. Les trois unités qui la composent se fondent parfaitement dans cet environnement rocailleux dominé par les cactus qui se dressent çà et là.

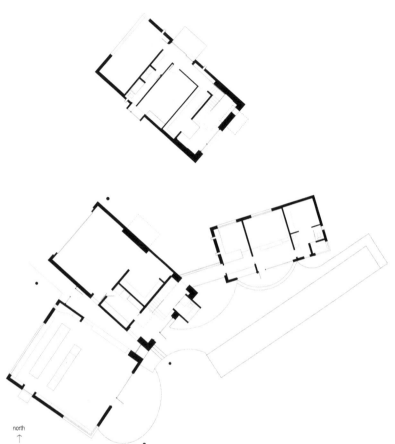

north
↑

left: Floor plan_Living space with open kitchen_Stairs. right: Exterior view_Exterior view at night Infinity pool with view of mountains.
links: Grundriss_Wohnraum mit offener Küche_Treppenaufgang. rechts: Außenansicht_Ansicht bei Nacht_Infinity Pool mit Blick auf die Berge.
à gauche: Plan_Salon et cuisine ouverte_Escalier. à droite: La villa dans son environnement naturel_La villa la nuit_Piscine extra-longue avec colline à l'arrière plan.

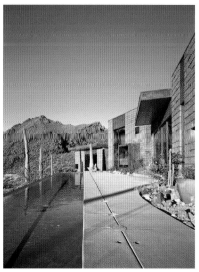

# BIG SUR_CA **JACKSON FAMILY RETREAT**

**ARCHITECTS:** FOUGERON ARCHITECTURE
**COMPLETION:** 2000_**TYPOLOGY:** LIVING
**PHOTOS:** RICHARD BARNES PHOTOGRAPHY

Located in the Big Sur area of Northern California, this 2,500 square foot two bedroom house was built for a family to enjoy together on the weekends and holidays. It is a modernist structure that sits lightly on the land acknowledging the ecologically fragile nature of the site. The house is composed of four volumes all made of different materials that are interwoven and interconnected to create visually and spatially complex exterior and interior spaces. The main volume of the house runs parallel to the canyon with a butterfly roof and glass corners at both ends that reach out to the blue sky and natural light.

Im Gebiet von Big Sur in Nordkalifornien entstand dieses 232 Quadratmeter große Zwei-Schlafzimmer-Haus für die gemeinsamen Wochenenden und Ferien einer Familie. Mit Rücksicht auf den ökologisch empfindlichen Standort ist die moderne Konstruktion dem Boden nur leicht aufgesetzt. Ihre vier Baukörper bestehen aus unterschiedlichen, miteinander verflochtenen und verbundenen Materialien, sodass sich optisch und räumlich komplexe Innen- und Außenräume ergeben. Der Hauptbau verläuft parallel zum Canyon. Sein Flügeldach und seine verglasten Ecken an beiden Enden weisen zum blauen Himmel und natürlichen Licht.

Cette villa de 232 mètres carrés située à Big Sur, dans le nord de la Californie, a été construite pour qu'une famille vienne s'y réunir le week-end et pendant les vacances. Il s'agit d'un bâtiment moderniste posé légèrement sur le sol de manière à respecter un écosystème fragile. Ses quatre volumes sont réalisés dans des matériaux différents et reliés entre eux de manière à créer des espaces intérieurs et extérieurs d'une structure complexe. Le volume principal, parallèle au canyon qui se trouve à proximité, est couvert par un toit ultraléger reposant sur une bande vitrée qui laisse entrer la lumière naturelle et permet aux occupants d'apprécier le bleu du ciel de l'intérieur.

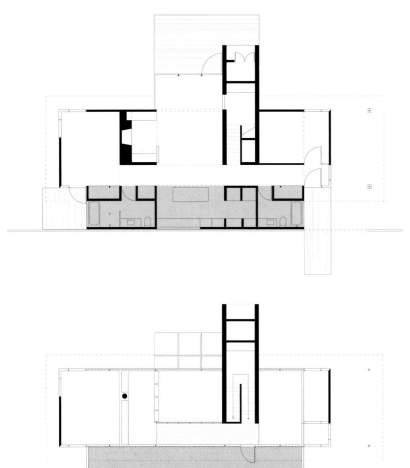

left: Ground floor and first floor plan_Elevation entrance_Sundeck_Rear view. right: Terrace and living room_Garden elevation_Northeast elevation.
links: Grundriss Erdgeschoss und erstes Obergeschoss_Eingangsansicht_Terrasse_Rückansicht.
rechts: Terrasse und Wohnbereich_Gartenansicht_Nordostansicht.
à gauche: Plans du rez-de-chaussée et du premier étage_Façade du côté de l'entrée_Deux vues de la terrasse. à droite: Séjour vu de l'extérieur_Façade côté jardin_Façade nord-est.

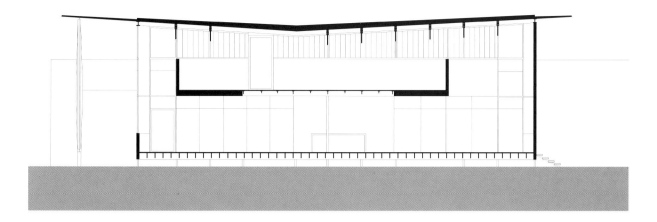

left: View down into living room. right: Section_Corridor, kitchen and living area_Interior of upper level.
links: Blick von oben ins Wohnzimmer. rechts: Schnitt_Flur, Küche und Wohnbereich_Interieur im Obergeschoss.
à gauche: Séjour. à droite: Vue en coupe_Cuisine, couloir et séjour_Mezzanine.

# BRENTWOOD_CA **TIGERTAIL**

**ARCHITECTS:** TIGHE ARCHITECTURE
**COMPLETION:** 2006_**TYPOLOGY:** LIVING
**PHOTOS:** ART GRAY PHOTOGRAPHY

The architecture of this 3,200-square-feet residence is a result of various conditions inherent within the site and the existing building. Current building setback regulations, openings to the view and the need for solid walls for shear and privacy had an effect on the peculiar geometry of the two-story volume. Three bent steel moment frames straddle the existing one-story structure, while the folded planes of the walls and roof act as an extension of the rolling topography. The exterior of the folded planes is sheathed in metal, while the interior is lined with wood blurring the distinction between wall, ceiling and floor plane.

Die Architektur dieses 297 Quadratmeter großen Wohnhauses resultiert aus den Grundstücksgegebenheiten und dem vorhandenen Gebäude. Vorgeschriebene Baugrenzen, Fenster zur Aussicht und massive Mauern, die vor Erddruck schützen und Privatsphäre bieten, wirkten sich auf die spezifische Geometrie des zweigeschossigen Baukörpers aus. Drei Stahlrahmentragwerke überspannen die bestehende eingeschossige Konstruktion, wobei gefaltete Wand- und Dachebenen die sanft ansteigende Topografie erweitern. Außen sind die Faltungen mit Metall ausgekleidet, innen hebt eine Holztäfelung den Unterschied zwischen Wand, Decke und Fußboden auf.

La géométrie particulière de cette maison de 297 mètres carrés répartis sur deux niveaux a été largement déterminée par la législation locale, la topographie des lieux, le bâtiment préexistant et la nécessité de l'ouvrir sur le paysage tout en ménageant l'intimité des occupants. Trois cadres en acier complètent la structure d'origine de plain-pied. Les plis des murs et du toit renvoient aux sinuosités du terrain. Des plaques de métal ont été utilisées comme revêtement extérieur, tandis qu'à l'intérieur le bois se retrouve aussi bien sur les murs que sur le plafond ou le plancher.

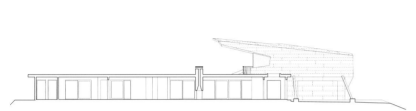

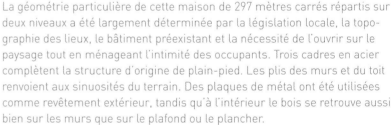

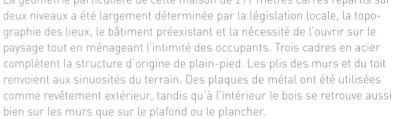

left: Sections_General view_Roof construction, glazed façade. right: Exterior sheather in metal Detail window_Exterior with view of city.
links: Schnitte_Gesamtansicht_Dachkonstruktion, verglaste Fassade. rechts: Ummantelung aus Metall_Fensterdetail_Außenansicht mit Blick in die Stadt.
à gauche: Vues en coupe_Vue d'ensemble côté jardin_Auvent et façade vitrée. à droite: vue d'ensemble côté rue_Gros plan sur une fenêtre_Toit avec revêtement métallique et vue de la ville à l'arrière plan.

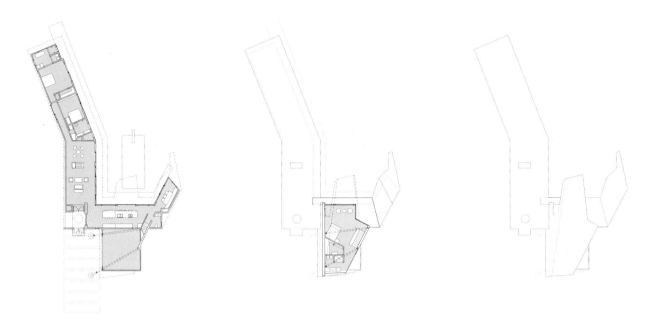

left: Exterior view of garden and pool. right: Floor plans_Exterior view with folded planes by night.
links: Ansicht von Garten und Pool. rechts: Grundrisse_Gefaltetes Dach.
à gauche: Le bâtiment et la piscine la nuit. à droite: Plan des différents niveaux_Vue du toit angulaire la nuit.

BURBANK_CA **WOODBURY UNIVERSITY**
**NEW STUDIO BUILDING**

**ARCHITECTS:** RIOS CLEMENTI HALE STUDIOS
**COMPLETION:** 2008_**TYPOLOGY:** EDUCATION
**PHOTOS:** TOM BONNER

Woodbury University required a new studio building to complete the architecture department, comprising of five, one-story buildings. RCHS designed the new, two-story building to house architectural studios, critique spaces, support spaces, and a double-height multi-purpose room. While the south façade creates a buffer zone, the north façade opens the studio building to the department complex, providing a porous edge to a courtyard formed by the existing studio building. To connect the new structure to the existing complex, the north façade employs smaller-scale layering of vertical elements.

Die Architekturschule der Woodbury University mit ihren fünf eingeschossigen Bauten sollte um ein Studiogebäude ergänzt werden. Der zweigeschossige Neubau von RCHS umfasst Architekturstudios, Besprechungs- und Serviceflächen und einen zwei Etagen hohen Mehrzweckraum. Während seine Südfassade eine Pufferzone schafft, öffnet sich die poröse Nordfassade zum bestehenden Gebäudeensemble und einem Hof, den ein vorhandenes Studiogebäude bildet. Um den Neubau an den Bestand anzubinden, sind an der Nordfassade die Schichten mit vertikalen Elementen kleiner dimensioniert.

L'université de Woodbury avait besoin d'un nouveau bâtiment venant compléter les cinq édifices de plain-pied de sa faculté d'architecture. Les architectes ont conçu un immeuble sur deux niveaux abritant des ateliers, des espaces critiques, des locaux techniques et une salle polyvalente haute de plafond. La façade sud donne sur une zone tampon, tandis que la façade nord s'ouvre sur une cour et divers bâtiments préexistants par l'intermédiaire d'une surface poreuse à base de lattes verticales de petit format.

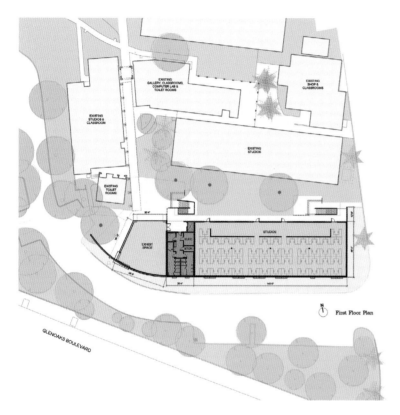

left: Site plan_Exhibition space_Interior, studio. right: Exterior view_Brick façade_Street side view. links: Lageplan_Ausstellungsfläche_Innenansicht Studio_Verglaste Fassade. rechts: Außenansicht_Backsteinfassade_Straßenansicht. à gauche: Plan de situation_Salle d'exposition_Atelier. à droite: Extérieur_Façade en briques_Le bâtiment vu de la rue.

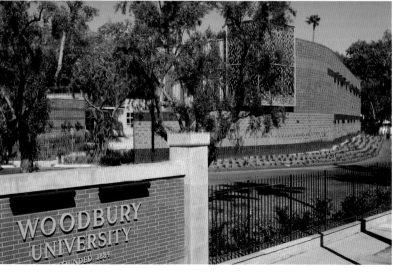

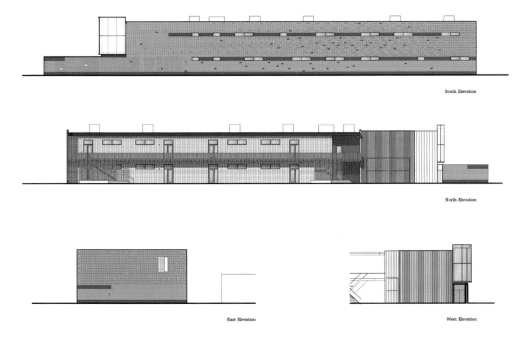

South Elevation

North Elevation

East Elevation

West Elevation

left: Wall with varying patterns of concrete masonry units. right: Elevations_Bi-fold hangar door opens into the north courtyard.

links: Betonfassade. rechts: Ansichten_Gefaltete Hangartür zum Hof.

à gauche: Murs en parpaings de types divers. à droite: Trois vues en élévation_Cour nord avec hangar muni d'une porte en deux éléments horizontaux.

# CARMEL VALLEY_CA **FALCON HOUSE**

**ARCHITECTS:** DESIGNARC
**COMPLETION:** 2007_**TYPOLOGY:** LIVING
**PHOTOS:** EMILY HAGOPIAN PHOTOGRAPHY

Designed for a young couple with a child, Falcon House responds to the family's desire to live a more modest lifestyle, eschewing overt displays of extravagance for an intimate and deferential relation to nature. The 3,200-square-foot residence occupies a difficult portion of the northern slope of a hillside, overlooking a verdant valley and oriented toward Castle Rock in the distance. A corridor as bridge spans two pieces of the house, uniting living and sleeping spaces, and allowing an existing watercourse to flow essentially through the house unobstructed.

Das für ein junges Paar mit Kind entworfene Falcon House korrespondiert mit dem Wunsch der Familie nach einem bescheideneren Lebensstil. Es verzichtet zugunsten einer intimen und respektvollen Beziehung zur Natur auf eine offen zur Schau gestellte Extravaganz. Das 297 Quadratmeter große Wohnhaus nimmt den schwierigen Teil eines Nordhangs ein, der eine Sicht auf ein dicht begrüntes Tal bietet und zum entfernten Castle Rock weist. Ein Korridor in Form einer Brücke überspannt zwei Räume des Hauses und vereint Wohn- und Schlafzimmer. Dadurch kann ein vorhandener Wasserlauf das Haus nahezu ungehindert passieren.

Un jeune couple avec enfant a demandé aux architectes de concevoir une villa où la famille pourrait vivre modestement, en privilégiant une relation étroite avec la nature par rapport à un mode de vie extravagant. Le bâtiment, qui couvre une superficie totale de 297 mètres carrés, est construit sur le versant nord d'une colline qui domine une vallée verdoyante orientée vers Castle Rock. Il se compose de deux volumes distincts, l'un abritant les pièces de séjour, l'autre les chambres. Ces deux unités sont reliées entre elles par un couloir vitré qui enjambe un ruisseau.

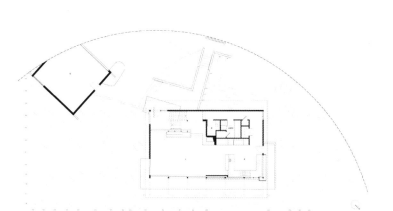

left: Floor plan lower level_Hillside view_Driveway. right: Sundeck, view into open kitchen and living room.
links: Grundriss Erdgeschoss_Gesamtansicht_Auffahrt. rechts: Terrasse, Ansicht der offenen Küche und des Wohnzimmers.
à gauche: Plan du niveau inférieur_Vue d'ensemble_Route d'accès. à droite: Terrasse prolongeant le salon avec cuisine ouverte.

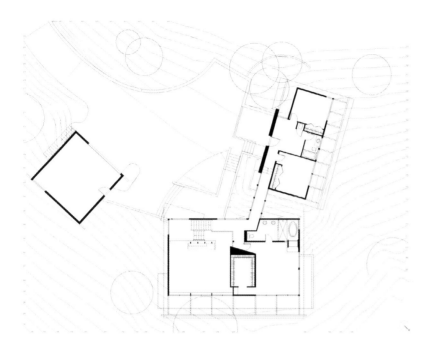

left: Exterior view. right: Ground floor plan_Bridge between the volumes_Sundeck_Entrance view_Kitchen.
links: Außenansicht. rechts: Grundriss Erdgeschoss_Brückenübergang zwischen den Gebäuden_ Terrasse_Eingangsansicht_Küche.
à gauche: Extérieur. à droite: Plan du rez-de-chaussée_Couloir vitré reliant les deux volumes_Ter-rasse_Esplanade d'entrée_Cuisine.

# CULVER CITY_CA **MODAA BUILDING**

**ARCHITECTS:** SPF :ARCHITECTS STUDIO PALI FEKETE ARCHITECTS
**COMPLETION:** 2005_**TYPOLOGY:** LIVING / WORK
**PHOTOS:** JOHN EDWARD LINDEN

Seven live/work artist lofts occupy the upper floor of the MODAA building in Culver City. On the ground floor the building houses the architects' own studios, WILSON restaurant, and the Museum of Design Art and Architecture (MODAA) – a 2,000-square-foot dedicated art gallery exploring the symbiotic relationship between art and architecture. Each loft features 16-foot high ceilings, two mezzanines and two private terrace decks. Tri-panel Fleetwood sliding glass doors are used in place of windows, and the residence's exposed ceiling timbers and open floor plan represents loft living in its purest sense.

Sieben Künstlerlofts zum Wohnen und Arbeiten belegen das Obergeschoss des MODAA Gebäudes in Culver City. Im Erdgeschoss befinden sich die eigenen Büros der Architekten, das Restaurant WILSON und das Museum of Design Art and Architecture (MODAA) – eine 185 Quadratmeter große Galerie erforscht die symbiotische Beziehung zwischen Kunst und Architektur. Jedes Loft verfügt über 4,9 Meter hohe Decken, zwei Zwischengeschosse und zwei eigene Terrassendecks. Anstelle von Fenstern kamen Fleetwood-Glasschiebetüren mit einer Dreifachverglasung zum Einsatz. Exponierte Holzdeckenunterseiten und ein offener Grundriss repräsentieren geradezu das Leben in einem Loft.

Sept lofts pour artistes se trouvent au niveau supérieur de cet immeuble construit à Culver City. Le rez-de-chaussée est occupé par les bureaux des architectes, le restaurant Wilson et le Museum of Design Art and Architecture (MODAA), galerie de 185 mètres carrés consacrée à la relation symbiotique entre l'art et l'architecture. Chaque loft dispose de deux mezzanines, de deux terrasses et de portes-fenêtres coulissantes à tripe vitrage. La hauteur de plafond exceptionnelle (4,80 mètres) et le plan résolument ouvert en font la quintessence même de ce type de logements.

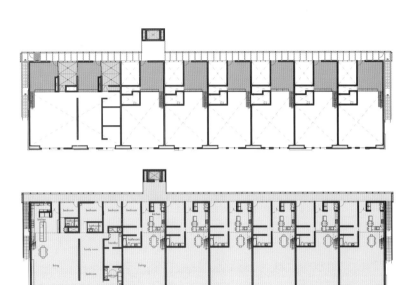

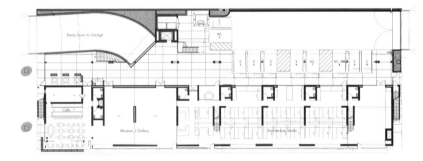

left: Loft, unit, and ground level floor plans_Stairs to live / work artist lofts_Façade detail. right: Exterior view by night_Street side view_Detail façade.
links: Grundriss Dachgeschoss, mittlere Wohneinheit und Erdgeschoss_Treppe zum Arbeits-und Wohnbereich im Dachgeschoss_Fassadendetail. rechts: Außenansicht bei Nacht_Straßenansicht_Fassadendetail.
à gauche: Plans des lofts et du rez-de-chaussée_Escalier extérieur_Détail de la façade. à droite: l'immeuble la nuit_L'immeuble vu de la rue_Autre détail de la façade.

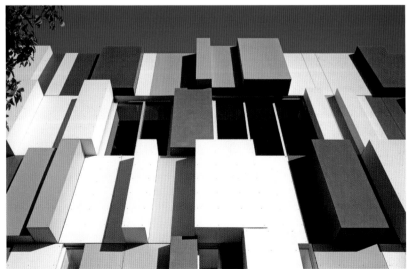

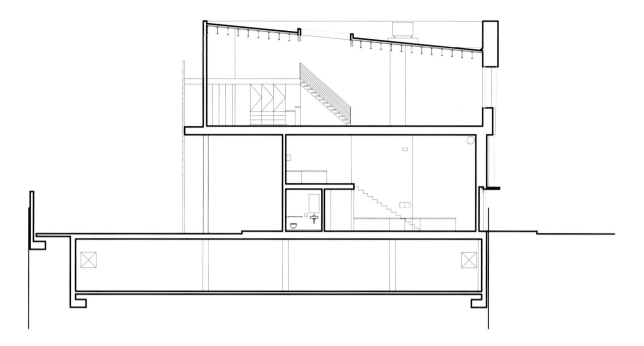

left: Workspaces. right: Section_Interior art gallery_Exhibition_Lounge_Interior.
links: Arbeitsplätze. rechts: Schnitt_Kunstgalerie_Ausstellung_Sitzecke_Ausstellung_Interieur.
à gauche: Espace de travail. à droite: Vue en coupe_Galerie d'art_Hall d'entrée_Deux autres vues de la galerie.

# CULVER CITY_CA **JACKSON HOUSE**

**ARCHITECTS:** DESIGN FIRM: DLFSTUDIO
**COMPLETION:** 2007_**TYPOLOGY:** LIVING
**PHOTOS:** DLFSTUDIO

The project is located within walking distance of downtown Culver City, a small municipality on the west side of LA, California. The two-story house is situated on a sub-standard, trapezoid-shaped lot and replaced an existing dilapidated house. The program consists of a "Great Room" (entry, living area, dining and kitchen), powder room, secondary bathroom, master suite, terrace and a studio, which could be converted into two future bedrooms. Within the clean lines and simple materials of the shell, the goal was to create light, interconnected, open spaces that were defined by shape and volume.

Das Projekt liegt in fußläufiger Entfernung zur Innenstadt von Culver City, einer kleinen Gemeinde auf der Westseite von Los Angeles. Das zweigeschossige Gebäude auf einem minderwertigen trapezförmigem Grundstück ersetzt ein baufällig gewordenes Haus. Sein Raumprogramm beinhaltet ein „Großes Zimmer" (Eingang, Wohnbereich, Esszone und Küche), ein Badezimmer, ein zweites Bad, ein Hauptschlafzimmer sowie Terrasse und ein Studio, die sich in zwei weitere Schlafräume umwandeln lassen. Eine mit klaren Linien und einfachen Materialien gestaltete Gebäudehülle beherbergt helle, miteinander verbundene, offene Räume, die von ihrer Form und ihrem Volumen definiert werden.

Cette maison se trouve près du centre ville de Culver City, commune de la banlieue ouest de Los Angeles. Elle a été construite sur un terrain trapézoïdal en remplacement d'un édifice endommagé. On trouve à l'intérieur une grande salle qui rassemble l'entrée, le séjour et la cuisine/salle à manger, ainsi que des toilettes avec lavabo, une salle de bain, une chambre principale et un espace disponible pour y aménager deux chambres supplémentaires, le tout étant complété par une terrasse au sud-ouest. Privilégiant les lignes claires et les matériaux simples, les architectes ont cherché à créer des volumes ouverts, lumineux et interconnectés s'adaptant à la forme particulière du terrain.

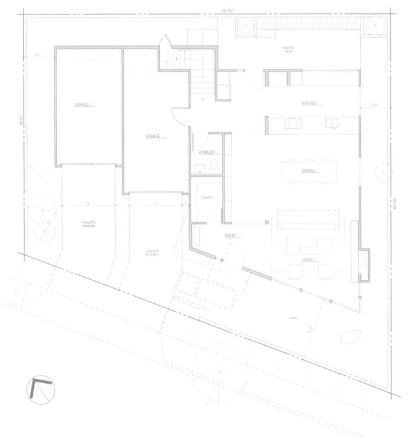

left: First floor plan_Front view of house_Kitchen and dining area. right: Glass corner of house.
links: Grundriss erstes Obergeschoss_Vorderseite des Hauses_Küche und Essbereich. rechts: Verglaste Ecke.
à gauche: Plan du rez-de-chaussée_Façade principale_Cuisine/salle à manger. à droite: Façade partiellement vitrée.

GALLERY

BATH

TERRACE

BEDROOM

STUDIO/BEDROOM

BATH

CLOSET

OPEN

left: Living room. right: Second floor plan_Kitchen_Gallery.
links: Wohnzimmer. rechts: Grundriss zweites Obergeschoss_Küche_Galerie.
à gauche: Séjour. à droite: Plan du premier étage_Cuisine_Galerie.

HERCULES_CA **HERCULES PUBLIC LIBRARY**

**ARCHITECTS:** HGA ARCHITECTS AND ENGINEERS (EXECUTIVE AR-
CHITECTS) / WILL BRUDER+PARTNERS (DESIGN ARCHITECTS)
**COMPLETION:** 2007_**TYPOLOGY:** PUBLIC
**PHOTOS:** BILL TIMMERMAN PHOTOGRAPHY

The development of the Hercules Public Library houses a circulation of approximately 800,000 books and periodicals, as well as other learning resources
such as multi-use computer stations with Internet research capabilities.
One feature that the Hercules Library is well known for is its teen homework
center, which gives students the opportunity to take advantage of after-school
tutoring programs.  Some of the library's other highlights include the "Story
Cove", meant for the purpose of children's reading events, a café, an extensive
reading area with a fireside seating, as well as several meeting and study
rooms.

Das Gebäude der Hercules Public Library beherbergt einen Bestand von etwa
800.000 Büchern und Zeitschriften sowie andere Lernressourcen wie vielseitig
nutzbare Computerarbeitsplätze mit Internetzugang. Bekannt ist die Hercules
Library für ihr Hausaufgabenzentrum, in dem Schüler nach der Schule Nach-
hilfeprogramme nutzen können. Zu den weiteren Glanzlichtern der Bibliothek
zählen die Kindern zugedachte „Lesehöhle" für Leseveranstaltungen, ein
Café, ein weitläufiger Lesebereich mit Sitzmöglichkeiten am Kamin sowie
mehrere Besprechungs- und Arbeitszimmer.

Cette bibliothèque abrite quelque 800 000 livres et périodiques ainsi que diverses autres ressources éducatives, notamment des ordinateurs avec accès
Internet. Elle est célèbre pour son espace réservé aux ados, qui peuvent y bénéficier de cours de soutien à l'apprentissage scolaire. Citons encore parmi
ses particularités le « Coin des conteurs » qui attire de nombreux enfants,
la cafétéria, la grande salle de lecture avec cheminée, et plusieurs salles de
réunion et d'étude.

left: Floor plan_Solar glazing_Reading area. right: Library interior_Skygarden_Courtyard.
links: Grundriss_Solarfenster_Leseraum. rechts: Innenansicht der Bibliothek_Kinderbereich
Innenhof.
à gauche: Plan_Fenêtres solaires_Salle de lecture. à droite: Intérieur de la bibliothèque_Espace
pour enfants_Cour intérieure.

# HERMOSA BEACH_CA **SURFHOUSE**

**ARCHITECTS:** XTEN ARCHITECTURE
**COMPLETION:** 2007_**TYPOLOGY:** LIVING
**PHOTOS:** ART GRAY PHOTOGRAPHY

The Surfhouse appears as an abstract block of ebonized cedar a few blocks from the Pacific Ocean in Hermosa Beach. The site is very small. While typical lots in the area measure 120 x 40 feet, the allowable building area for the Surfhouse measures just 33 x 24 feet. The architects approached the project by subtracting the larger program areas from a solid volumetric form that conformed to the zoning regulations and sought to maximize space, light, and views while also creating a sense of privacy and retreat for the young owners on a busy beachside street. The top floor and decks are completely open as continuous indoor/outdoor living spaces open to the beach and ocean.

Das Surfhouse steht wie ein abstrakter Klotz aus ebenholzschwarz gebeiztem Zedernholz wenige Häuserblöcke vom Pazifischen Ozean entfernt in Hermosa Beach. Sein Grundstück ist sehr klein. Während typische Parzellen in dieser Gegend 37 x 12 Meter messen, beträgt die zulässige bebaute Fläche für das Surfhouse gerade einmal 10 x 7 Meter. Daher substrahierten die Architekten die größeren Flächen des Programms von einer massiven volumetrischen Form, die den Bebauungsvorschriften entsprach. Auf diese Weise nutzten sie den Raum, das Licht und die Aussichten bestmöglich aus. Dabei schufen sie an der belebten Strandstraße Privatsphäre und einen Zufluchtsort für die jungen Eigentümer. Das Obergeschoss und die Terrassen sind als durchgehende Innen-/Außenräume zum Strand und Ozean geöffnet.

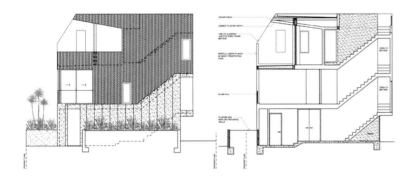

Ce bâtiment qui se dresse à quelque distance de l'océan Pacifique apparaît comme un bloc abstrait en cèdre noir. Il a été construit sur un terrain exigu, qui ne mesure que sept mètres sur dix alors que la moyenne à Hermosa Beach est de douze mètres sur trente-six. Les architectes se sont adaptés à cette situation difficile — à laquelle venaient encore s'ajouter les contraintes du zonage — en concevant un volume compact qui optimise l'espace disponible ainsi que l'éclairage naturel et les vues sur l'océan, tout en offrant aux jeunes propriétaires une maison où ils disposent de l'intimité nécessaire dans ce quartier agité du bord de mer. Le bâtiment dispose de terrasses et d'un dernier étage qui s'ouvrent entièrement sur la plage et l'océan, formant ainsi un continuum intérieur/extérieur.

left: Section_Balcony with ocean view_Street side view. right: Detail balcony.
links: Schnitt_Balkon mit Blick auf den Ozean_Straßenansicht. rechts: Balkondetail.
à gauche: Vue en coupe_Balcon avec vue sur l'océan_Le bâtiment vu de la rue. à droite: Balcon.

left: Exterior. right: Floor plans_Living space_Living room and balcony_Living room.
links: Außenansicht. rechts: Grundrisse_Wohnbereich_Wohnzimmer und Balkon_Wohnzimmer.
à gauche: Le bâtiment la nuit. à droite: Plans_Séjour_Séjour et balcon_Autre vue du séjour.

# HERMOSA BEACH_CA **STRAND RESIDENCE**

**ARCHITECTS:** KAA DESIGN GROUP, INC.
**COMPLETION:** 2005_**TYPOLOGY:** LIVING
**PHOTOS:** FARSHID ASSASSI, WELDON BREWSTER (317)

Meeting the specific requirements of an active retired couple, this project's design addresses conceptual notions of merging natural light with the erosion of spatial boundaries. The result is a building that incorporates overlapping, interlocking volumes and planes, both horizontally and vertically. Spaces unite to allow for boundless ocean views or more private vistas into introspective areas without compromising privacy amidst the density. A contextual and sturdy material palette, needed in salty coastal environments, differentiates the building's massing as it cascades along the structure's primary axis.

Der Entwurf des Projekts wird dem spezifischen Bedarf eines aktiven pensionierten Paars gerecht, indem er die konzeptionellen Vorstellungen von lichtdurchfluteten Räumen mit einer Auflösung der Raumgrenzen umsetzt. Das Ergebnis ist ein Gebäude mit sich horizontal und vertikal überschneidenden und gegenseitig durchdringenden Volumen und Ebenen. Miteinander verbundene Räume gewähren grenzenlose Aussichten auf den Ozean oder private Einblicke in beschauliche Bereiche, ohne die Privatsphäre im dichten Umfeld zu gefährden. Eine auf die Umgebung abgestimmte, robuste Materialpalette, die bei salzhaltiger Luft erforderlich ist, gliedert die einzelnen Gebäudevolumen kaskadenartig entlang der Hauptachse.

Le concept de base de cette villa destinée à un couple de retraités actifs utilise au mieux l'éclairage naturel pour éroder les limites spatiales. Avec pour résultat un bâtiment où les volumes et les plans se superposent et s'interpénètrent horizontalement et verticalement. Certains espaces offrent des vues panoramiques sur l'océan tandis que d'autres, plus intimistes, sont propices à l'introspection dans un tissu urbain pourtant dense. Cette villa en cascade selon un axe primaire figure toute une palette de matériaux différents, aptes à résister à l'atmosphère saline du bord de mer.

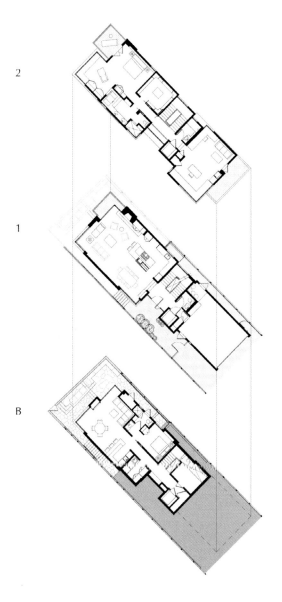

left: Floor plans_Living space with ocean view_Glazed hall with private vista_Main entrance from street. right: Beach façade.
links: Grundrisse_Wohnraum mit Blick auf den Ozean_Verglaster Flur_Straßenansicht Haupteingang. rechts: Strandfassade.
à gauche: Plans_Séjour avec vue sur l'océan_Couloir vitré_Entrée sur la rue. à droite: Façade du côté de l'océan.

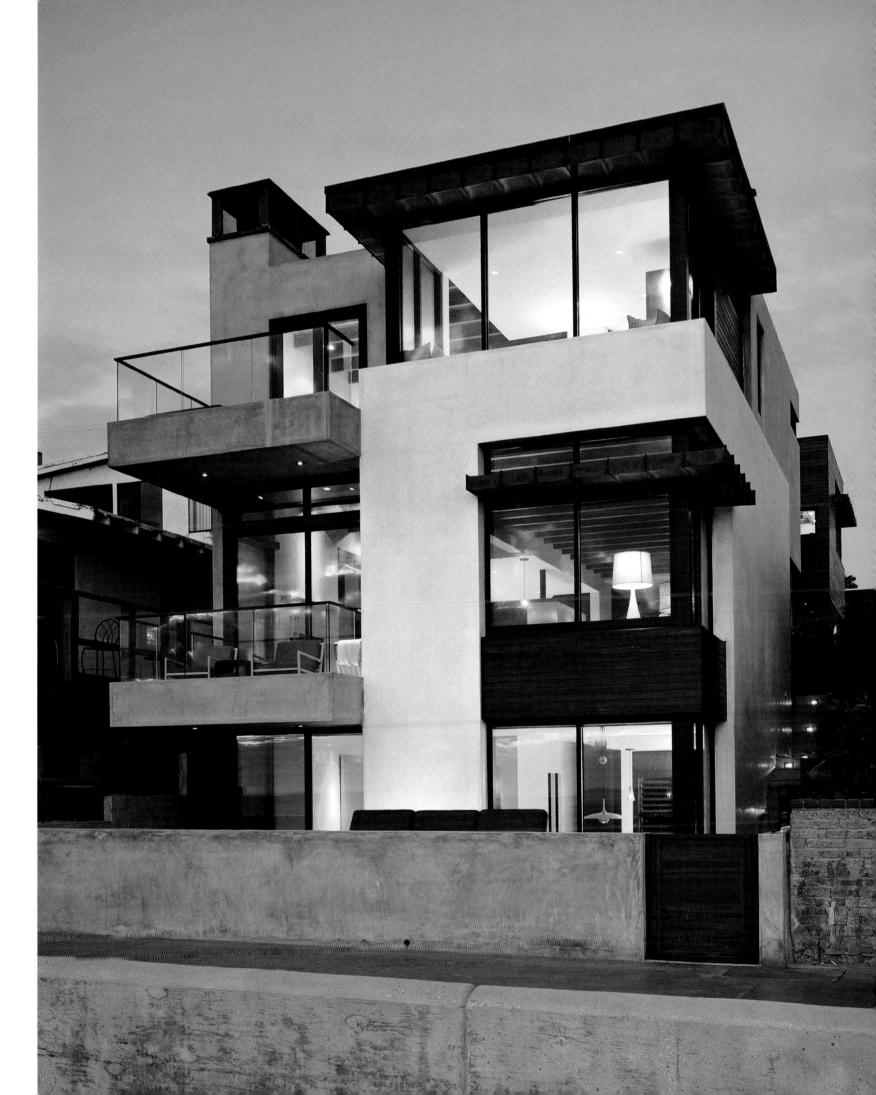

# HOLLYWOOD HILLS_CA **OPENHOUSE**

**ARCHITECTS:** XTEN ARCHITECTURE
**COMPLETION:** 2007_**TYPOLOGY:** LIVING
**PHOTOS:** ART GRAY PHOTOGRAPHY

The house is embedded into a narrow and sharply sloping property in the Hollywood Hills. Large steel spans and double cantilevers allow the front, side and rear elevations to slide open and erase all boundaries between indoors and out, opening the architecture to gardens and terraces on two levels. The glazed open spaces are visually counterweighted by sculptural, solid elements rendered in stacked granite and dark stained oak. With the glass walls completely open, the house becomes a platform defined by an abstract roof plane, a palette of natural materials, the gardens and the views.

Das Haus liegt eingebettet in einem schmalen, stark abfallenden Gelände in den Hollywood Hills. Weit gespannte Stahltragwerke und doppelte Auskragungen gestatten das Aufschieben der Front-, Seiten- und Rückfassaden. Dadurch werden die Grenzen zwischen Innen und Außen aufgehoben und die Architektur zu Gärten und Terrassen auf zwei Ebenen geöffnet. Zu den verglasten freien Räumen bilden plastische, robuste Elemente in Form von gestapeltem Granit und dunkel gebeiztem Eichenholz ein optisches Gegengewicht. Bei vollständig geöffneten Glaswänden wird das Haus zu einer Plattform, die sich durch eine abstrakte Dachfläche, eine Palette natürlicher Materialien, Gärten und Aussichten auszeichnet.

Cette villa a été construite sur un terrain étroit et en forte pente des collines d'Hollywood. Sur les faces avant et arrière ainsi que sur les côtés, des porte-à-faux et de larges ouvertures atténuent la distinction habituelle entre intérieur et extérieur. Cette impression se trouve encore renforcée par les jardins et terrasses sur deux niveaux qui prolongent les espaces créés par les architectes. La transparence et la légèreté des nombreuses baies vitrées contrastent avec les aménagements intérieurs utilisant le granite ou le bois de chêne. Lorsque toutes les vitres sont ouvertes, la maison prend l'aspect d'une plate-forme définie par son toit abstrait, sa palette de matériaux naturels et les jardins qui l'entourent.

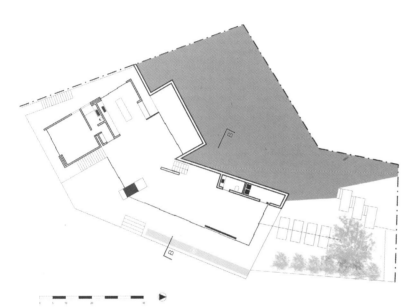

left: Ground floor plan_Exterior view from pool terrace_Detail roof_Sundeck with city view. right: Exterior view from entry drive_General view.
links: Grundriss Erdgeschoss_Außenansicht Pool und Terrasse_Dachdetail_Balkon mit Blick auf die Stadt. rechts: Straßenansicht_Gesamtansicht.
à gauche: Plan du rez-de-chaussée_Façade du côté de la piscine_Détail du toit_Terrasse avec vue sur la ville. à droite: Façade du côté de l'entrée_La villa avec la ville à l'arrière plan.

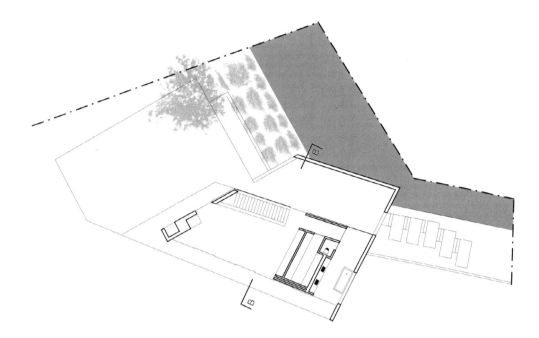

left: Exterior fireplace. right: First floor plan_Glazed staircase_Open living room_Living room with city view.
links: Außenkamin. rechts: Grundriss erstes Obergeschoss_Verglaster Treppenaufgang_Offenes Wohnzimmer_Wohnzimmer mit Blick auf die Stadt.
à gauche: Cheminée extérieure. à droite: Plan du rez-de-chaussée_Escalier vitré_Séjour entièrement vitré_Vue du séjour avec la ville à l'arrière plan.

INVERNESS_CA **ARCHITECT'S POINT REYES RESIDENCE**

**ARCHITECTS:** STUDIOS ARCHITECTURE
**COMPLETION:** 2004_**TYPOLOGY:** LIVING
**PHOTOS:** MICHAEL O'CALLAHAN,
TIM GRIFFITH PHOTOGRAPHY (322 L., 323)

The residence is located on a steeply sloped, heavily forested site near To-males Bay on California's Point Reyes National Seashore, an area known for its seaside woodlands and dairy farms. Wooden decks and an enclosed glass dining area thrust out from the base shed and appear to float amongst the trees. Strong, earthy materials were selected to stand up to the harsh coastal elements and to respond to the dynamics of the site. An eroded wooden shell encloses the space and positions the open-glazed steel skeleton, while an ensemble of garden walls, decks, the garage and gate house engage the site forming an outdoor compound.

Das Wohnhaus liegt auf einem dicht bewaldeten Steilhang in der Nähe von Tomales Bay an der kalifornischen Point Reyes National Seashore, einem für seine Küstenwälder und Milchbauernhöfe bekannten Gebiet. Aus dem Hauptgebäude vorspringende Stockwerke aus Holz und ein verglaster Ess-bereich scheinen zwischen den Bäumen zu schweben. Robuste, erdfarbene Materialien sollen dem rauen Küstenklima standhalten und mit der Dynamik des Standorts korrespondieren. Eine erodierte hölzerne Hülle umschließt den Raum und passt ein offenes, verglastes Stahlskelett ein. Ein Ensemble aus Gartenmauern, Plattformen, Garage und Pförtnerhaus schafft durch seinen Dialog mit dem Gelände einen Außenbereich.

Cette villa est construite sur un terrain boisé en forte pente près de la baie de Tomales, en Californie, dans le parc national de Point Reyes, célèbre pour ses forêts littorales et sa production laitière. Des plates-formes en bois et une salle à manger entièrement vitrée semblent jaillir du sol et flotter dans les arbres. Les architectes ont privilégié les matériaux naturels à la fois pour leur adéquation au dynamisme du site et leur bonne résistance à la rigueur du climat dans cette partie de la côte californienne. Le squelette en acier est revêtu d'une enveloppe en bois et en verre. Le bâtiment principal se complète par un garage, des terrasses, un portail et des murets dans le jardin.

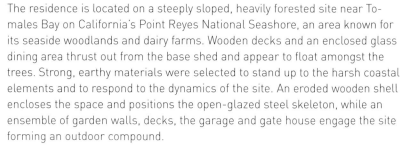
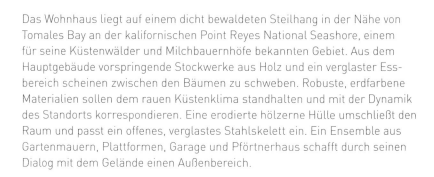
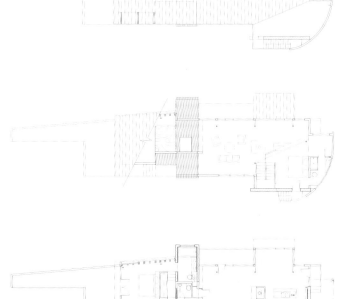

left: Floor plans_General view_Wooden façade_Open living space. right: Enclosed glass dining area.
links: Grundrisse_Gesamtansicht_Hölzerne Fassade_Offener Wohnraum. rechts: Esszimmer mit Glasfassade.
à gauche: Plans des différents niveaux_Vue d'ensemble_Façade en bois_Séjour vitré. à droite: Extérieur avec l'oriel de la salle à manger.

# LA JOLLA_CA **2-INNS**

**ARCHITECTS:** SEBASTIAN MARISCAL STUDIO
**COMPLETION:** 2006_**TYPOLOGY:** LIVING
**PHOTOS:** HISAO SUZUKI

The hotel explores the qualities of a continuous interior-exterior space in the private realms of two identical adjacent houses. Stepped back from the street, the houses carve into the existing topography. The exposed concrete sub-level forms the base that extends from the front lawn to the hill in the back. Elevated from the street, the main level is enclosed by twenty-five full-height glass panels, which slide away on an automated track, creating a continuous open plane that connects the back garden to the ocean views. This feature transforms the public areas into an exterior space while maintaining privacy from the street.

Das Hotel schafft einen durchgängigen Innen-Außen-Raum in den Privat-bereichen zweier identischer Nachbargebäude. Die von der Straße zurück-gesetzten Häuser sind in die Topografie eingelassen. Die untere Ebene aus Sichtbeton bildet den Sockel, der sich von der Rasenfläche vor dem Haus bis zum Hügel auf der Rückseite erstreckt. Die über das Straßenniveau ange-hobene Hauptebene wird von 25 raumhohen Glasplatten umschlossen, die auf einer selbsttätigen Führung gleiten. Die so entstandene durchgehende offene Fläche verbindet den rückseitigen Garten mit der Sicht auf den Ozean. Dadurch werden die öffentlichen Bereiche zu einem Außenraum und sind dennoch von der Straße abgeschottet.

Cet hôtel composé de deux immeubles identiques et adjacents explore les avantages de la continuité entre intérieur et extérieur. Les bâtiments, situés en retrait par rapport à la rue, tiennent compte de la configuration du terrain. Ils se composent d'une base en béton brut de coffrage qui se dresse sur une pelouse, et d'un volume avec revêtement en bois posé sur un niveau intermé-diaire entièrement vitré. Des portes-fenêtres coulissantes permettent d'ouvrir totalement cet espace sur le jardin et l'océan tout proche, alors que la face arrière reste à l'abri des regards indiscrets.

left: Terrace_Night view of terrace with fire pit _View into the glazed kitchen by night. right: View from the garden_Rear view_Terrace.
links: Terrasse_Ansicht der Terrasse mit Feuerstelle_Verglaste Küche. rechts: Gartenansicht_Rückansicht_Terrasse.
à gauche: Terrasse_La terrasse avec brasero la nuit_La cuisine vitrée vue de l'extérieur la nuit. à droite: L'hôtel côté jardin_Face arrière_Terrasse.

# LOS ANGELES_CA **CANYON VIEW OFFICE / GUEST HOUSE**

**ARCHITECTS:** KANNER ARCHITECTS
**COMPLETION:** 2004_**TYPOLOGY:** LIVING / OFFICE
**PHOTOS:** JOHN EDWARD LINDEN

Located on a lush hillside behind a main residence, this small structure is a psychologist's office and guest house. The building offers privacy, convenience, and enhances the value of the property. The owners insisted on a minimalist design – flexible, modern, private, warm and contextual. The highly articulated form is composed of a series of angled cedar wall planes. By breaking the box into a series of angled walls the building more effectively blends into its environment. Each plan angle responds to room function, view corridors, light quality and programmatic flexibility.

Auf einem grünen Hang hinter dem Hauptwohnhaus gelegen beherbergt diese kleine Konstruktion die Praxis eines Psychologen und ein zukünftiges Gästehaus. Das Gebäude bietet neben Privatsphäre auch Komfort und wertet das Anwesen auf. Den Eigentümern lag an einem minimalistischen Entwurf, der flexibel, modern, privat, behaglich und an das Umfeld angepasst sein sollte. Die stark gegliederte Form besteht aus einer Reihe winklig angeordneter Wandplatten aus Zedernholz. Durch das Aufbrechen des Kubus in mehrere Platten lässt sich der Bau besser in seine Umgebung einfügen. Jeder ebene Winkel korrespondiert mit der Raumfunktion, den Sichtachsen, der Lichtqualität und der programmatischen Flexibilität.

Ce pavillon construit sur une colline boisée est l'annexe de la résidence principale d'un psychologue, qui y a installé son bureau et un appartement pour invités. Confortable et intimiste, le pavillon augmente la valeur totale de la propriété. Le client a expressément demandé aux architectes de concevoir un bâtiment minimaliste, flexible, moderne, chaleureux et bien intégré à son contexte spatial. Les différents volumes, caractérisés par leurs angles aigus, présentent des surfaces avec bardage en cèdre et s'intègrent bien à l'environnement. Chacun des angles correspond à une fonction, une perspective, une lumière et une flexibilité programmatique qui lui sont propres.

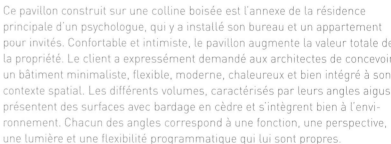

left: Site plan_Entrance view_Glass and wood exterior_Detail courtyard. right: General view of wooden cladding.
links: Lageplan_Eingangsansicht_Außenseite aus Glas und Holz_Detail Innenhof. rechts: Gesamtansicht der hölzernen Verkleidung.
à gauche: Plan de situation_Entrée_Façade en verre et bois_Détail de la cour. à droite: Gros plan sur le revêtement en bois.

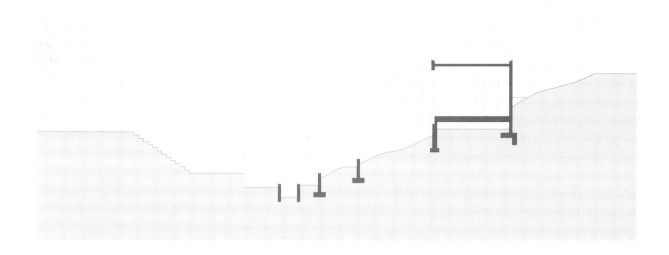

left: Exterior. right: Section_View inside_Interior_Living space.
links: Außenansicht. rechts: Schnitt_Wohnraumansicht_Interieur_Wohnzimmer.
à gauche: Extérieur. à droite: Vue en coupe_L'intérieur vu de l'entrée_Intérieur_Séjour.

## LOS ANGELES_CA **INNER-CITY ARTS**

**ARCHITECTS:** MICHAEL MALTZAN ARCHITECTURE
**COMPLETION:** 2008_**TYPOLOGY:** EDUCATION
**PHOTOS:** MICHAEL MALTZAN ARCHITECTURE, INC. / IWAN BAAN

Inner-City Arts serves over 30,000 at-risk youth from LA's public schools each year, providing a range of art facilities and services. Built in three phases over 15 years, the one-acre campus was conceived as a contemporary open-air village, an indoor/outdoor tradition perfectly suited to the Southern California climate. The past fall 2008, Phase III of the campus expansion project was completed. New additions include a theater, visual arts complex, performing arts studios, parent-teacher resource center, gardens, and gathering spaces, enabling Inner-City Arts to serve students and teachers each year.

Inner-City Arts bietet den jährlich 30.000 Risikojugendlichen aus den öffentlichen Schulen von Los Angeles Kunsteinrichtungen und Dienstleistungen. Das in drei Bauabschnitten über einen Zeitraum von 15 Jahren entstandene, 4.000 Quadratmeter große Campusgelände ist als modernes Dorf im Freien konzipiert. Dieses traditionelle Innen/Außen-Konzept passt hervorragend zu dem südkalifornischen Klima. Seit Herbst 2008 ist der dritte Bauabschnitt der Campuserweiterung fertiggestellt. Zu den neuen Anbauten zählen ein Theater, ein Komplex für bildende Kunst, Studios für darstellende Kunst, ein Lehrer-Eltern-Informationszentrum, Gärten und Versammlungsräume, sodass Inner-City Arts Schülern und Lehrern ganzjährig zur Verfügung steht.

Ce centre culturel d'une superficie totale de quatre mille mètres carrés accueille plus de trente mille jeunes à risques chaque année. Construit en trois phases sur une durée de quinze ans, il a été conçu comme un village contemporain qui privilégie les espaces de plein air, conformément à l'interconnexion traditionnelle des espaces intérieurs et extérieurs rendue possible par le climat du sud de la Californie. La phase III du projet, terminée à l'automne 2008, a porté sur la construction d'une salle de spectacles, d'un complexe consacré aux arts visuels, d'ateliers d'expression corporelle, d'un centre d'information pour parents et enseignants, ainsi que sur l'aménagement de jardins et d'espaces de rencontre.

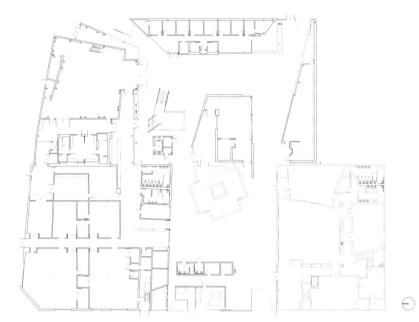

left: Floor plan_Wooden roof construction_Glass façade and wall facing_Inner courtyard. right: View from street side_Aerial view_Courtyard.
links: Grundriss_Hölzerne Dachkonstruktion_Glasfassade und Wandverkleidung_Innenhof. rechts: Straßenansicht_Luftbild_Innenhof.
à gauche: Plan_Plafond en bois_Mur et façade en verre_Cour intérieure. à droite: Le bâtiment vu de la rue_Le bâtiment vu de haut_Autre vue de la cour.

## LOS ANGELES_CA **BARSKY RESIDENCE**

**ARCHITECTS:** ASSEMBLEDGE+
**COMPLETION:** 2005_**TYPOLOGY:** LIVING
**PHOTOS:** MICHAEL WESCHLER

This small addition attaches itself to the rear of a quaint Spanish-style house in the Melrose area of Los Angeles, California. The modernist character of the addition creates a harmonious and elegant connection between old and new, where the architects designed a cantilevered foundation so that the box would appear to float off the ground. On a very limited budget, the project tried to make use of rather simple materials and formulate their uniqueness. The standard material of Stucco was translated into a lively material by creating a vertically combed finish that allows for a dynamic play of light and shadow throughout the day.

Dieser kleine Anbau ergänzt die Rückseite eines idyllischen Hauses im spanischen Stil im Melrose Viertel von Los Angeles in Kalifornien. Sein moderner Charakter schafft eine harmonische und elegante Verbindung zwischen Alt und Neu. Da die Architekten einen zurückgesetzten Sockel vorsahen, scheint der kubische Baukörper über dem Gelände zu schweben. Aufgrund des sehr begrenzten Budgets kamen eher einfache Materialien zum Einsatz, deren Besonderheiten ausgearbeitet wurde. Aus marktgängigem Putz entstand durch eine gekämmte Oberfläche ein lebendiges Material, das tagsüber ein dynamisches Licht- und Schattenspiel ergibt.

Ce petit édifice a été rajouté à l'arrière d'une vieille maison en style espagnol du quartier de Melrose, à Los Angeles. Son apparence futuriste — un volume en porte-à-faux sur ses fondations, qui semble ainsi flotter dans l'air — établit un lien à la fois élégant et harmonieux entre l'ancien et le moderne. Les architectes, qui disposaient d'un budget très limité, ont tiré le meilleur parti possible de matériaux assez simples. Ils ont notamment réinterprété le stuc, un matériau parfaitement traditionnel, en le dynamisant par des ondulations verticales qui créent des jeux d'ombre et de lumière très vivants tout au long de la journée.

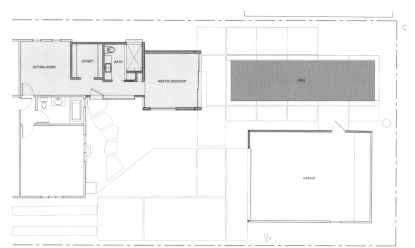

left: Floor plan_View inside bedroom_Vertically combed façade_Bathroom. right: Sliding glass door.
links: Grundriss_Blick ins Schlafzimmer_Vertikal gerillte Fassade_Badezimmer. rechts: Schiebetür aus Glas.
à gauche: Plan_La chambre à coucher vue de l'extérieur_Revêtement de façade avec ondulations verticales_Salle de bain. à droite: Chambre avec porte coulissante permettant d'accéder à la piscine.

# LOS ANGELES_CA **SKYLINE RESIDENCE**

**ARCHITECTS:** BELZBERG ARCHITECTS
**COMPLETION:** 2007_**TYPOLOGY:** LIVING
**PHOTOS:** BELZBERG ARCHITECTS

Perched atop a ridgeline in the Hollywood hills, the Skyline Residence has been transformed into a modern home with spectacular views of downtown Los Angeles, Laurel Canyon, and the San Fernando Valley. The ambitions of the project were to use the prominence of the location as the impetus for the design, resulting in an architecture that is gracefully complimented by its surroundings. The linear nature of the site encouraged a layout in which each room was defined by at least one fully glazed wall. The infinity-edge pool brings the valley to the edge of the pool enhancing the vastness and immediacy of the city below.

Die auf einer Kammlinie in den Hollywood Hügeln gelegene Skyline Residence wurde zu einem modernen Wohnhaus umgebaut, das eine spektakuläre Sicht auf das Stadtzentrum von Los Angeles, den Laurel Canyon und das San Fernando Valley bietet. Ziel des Projekts war, den prominenten Standort als Ansatzpunkt für eine elegante Architektur zu nutzen, die ihrer Umgebung alle Ehre macht. Das lineare Grundstück ermöglichte eine Anordnung, bei der jeder Raum von mindestens einer Glaswand definiert wird. Der Infinity Pool holt das Tal an den Rand des Beckens, wodurch die riesigen Ausmaße und die unmittelbare Nähe der Stadt betont werden.

Une maison construite sur les collines d'Hollywood a été transformée en une villa moderne offrant des vues spectaculaires sur Los Angeles, le Laurel Canyon et la vallée de San Fernando. Les architectes ont cherché à tirer profit de la position surélevée du terrain et à réaliser un bâtiment dont les alentours constituent un complément harmonieux. La nature linéaire du site les a incités à concevoir des pièces où au moins l'un des murs est entièrement vitré. Le vaste paysage composé par la ville en contrebas et la chaîne de montagnes qui se profile à l'horizon se reflète dans la piscine à débordement, soulignant ainsi la sensation d'étendue, voire d'infini, qui se dégage du lieu.

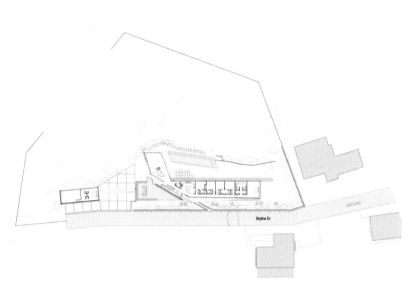

left: Site plan_Glazed front entrance_Living room with fire place, view towards pool and sundeck.
right: Movie projection onto guest house with the city below_View from entry drive.
links: Lageplan_Verglaster Vordereingang_Wohnzimmer mir Kamin, Blick auf Pool und Terrasse.
rechts: Filmvorführung auf Gästehaus mit Blick auf Stadt_Auffahrt.
à gauche: Plan de situation_Hall d'entrée vitré_Séjour avec cheminée et vue sur la piscine. à droite:
Mur servant d'écran de projection avec la ville à l'arrière plan_La villa vue de la route d'accès.

LOS ANGELES_CA

# CENTRAL LOS ANGELES AREA HIGH SCHOOL #9 FOR THE VISUAL AND PERFORMING ARTS

**ARCHITECTS:** COOP HIMMELB(L)AU
**COMPLETION:** 2008_**TYPOLOGY:** EDUCATION
**PHOTOS:** LANE BARDEN

With its professional performing arts theater, equipped with a full stage, orchestra pit, back stage, and fly-loft, the Central Los Angeles Public High School for the Visual and Performing Arts can take its place alongside the Disney Concert Hall and the Museum of Contemporary Art on the Grand Avenue cultural corridor. The tower and 9-shaped spiral ramp, housing an event, conference, and exhibition space, will become a new landmark representing the arts in Los Angeles. The school's design creates a public space that allows both students and the community to enjoy the new educational and cultural center.

Dieses als „Schule für die Zukunft" bezeichnete aufsehenerregende Schulprojekt für den Los Angeles Unified School District liegt in der gleichen innerstädtischen Trasse wie die Disney Concert Hall, das Museum of Contemporary Art und die Cathedral of Our Lady of the Angels. Als Aushängeschild für die künstlerisch ausgerichtete High School wird auf dem Schulcampus eine Ausbildung in Musik, Tanz, Theater und visueller Kunst geboten. Der deutlich sichtbare Turm symbolisiert die Bedeutung der Kunst für die Stadt und ist mit einer spiralförmigen Rampe in Form der Zahl 9 ausgestattet.

Ce projet de complexe universitaire baptisé « Une école pour le futur » doit être construit dans le centre ville de Los Angeles, à proximité du Disney Concert Hall, du Museum of Contemporary Art et de la cathédrale Notre-Dame des Anges. Il s'agit d'un établissement consacré à l'enseignement artistique, c'est-à-dire à la musique, la danse, le théâtre et les beaux-arts. Son élément emblématique est une tour qui symbolise l'importance de l'art dans la ville. On y accède à l'extérieur par une rampe en spirale qui l'entoure en formant le chiffre 9. Divers panneaux assurent la signalisation et permettent de diffuser des informations relatives à l'école.

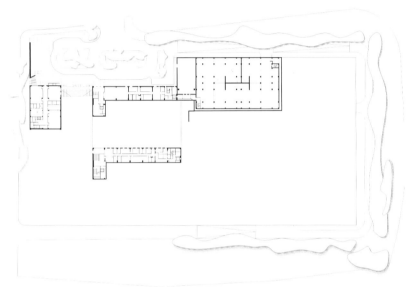

left: Floor plan_Front view at night_Spiral in form of a 9. right: Spiral ramp on theater's fly loft_Inner courtyard_View of three sculptural buildings.
links: Grundriss_Vorderansicht bei Nacht_Spirale in Form einer 9. rechts: Spirale über Theaterbühne_Innenhof_Drei plastische Gebäude.
à gauche: Plan_Façade principale la nuit_Tour et rampe en spirale. à droite: Autre vue de la spirale au-dessus de la salle de spectacles_Cour intérieure_Vue des trois bâtiments du complexe.

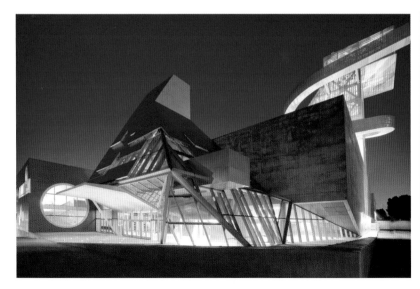

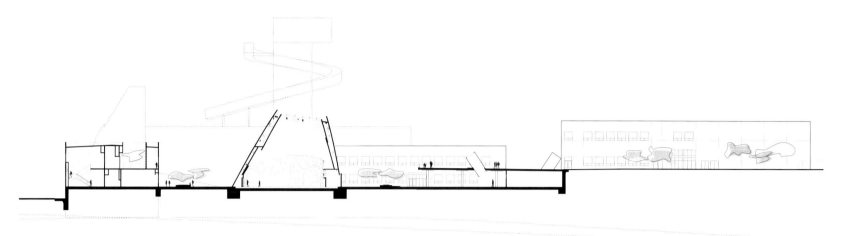

left: Entrance hall, steel roof construction. right: Section_Theater, stage view_Street side view Skylight_Detail façade.
links: Eingangshalle, Dachkonstruktion aus Stahl. rechts: Schnitt_Theater, Blick zur Bühne Straßenansicht_Oberlicht_Fassadendetail.
à gauche: Hall d'entrée avec vue du squelette en acier. à droite: Vue en coupe_Salle de spectacles Le bâtiment vu de la rue_Puits de lumière_Gros plan sur la façade.

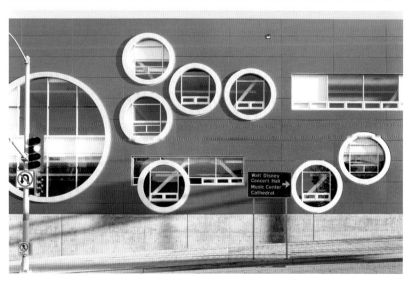

LOS ANGELES_CA **NOONAN RESIDENCE**

**ARCHITECTS:** FUNG + BLATT ARCHITECTS, INC
**COMPLETION:** 2005_**TYPOLOGY:** LIVING
**PHOTOS:** JOSH PERRIN

Accommodating diverse living arrangements, the Noonan Residence's cubic form offers multiple levels that open to views of the city and relate one interior space to another. The second level houses the main living areas, as well as the master bedroom and a future elevator that provides for single-level living should accessibility issues becomes necessary later. The first level houses a suite, which, with its own exterior entry, can function as a caretaker's apartment or additional workspace. Carved into the third level is a roof terrace that allows southern light to penetrate the living space below.

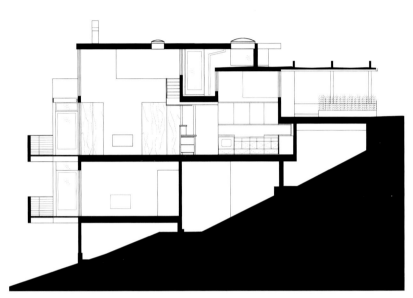

Der auf verschiedene Wohnbedürfnisse ausgelegte Kubus der Noonan Residence bietet unterschiedliche Ebenen, die Aussichten auf die Stadt eröffnen und die einzelnen Innenräume miteinander in Beziehung bringen. Die zweite Ebene beherbergt die Hauptwohnbereiche und das Schlafzimmer mit einem integrierbaren Aufzug, falls sich bei einer späteren eingeschossigen Belegung Zugangsfragen stellen sollten. In der ersten Ebene kann eine Zimmerflucht mit einem eigenen Außeneingang als Hausmeisterwohnung oder zusätzlicher Arbeitsbereich genutzt werden. In die dritte Ebene ist eine Dachterrasse eingelassen, über die Südlicht in den Wohnraum darunter gelangen kann.

Ce bâtiment résidentiel aux formes cubiques contient des pièces sur plusieurs niveaux qui sont reliées entre elles et offrent de belles vues sur la ville en contrebas. Au niveau supérieur se trouvent les espaces de séjour ainsi que la chambre principale. Les architectes ont prévu l'emplacement d'un ascenseur qui pourrait devenir nécessaire à l'avenir. L'appartement du niveau inférieur abrite un espace de travail mais peut aussi être occupé par un gardien puisqu'il dispose d'une entrée indépendante. L'ouverture aménagée dans le toit en terrasse assure un bon éclairage naturel du séjour situé en dessous.

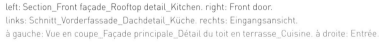

left: Section_Front façade_Rooftop detail_Kitchen. right: Front door.
links: Schnitt_Vorderfassade_Dachdetail_Küche. rechts: Eingangsansicht.
à gauche: Vue en coupe_Façade principale_Détail du toit en terrasse_Cuisine. à droite: Entrée.

## LOS ANGELES_CA **VIENNA WAY**

**ARCHITECTS:** MARMOL RADZINER AND ASSOCIATES
**COMPLETION:** 2007_**TYPOLOGY:** LIVING
**PHOTOS:** JOE FLETCHER

This 4,000-square-foot residence is located on a large lot that divides into thirds. The two main structures exist on the outer edges of the property and maximize the interaction between the indoor-outdoor space as well as the available land. A kitchen spans the two structures and is covered by a green roof. The northern wing contains the private living space with a fireplace. The southern wing contains the formal, public spaces that begin in the front of the property and conclude in an outdoor dining area.

Dieses 342 Quadratmeter große Wohnhaus liegt auf einem großen, in Drittel aufgeteilten Areal. Die zwei Hauptkonstruktionen an den Außenrändern des Grundstücks nutzen die Wechselbeziehung zwischen dem Innen- und Außenraum sowie dem verfügbaren Land maximal aus. Eine sich über beide Bauten erstreckende Küche ist mit einem begrünten Dach versehen. Im nördlichen Gebäudeflügel sind der private Wohnraum und ein offener Kamin untergebracht. Der Südflügel beherbergt die öffentlichen Räume, die an der Vorderseite des Anwesens beginnen und mit einem Essbereich im Freien abschließen.

Cette résidence d'environ 342 mètres carrés est située sur un terrain divisé en trois parties. Les deux volumes principaux sont construits aux extrémités de manière à optimiser l'utilisation de l'espace et l'interaction entre intérieur et extérieur. La cuisine qui relie les deux volumes est couverte par un toit végétalisé. Au nord se trouve un séjour avec cheminée, au sud des pièces moins intimistes qui se succèdent depuis l'entrée jusqu'à une salle à manger de plein air.

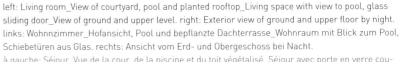

left: Living room_View of courtyard, pool and planted rooftop_Living space with view to pool, glass sliding door_View of ground and upper level. right: Exterior view of ground and upper floor by night.
links: Wohnzimmer_Hofansicht, Pool und bepflanzte Dachterrasse_Wohnraum mit Blick zum Pool, Schiebetüren aus Glas. rechts: Ansicht vom Erd- und Obergeschoss bei Nacht.
à gauche: Séjour_Vue de la cour, de la piscine et du toit végétalisé_Séjour avec porte en verre coulissante donnant sur la piscine. à droite: L'extérieur la nuit.

left: Glazed kitchen. right: Kitchen_Interior.
links: Verglaste Küche. rechts: Küche_Interieur.
à gauche: Cuisine entièrement vitrée. à droite: Cuisine_Intérieur.

# LOS ANGELES_CA **GREENFIELD RESIDENCE**

**ARCHITECTS:** MINARC
**COMPLETION:** 2007_**TYPOLOGY:** LIVING
**PHOTOS:** RALF SEEBURGER, TORFI AGNARSSON (346 R.)

This development is a simplistic, eco-conscious design that is focused on functionality and creating a breathing family environment, with an effort in using materials in their most organic form. Maximum use of natural light cuts down electrical cost, and a heated patio for outdoor dining maximizes outdoor / indoor living. Floor material connected in an unobtrusive manner increases the floor plan flow and space. The design and use of color inspired by a dramatic landscape creates a contrasting stimulating interior, while the kitchen island creates a multi-functional gathering point in the heart of the house.

Der schlichte, umweltbewusste Gebäudeentwurf setzt auf Funktionalität und ein familiengerechtes Umfeld, wobei nach Möglichkeit Materialien in ihrer elementarsten Form zum Einsatz kommen. Ein Höchstmaß an natürlichem Licht senkt die Stromkosten, ein beheizter Hof für Mahlzeiten im Freien maximiert das Wohnen innen und draußen. Dezent miteinander verbundene Fußbodenbeläge schaffen fließende Übergänge und lassen die Räume größer wirken. Gestaltung und Verwendung der Farben sind von einer aufsehenerregenden Landschaft inspiriert, wodurch kontrastierende, belebte Innenräume entstehen. In der Mitte des Hauses bildet die Kücheninsel einen multifunktionalen Treffpunkt.

Cette maison individuelle simple et écologique met l'accent sur le fonctionnalisme et crée un environnement familial qui accorde une large part aux matériaux naturels. L'optimisation de l'éclairage solaire permet de réduire les factures d'électricité, tandis qu'une terrasse couverte augmente vers l'extérieur la surface habitable. La jonction discrète entre les différents revêtements de sol contribue à agrandir l'espace visuellement. L'utilisation de couleurs naturelles contrastées crée un intérieur stimulant, avec au centre l'îlot cuisine comme point de rencontre multifonctionnel.

N

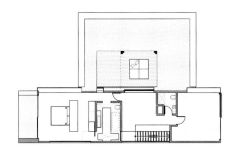

left: First and second floor plan_Terrace_Fireplace and kitchen. right: Outdoor sleeping area_Rear view.
links: Grundriss erstes und zweites Obergeschoss_Terrasse_Kamin und Küche. rechts: Schlafplatz im Freien_Rückansicht_Terrasse.
à gauche: Plan du rez-de-chaussée et du premier étage_Terrasse_Cuisine avec cheminée. à droite: Chambre en plein air_Vue de la face arrière.

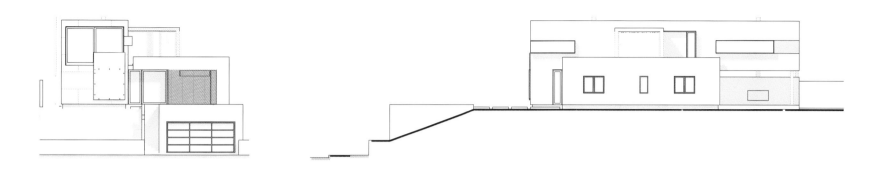

left: Interior. right: Elevations_Living room.
links: Interieur. rechts: Ansichten_Wohnzimmer.
à gauche: Intérieur. à droite: Vues en élévation_Séjour.

# LOS ANGELES_CA **ALAN-VOO FAMILY HOUSE**

**ARCHITECTS:** NEIL M. DENARI ARCHITECTS, INC.
**COMPLETION:** 2007_**TYPOLOGY:** LIVING
**PHOTOS:** BENNY CHAN, FOTOWORKS

The goal of this renovation and extension project was the addition of 1,000-square-foot space to the existing 1,000-square-foot house. The scheme leaves half of the house for the daughter's bedrooms and incorporates the other half plus new extensions in front and back into a public zone and a private bedroom for the parents. This strategy amounts to a new 16-foot wide linear house being inserted into the existing house. Multi-toned, bright colors accentuate the new pieces, which suggests a graphic expression representative of the family's interests.

Mit dem Umbau- und Erweiterungsprojekt sollte das 304 Quadratmeter große Haus um die gleiche Fläche vergrößert werden. Der Entwurf sieht eine Hälfte des Hauses für die Schlafräume der Töchter vor und berücksichtigt die neuen Anbauten. Im hinteren Gebäudeteil befinden sich die öffentlichen Räume und das Elternschlafzimmer. Aus der Erweiterung resultiert ein neues, 4,90 Meter breites Haus, das in das bestehende Gebäude eingefügt ist. Helle Farben in unterschiedlichen Tönen akzentuieren die neuen Räume, welche die einzelnen Interessen der Familie grafisch artikulieren.

La rénovation de cette maison individuelle a été l'occasion de doubler la surface habitable, qui s'élevait à environ 304 mètres carrés avant les travaux. La moitié de la maison d'origine est maintenant à la disposition des enfants, tandis que les parents peuvent utiliser l'autre moitié ainsi que l'extension où se trouvent les pièces de séjour et des chambres. Dans la structure linéaire de cinq mètres de large ainsi rajoutée, des éléments multicolores et lumineux mettent l'espace en valeur et reflètent les centres d'intérêt des divers membress de la famille.

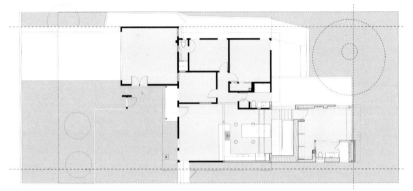

left: Floor plan_New house insertion into existing_Exterior. right: View inside living room.
links: Grundriss_Schnittstelle zwischen Erweiterungsbau und bestehendem Haus_Außenansicht.
rechts: Blick ins Wohnzimmer.
à gauche: Plan_Vue du volume rajouté au bâtiment préexistant_Extérieur. à droite: Séjour du rez-de-chaussée vu de l'extérieur.

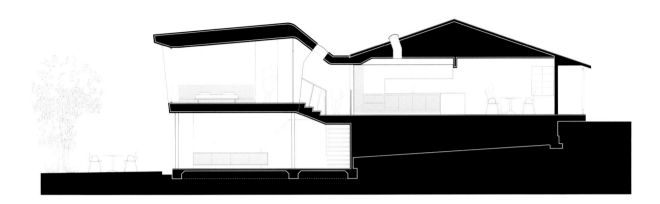

left: Interior structural detail. right: Section_Kitchen.
links: Detail der Inneneinrichtung. rechts: Schnitt_Küche.
à gauche: Détail de l'intérieur. à droite: Vue en coupe_Cuisine.

LOS ANGELES_CA **COURTYARD HOUSE**

**ARCHITECTS:** RIPPLE DESIGN
**COMPLETION:** 2006_**TYPOLOGY:** LIVING
**PHOTOS:** MARLA AUFMUTH PHOTOGRAPHER

This house creates all of its own power, offering financial benefits, reduced ecological waste, and a premium quality of life. One example of this is the courtyard door systems. Various combinations of these doors opened and closed can regulate comfort via breezes and heat gain. Designing this type of home requires careful attention to detail. The thickening of specific walls and ceilings and the exploitation of dense or reflective materials modulate heat gain and eliminate the need for air conditioning systems. The emphasis here is that the choice to reduce the ecological footprint can start in the home.

Dieses Haus schafft alles aus eigener Kraft. Es bringt finanzielle Vorteile, vermeidet ökologische Belastungen und bietet ein Höchstmaß an Lebensqualität. Ein Beispiel hierfür ist das Türsystem des Innenhofs. Mit einer Kombination aus offenen und geschlossenen Türen lassen sich Frischluft und Wärmegewinne und damit das Raumklima regulieren. Der Entwurf eines solchen Wohntyps erfordert Detailsorgfalt. Die Dicke ausgewählter Wände und Decken sowie der Einsatz dichter oder reflektierender Materialien bestimmen die Wärmezufuhr und machen Klimaanlagen unnötig. Im Vordergrund steht dabei, mit der Verkleinerung des ökologischen Fußabdrucks bereits im Haus zu beginnen.

Cette villa intègre des solutions économiques qui permettent de réduire les déchets et d'améliorer la qualité de vie. Citons notamment la cloison vitrée rétractable qui donne sur la cour et assure la régulation thermique en réchauffant l'intérieur lorsqu'elle est fermée et le ventilant lorsqu'elle est ouverte. Parmi les détails « écologiques » de la villa, citons encore l'épaisseur renforcée de certains murs et plafonds, ainsi que l'utilisation de matériaux denses ou réfléchissants qui rendent une climatisation conventionnelle superflue. Les architectes ont voulu montrer ainsi que le choix de réduire l'impact sur l'environnement est une affaire personnelle qui commence là où l'on habite.

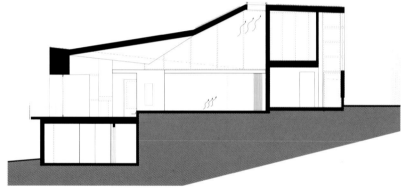

left: Section_Exterior view by night_Indoor outdoor space. right: View into courtyard.
links: Schnitt_Außenansicht bei Nacht_Räumliche Verbindung zwischen Innen und Außen. rechts: Blick in den Innenhof.
à gauche: Vue en coupe_Villa la nuit_Espace intérieur/extérieur. à droite: Vue de la cour.

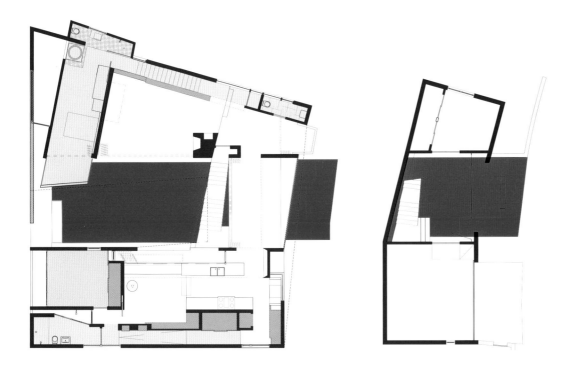

left: Wooden interior. right: Ground floor plan_Entrance_Interior with bookcase.
links: Hölzerne Inneneinrichtung. rechts: Grundriss Erdgeschoss_Eingang_Inneneinrichtung mit eingebauten Bücherregalen.
à gauche: Intérieur avec revêtement de mur en bois. à droite: Plan du rez-de-chaussée_Entrée_Intérieur avec bibliothèque.

# MALIBU_CA **POINT DUME RESIDENCE**

**ARCHITECTS:** GRIFFIN ENRIGHT ARCHITECTS
**COMPLETION:** 2007_**TYPOLOGY:** LIVING
**PHOTOS:** BENNY CHAN, FOTOWORKS

This project explores the nature of fluidity and sequence in the context of space, circulation, and landscape. The site rests atop one of the highest points in Point Dume, Malibu, and offers stunning panoramas, making the organization of views a paramount concern for the project. The home both captures and is captivated by these vistas, creating spaces that flow in to one another and in to the landscape. The smooth, sinuous surfaces that organize the spaces are punctured and intersected in such a way as to break down the barriers that visually and psychologically separate the inside from the outdoors.

Dieses Projekt erforscht den fließenden und kontinuierlichen Charakter von Räumen, Wegeführung und Landschaft. Da das Grundstück an einer der höchsten Stellen Malibus in Point Dume liegt und ein überwältigendes Panorama bietet, hatte die Organisation der Aussichten höchste Priorität. Das Wohnhaus fängt diese Sicht nicht nur ein, sondern wird auch von ihrem Reiz eingenommen, indem seine Zimmer ineinander und in die Landschaft übergehen. Die glatten, gewundenen Flächen, welche die Räume organisieren, sind so ausgespart und durchschnitten, dass sie die optischen und psychologischen Grenzen zwischen Innen und Außen aufheben.

Ce bâtiment explore les concepts de fluidité et de succession en matière d'espace, de circulation et de paysage. Situé à Point Dume, sur les hauteurs de Malibu, il offre de superbes panoramas sur les environs, que les architectes se sont efforcés d'intégrer à leur projet. Les différents espaces de la villa sont ainsi en interaction continuelle non seulement entre eux, mais aussi avec le paysage. Leurs surfaces souples et ondulantes s'entrecoupent de manière à supprimer les barrières tant visuelles que psychologiques entre l'intérieur et l'extérieur.

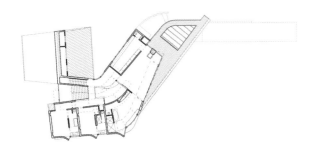
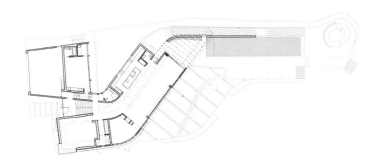

left: Floor plans_Living room with open kitchen_Living area. right: Sundeck and pool_Entrance view_Patio.
links: Grundrisse_Wohnzimmer mit offener Küche_Wohnbereich. rechts: Terrasse and Pool_Eingang_Innenhof.
à gauche: Plans_Séjour avec cuisine ouverte_Autre vue du séjour. à droite: Trois vues du bâtiment, de la terrasse et de la piscine.

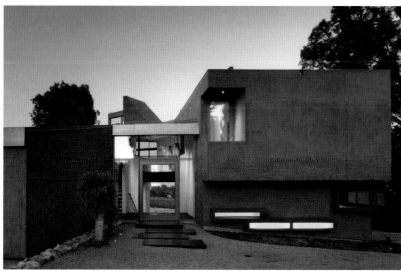

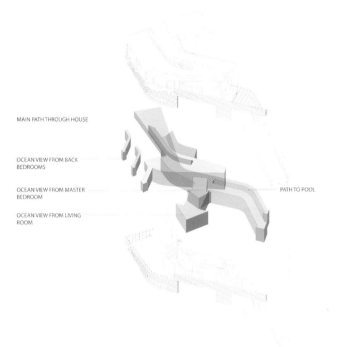

MAIN PATH THROUGH HOUSE

OCEAN VIEW FROM BACK
BEDROOMS

OCEAN VIEW FROM MASTER
BEDROOM

OCEAN VIEW FROM LIVING
ROOM

PATH TO POOL

PATHS ALLOW NATURAL VENTILATION
AND ALIGH WITH PREVAILING WIND
DIRECTION

left: Interior upper level. right: Circulation and view diagram_View from upper level_Bathroom_Living area.
links: Innenansicht vom Obergeschoss. rechts: Auseinandergezogene Darstellung_Blick vom Obergeschoss_Badezimmer_Wohnbereich.
à gauche: Couloir au niveau supérieur. à droite: Diagramme de circulation_Le séjour vu du niveau supérieur_Salle de bain_Séjour avec baie vitrée.

# MANHATTAN BEACH_CA **FULLER RESIDENCE**

**ARCHITECTS:** DESIGNARC
**COMPLETION:** 2006_**TYPOLOGY:** LIVING
**PHOTOS:** BENNY CHAN, FOTOWORKS

Perched above a pedestrian street in an historic beach community, the house occupies a narrow seaside lot. Recalling nearby lifeguard towers and beach bungalows, the house takes its place among a lively landscape of building scales and housing styles, which has evolved over the last century. The lower floor of the house consists of social spaces – a ground floor family room and guest space opens directly onto the street across a small courtyard, participating in the life of the street. The main living spaces occupy the second level and are linked to their surroundings by large sliding pocket doors, letting in the ocean breeze.

Oberhalb einer Fußgängerstraße in einer historischen Strandgemeinde belegt das Haus ein schmales Grundstück am Meer. Es erinnert an die nahe gelegenen Strandwächtertürme und Sommerhäuser und steht inmitten einer lebhaften Landschaft aus unterschiedlichen Gebäudegrößen und -stilen, die sich im Laufe des letzten Jahrhunderts entwickelt haben. Das untere Geschoss des Hauses beherbergt die gemeinschaftlichen Räume – ein Mehrzweckraum und ein Gästezimmer im Erdgeschoss führen unmittelbar zur Straße über einen kleinen Hof und nehmen so am Straßenleben teil. In der zweiten Etage mit den Hauptwohnräumen lassen großzügige, verschiebbare Taschentüren die Meeresbrise herein.

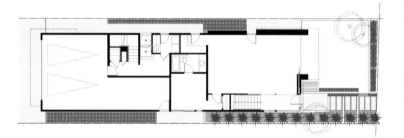

Cette maison est construite sur un terrain étroit, en haut d'une rue piétonne desservant une station balnéaire. Rappelant les bungalows ou les tours de maîtres-nageurs qu'on voit sur les plages, elle s'intègre bien dans un environnement urbain où l'on retrouve tous les styles qui se sont succédé depuis un siècle. Le séjour du rez-de-chaussée, qui se prolonge par une cour qui va jusqu'à la rue, permet à la famille et à ses amis de profiter de la vie de la station. Les pièces des deux niveaux supérieurs, plus intimistes, s'ouvrent sur l'extérieur par de grandes portes-fenêtres coulissantes qui donnent directement sur l'océan.

left: Floor plan lower level_Living area_Open kitchen with dining area. right: Front façade.
links: Grundriss Unter Geschoss_Wohnzimmer_Offene Küche mit Essbereich. rechts: Vorderfassade.
à gauche: Plan_Séjour_Cuisine/salle à manger. à droite: Façade principale.

left: Dining area. right: Floor plan main level and upper level_Kitchen.
links: Essbereich. rechts: Grundriss Erdgeschoss and Obergeschoss_Küche.
à gauche: Salle à manger. à droite: Plans_Autre vue de la cuisine/salle à manger.

# MARIN COUNTY_CA **EQUINOX HOUSE**

**ARCHITECTS:** BANTA DESIGN
**COMPLETION:** 2007_**TYPOLOGY:** LIVING
**PHOTOS:** MATTHEW MILLMAN PHOTOGRAPHY

The Equinox House is more of an evolution than a renovation. The sturdy existing house was transformed into a leaner, more flexible frame for its expansive views of San Francisco Bay. The house is named after the vernal and autumnal equinoxes, as the sun and moon are visible from rise to setting along the interior arc of its main living room and outdoor terraces. The interior space was extended to the outside to establish loop circulation wherever possible, while the exchange of materials and finishes for more durable surfaces was part of the transformation of the house from a suburban mansion into a museum of views.

Equinox House hat mehr mit einer Entwicklung als einer Erneuerung gemein. Das massive Haus wurde wegen seiner weiten Ausblicke auf die Bucht von San Francisco in eine schlankere, flexiblere Gestalt umgebaut. Benannt ist das Gebäude nach der Frühlings- und Herbst-Tagundnachtgleiche, da am inneren Bogen seines Wohnzimmers und der Außenterrassen der Auf- und Untergang von Sonne und Mond zu sehen sind. Der Innenraum wurde nach draußen ausgedehnt, um wo immer möglich eine schleifenförmige Erschließung herzustellen. Der Austausch von Materialien und Oberflächenbearbeitungen durch widerstandsfähigere Ausführungen gehörte zur Umgestaltung des Hauses von einer Villa am Stadtrand zu einem Panorama-Museum.

Les architectes ont conçu ce projet de rénovation comme une évolution: la villa d'origine, solide mais refermée sur elle-même, a été rendue plus flexible et plus souple de manière à tirer profit des vues magnifiques qu'on découvre ici sur la baie de San Francisco. Le nom « Equinox » a été choisi car il est désormais possible de suivre toute la course du soleil et de la lune à partir du grand salon et des terrasses lors des équinoxes de printemps et d'automne. D'autre part, les revêtements de surfaces ont été renouvelés et les espaces intérieurs et extérieurs interconnectés dans la mesure du possible. Avec pour résultat final un pavillon de banlieue transformé en un véritable « musée des vues panoramiques ».

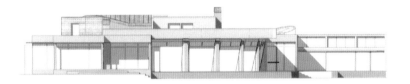

left: South elevation_Interior view, detail of living room. right: Balcony with bay view_Detail main façade_Main entrance view_Deck view.
links: Südansicht_Innenansicht, Wohnzimmer. rechts: Balkon mit Blick auf die Bucht_Detail Fassade_Eingang_Dachterrasse.
à gauche: Vue en élévation de la façade sud_Séjour. à droite: Balcon avec vue sur la baie_Gros plan sur la façade principale_Vue de l'entrée_Véranda.

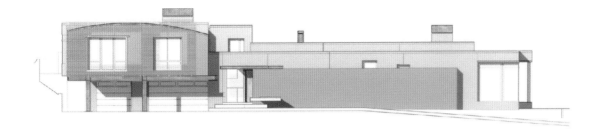

left: Interior. right: North elevation_Fireplace_Interior hallway with stairs_Exterior with city view.
links: Inneneinrichtung. rechts: Nordansicht_Kamin_Flur mit Treppenaufgang_Außenansicht mit Blick auf die Stadt.
à gauche: Intérieur. à droite: Vue en élévation de la façade nord_Cheminée_Couloir et escalier_Extérieur avec vue sur la ville.

MOUNTAIN VIEW_CA **COMMUNITY SCHOOL OF MUSIC AND ARTS**

**ARCHITECTS:** MARK CAVAGNERO ASSOCIATES
**COMPLETION:** 2004_**TYPOLOGY:** EDUCATION
**PHOTOS:** TIM GRIFFITH

This building is the first permanent home of the Community School of Music and Arts, which is a 35-year-old non-profit organization located in Mountain View, California. The project was built to be a state-of-the-art education facility, and includes features that typify what the school and its community represent and work towards achieving. Two of the main space components of the building comprise of music classrooms and private music studios, which provide an opportunity for growth. In addition to that, the building provides visual arts studios, an administration space, a recital hall, and an outdoor performance space.

Dieses Gebäude ist der erste feste Standort der Community School of Music and Arts, einer 35 Jahre alten gemeinnützigen Organisation im kalifornischen Mountain View. Das Projekt einer modernen Bildungseinrichtung repräsentiert die Schule und ihre Gemeinschaft und zeigt die Ziele ihrer Arbeit auf. Zu den beiden wichtigsten räumlichen Komponenten der Schule zählen erweiterbare Unterrichtsräume für Musik und private Musikstudios. Darüber hinaus bietet die Schule Studios für bildende Kunst, einen Verwaltungsbereich, eine Konzerthalle und einen Aufführungsraum im Freien.

Il s'agit là de la première implantation durable dont bénéficie la Community School of Music and Arts, un organisme à but non lucratif fondé à Mountain View, en Californie, il y a trente-cinq ans. Le bâtiment constitue un modèle en matière de structure éducative moderne et illustre parfaitement les objectifs communautaires de l'association. Ses deux composants principaux sont les salles de cours et les espaces de musique susceptibles d'évoluer en fonction des besoins. Le conservatoire comprend également des ateliers d'arts plastiques, des bureaux, un auditorium et un espace pour concerts en plein air.

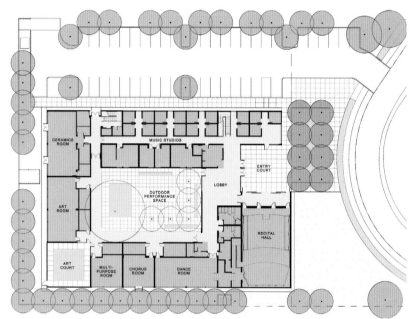

left: Site plan_North elevation. right: Entrance court.
links: Lageplan_Nordansicht. rechts: Eingangsbereich.
à gauche: Plan de situation_Façade nord. à droite: Cour d'entrée.

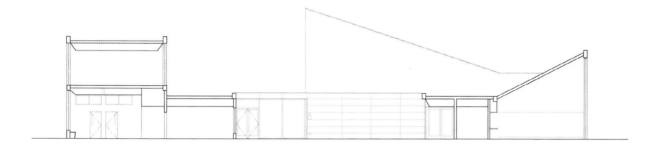

left: Interior of hall. right: North south section_School yard.
links: Eingangshalle. rechts: Nord-Südansicht_Schulhof.
à gauche: Hall d'entrée. à droite: Vue en élévation nord/sud_Cour intérieure.

# OAKLAND_CA **OAKLAND HOUSE**

**ARCHITECTS:** KANNER ARCHITECTS
**COMPLETION:** 2007_**TYPOLOGY:** LIVING
**PHOTOS:** TIM GRIFFITH

Located on a hill high above the San Francisco bay, this home is designed to capture the magnificent vistas spanning from the Bay Bridge to the Golden Gate Bridge. Floor-to-ceiling glass clears the way to unobstructed views. The predominantly south-southwest orientation requires deep overhangs to cut down glare and soften the light quality in the home. Spare and rigorously Modern in its aesthetic, the home has only a handful of materials and even fewer colors: pale blue scratch coat plaster, concrete floors, steel and glass window systems, and a mostly white and bleached wood composition of cabinetry and furnishings.

Dieses Wohnhaus auf einem Hügel hoch über der Bucht von San Francisco soll die herrlichen Aussichten zwischen der Bay Bridge und der Golden Gate Bridge einfangen. Raumhohes Glas ermöglicht eine freie Sicht. Die überwiegend südsüdwestliche Ausrichtung macht breite Dachüberstände erforderlich, die das Blendlicht einschränken und die Helligkeit im Haus mildern. Zu der reduzierten und konsequent modernen Ästhetik des Hauses gehören nur eine Handvoll Materialien und noch weniger Farben: blassblauer Unterputz, Betonfußböden, Fenstersysteme aus Stahl und Glas sowie überwiegend weißes und aufgehelltes Holz für Möbel und Ausstattung.

Située sur une colline qui domine la baie de San Francisco, cette villa offre une vue panoramique du Bay Bridge au Golden Gate Bridge, que les occupants peuvent apprécier de l'intérieur grâce à de grandes baies vitrées qui vont du sol au plafond. L'orientation générale au sud-ouest a rendu nécessaire de concevoir des surplombs au-dessus des ouvertures de manière à adoucir la lumière à l'intérieur. D'un style austère et résolument moderne, le bâtiment n'utilise que peu de matériaux différents (murs en béton, meubles en bois, fenêtres en acier et en verre), ainsi qu'une une palette de couleurs extrêmement réduite (enduit bleu clair, et aménagements intérieurs blancs ou en bois décoloré).

left: Ground floor plan_Areial view_Detail exterior. right: Fully glazed façade_Entrance.
links: Grundriss Erdgeschoss_Luftbild_Fassadendetail. rechts: Verglaste Fassade_Eingang.
à gauche: Plan du rez-de-chaussée_La villa vue de haut_Détail de l'extérieur. à droite: Façade entièrement vitrée_Vue de l'entrée.

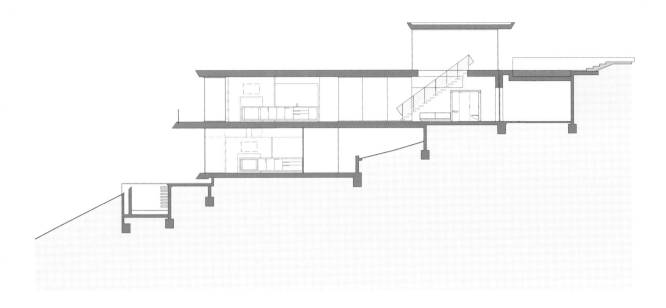

left: Exterior view. right: Section_Stair to upper floor_Living area_Sleeping room with open bathroom.
links: Außenansicht. rechts: Schnitt_Treppe ins Obergeschoss_Wohnbereich_Schlafzimmer mit offenem Badezimmer.
à gauche: Extérieur. à droite: Vue en coupe_Escalier_Séjour_Séjour avec salle de bain ouverte.

OAKLAND_CA **CATHEDRAL OF CHRIST THE LIGHT**

**ARCHITECTS:** SKIDMORE, OWINGS & MERRILL
**COMPLETION:** 2008_**TYPOLOGY:** ECCLESIASTICAL
**PHOTOS:** CESAR RUBIO (378 R., 379), TIMOTHY HURSLEY

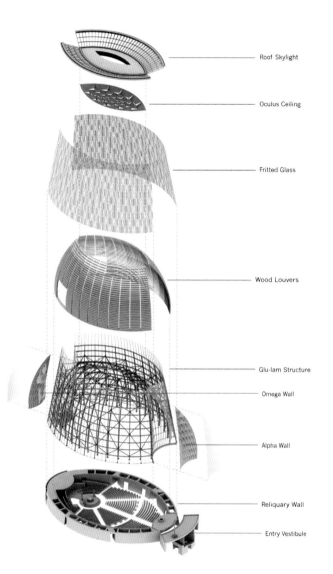

Roof Skylight

Oculus Ceiling

Fritted Glass

Wood Louvers

Glu-lam Structure

Omega Wall

Alpha Wall

Reliquary Wall

Entry Vestibule

The project was designed by Craig W. Hartman as a replacement for the cathedral of saint Francis de Sales, which was destroyed by an earthquake in 1989. The cathedral overlooks lake Merritt and has 1,350 seats. Inside there is also a mausoleum, conference center, offices, residences, a book store and a café. Outside, a landscaped plaza links the building with downtown Oakland. Rather than traditional iconography, the cathedral's design focuses on the experience of and space. The base of the building is concrete while wood ribs rise above featuring a glass enclosure and wooden louvers. The cathedral is also designed to withstand a 1000 year earthquake, making sure it will stand the test of time.

Craig W. Hartman entwarf das Projekt als Ersatz für die Kirche Saint Francis de Sales, die durch ein Erdbeben 1989 zerstört worden war. Die Kathedrale mit 1.350 Sitzen überblickt den See Merritt. Zur Anlage gehören auch ein Mausoleum, ein Konferenzzentrum, Büros, Wohnungen, ein Buchladen und ein Café. Außen verbindet ein landschaftlich gestalteter Platz das Gebäude mit der Innenstadt von Oakland. Anstelle einer traditionellen Ikonografie stellt der Entwurf auf Raumerfahrungen ab. Über einem Gebäudesockel aus Beton erheben sich Gewölberippen aus Holz mit einer gläsernen Umfassung und Holzlamellen. Um sicherzugehen, dass die Kathedrale die Zeiten übersteht, ist sie für ein Jahrtausenderdbeben ausgelegt.

Craig W. Hartman a conçu ce bâtiment en remplacement de la cathédrale Saint-François-de-Salle, détruite par un tremblement de terre en 1989. L'édifice se dresse au bord du lac Merritt et peut accueillir 1350 fidèles. Les espaces liturgiques se complètent par un mausolée, un centre de conférence, des bureaux et des appartements, une librairie et un café. Une esplanade paysagère assure la liaison entre la cathédrale et le centre ville d'Oakland. L'iconographie est réduite à un minimum à l'intérieur du bâtiment, la priorité ayant été accordée à l'impression d'ensemble générée par l'espace. Une armature en bois à claire-voie repose sur une base en béton et supporte une enveloppe en verre. Le bâtiment a par ailleurs été conçu pour résister à un tremblement de terre comme il n'en arrive dans la région qu'une fois par siècle.

left: Exploded view_Exterior view_Aerial view. right: View from water side.
links: Auseinandergezogene Darstellung_Außenansicht_Luftbild. rechts: Ansicht vom Wasser.
à gauche: Vue en éclaté_La cathédrale dans son contexte_Vue aérienne. à droite: La cathédrale vue du lac.

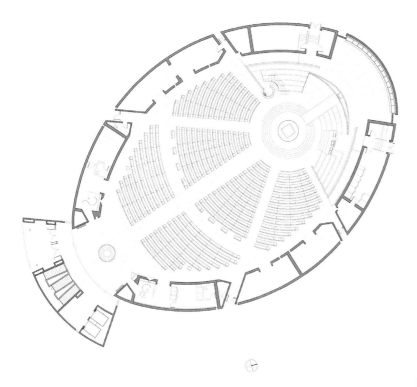

left: Interior. right: Floor plan_View towards exit_Interior detail_Decorated wall.
links: Innenansicht. rechts: Grundriss_Blick Richtung Ausgang_Detail der Inneneinrichtung_Verzierte Wand.
à gauche: Intérieur. à droite: Plan_Vue du chœur vers l'entrée_Détail de l'intérieur_Mur avec chemin de croix.

OJAI_CA **THACHER ARTS BUILDING**

**ARCHITECTS:** BARTON PHELPS & ASSOCIATES
**COMPLETION:** 2006_**TYPOLOGY:** EDUCATION
**PHOTOS:** BENNY CHAN, FOTOWORKS

Set between a mountain range and coastal valley, the hillside campus of this 115-year-old boarding school is an academic community of 235 students, 40 faculty members, and 140 horses. Insertion of the Arts Building into its historic core prompted an evaluation of the existing campus layout and the extraordinary power of the surrounding terrain. One of the goals was to demonstrate the new buildings' ability to maximize usefulness of the adjoining outdoor spaces and to enhance the campus experience. As a multiuse performing arts theater, the building promotes increased student participation in arts programs.

Zwischen einer Gebirgskette und einem Küstental gelegen beherbergt das Hanggrundstück des 115 Jahre alten Internats eine akademische Gemeinschaft aus 235 Schülern und 40 Dozenten sowie 140 Pferde. Da das Arts Building in den historischen Kern eingebunden werden sollte, wurden die Anordnung der vorhandenen Bauten und das umliegende Gelände in der Planung berücksichtigt. Eines der Ziele war, mit den Neubauten den Nutzen der angrenzenden Außenanlagen zu maximieren und die Erlebbarkeit des Campus zu steigern. Als vielseitig verwendbares Theater für darstellende Kunst fördert das Gebäude eine stärkere Teilnahme der Schüler an Kunstprogrammen.

Ce nouveau bâtiment fait partie d'un internat plus que centenaire situé à flanc de colline entre une chaîne de montagnes et une vallée côtière. Il peut accueillir 235 élèves, quarante professeurs et 140 chevaux. Avant de le construire, il a été nécessaire d'étudier la composition des bâtiments préexistants et d'évaluer le potentiel du terrain alentour, qui s'est révélé être phénoménal. Un des objectifs était d'optimiser l'utilisation des environs immédiats du nouveau bâtiment afin de rendre l'internat encore plus attrayant. D'autre part, le nouvel auditorium invite les élèves à participer plus activement aux programmes artistiques.

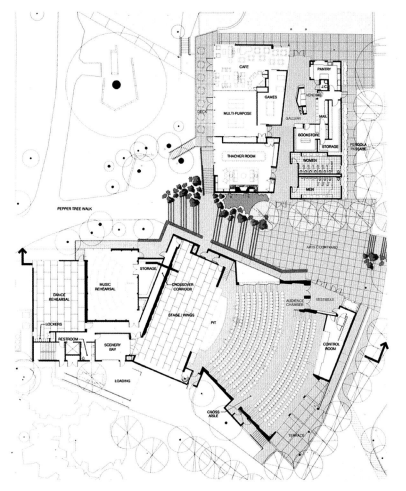

left: Site plan_Entrance view_Wooden wall panels. right: School yard.
links: Lageplan_Eingangsansicht_Hölzerne Wandpaneele. rechts: Schulhof.
à gauche: Plan de situation_Escalier_Façade avec bardage en planches. à droite: Vue de la cour.

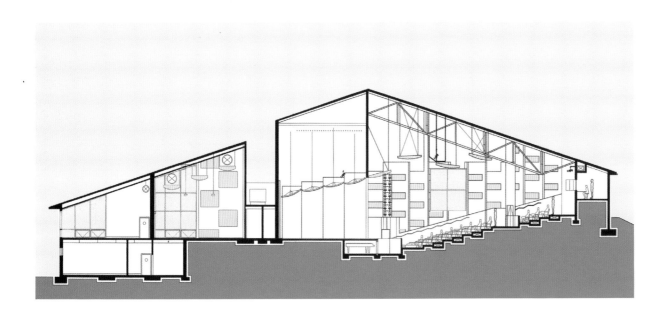

left: Gallery. right: Section_Auditorium_Pergola_Exterior.
links: Galerie. rechts: Schnitt_Aula_Überdachter Übergang_Außenansicht.
à gauche: Galerie. à droite: Vue en coupe_Auditorium_Pergola_Extérieur.

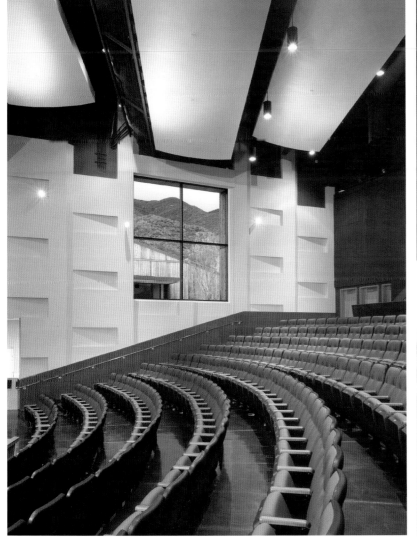

# PALM DESERT_CA **DIAMOND RESIDENCE**

**ARCHITECTS:** PATEL ARCHITECTURE
**COMPLETION:** 2007_**TYPOLOGY:** LIVING
**PHOTOS:** ARTHUR COLEMAN

In this signature streamlined modern desert home, architect Narendra Patel created a delicate pavilion, overlooking a golf course, valley, and mountains. The home's defining element is a daring inverted shell roof that lifts up towards the exterior, bringing light into airy interiors. The main living spaces including the great room, dining and family room, kitchen, and the master suite are located facing the pool as the primary choice view, while sheltered by the hovering roof. Circulation to the bedrooms is separate from the public areas, giving each bedroom its own access to private patios and views, while maximizing privacy.

In diesem zeichenhaften stromlinienförmigen Wohnhaus in der Wüste schuf Architekt Narendra Patel einen fein ausgearbeiteten Pavillon mit Blick auf einen Golfplatz, ein Tal und Berge. Das bestimmende Element des Hauses ist ein gewagtes, umgekehrtes Schalendach, das an den Außenrändern aufwärts gerichtet ist und Licht ins luftige Innere lässt. Der weitläufige Wohnraum, das Ess- und Mehrzweckzimmer, Küche und das Elternschlafzimmer weisen zum Pool mit der bevorzugten Aussicht und werden vom schwebenden Dach geschützt. Da die Privaträume und die gemeinschaftlichen Zonen getrennt zu erschließen sind, verfügt jedes Schlafzimmer über einen eigenen Zugang zu den privaten Höfen und Ausblicken.

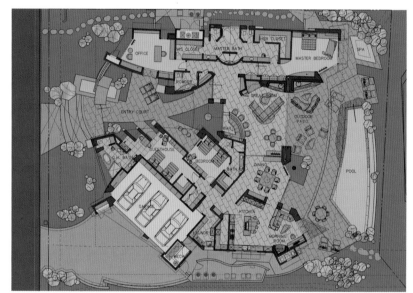

Dans un site de collines qui domine un terrain de golf et une vallée, l'architecte Narendra Patel a créé un bâtiment qui porte sa signature: un pavillon moderne aux lignes délicates bien adapté à un environnement désertique. Il se caractérise par un toit en forme de coquille renversée grâce auquel l'intérieur, bien aéré, est inondé de lumière. Les pièces principales (grand séjour, salle à manger, cuisine et chambres) donnent sur la piscine et bénéficient d'une vue magnifique tout en étant bien protégées par le toit suspendu. Chaque chambre dispose de sa propre terrasse avec vue sur les environs afin de garantir une intimité maximale à tous les occupants.

left: Site plan_Exterior with pool by night_View between buildings. right: Front entrance with gate.
links: Lageplan_Außenansicht vom Pool bei Nacht_Ansicht zwischen den Gebäuden. rechts: Eingangsbereich mit Eingangstor.
à gauche: Plan de situation_Bâtiments et piscine la nuit_Allée entre les bâtiments la nuit. à droite: Portail.

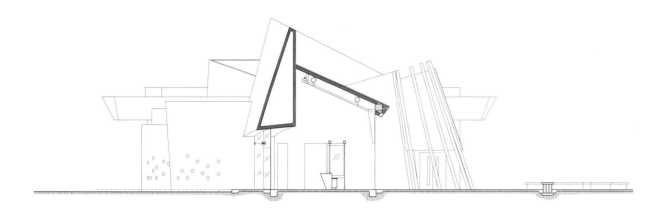

left: Bathroom with view outside. right: Elevation_Living area_Kitchen detail_Kitchen_Dining area.
links: Badezimmer mit Blick nach draußen. rechts: Ansicht_Wohnbereich_Küche_Detail der Küche_Essbereich.
à gauche: Salle de bain avec vue sur l'extérieur. à droite: Vue en élévation_Séjour_Cuisine ouverte_ Autre vue de la cuisine_Salle à manger.

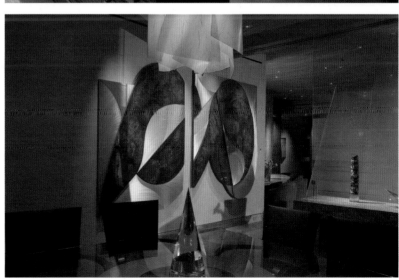

# PALM SPRINGS_CA **HENDERSON COMMUNITY CENTER**

**ARCHITECTS:** PATEL ARCHITECTURE
**COMPLETION:** 2009_**TYPOLOGY:** EDUCATION
**PHOTOS:** DAVID GLOMB /COURTESY PATEL ARCHITECTURE

The Henderson Community Center – named for city founders Clifford and Randall Henderson and completed last fall – serves as the chamber of commerce home and a place for community groups to meet. The city's first Leadership in Energy and Environmental Design building – the adjacent visitor center – is certified Silver. The center is certified Gold. "'Going green' might be the buzz phrase today, but ultimately it will become a survival skill," Patel believes. He designed the 6,300-square-foot building with an eye toward solar energy, natural air circulation, resource conservation, and minimal waste.

Das nach den Stadtgründern Clifford und Randall Henderson benannte, im letzten Herbst fertiggestellte Henderson Community Center dient als Handelskammer und Bürgerhaus. Als erstes Gebäude der Stadt erhielt das benachbarte Bürgerzentrum das LEED (Leadership in Energy and Environmental Design-)- Zertifikat für Nachhaltigkeit mit der Bewertung Silber. Das Henderson Community Center ist mit Gold ausgezeichnet. „'Going Green' mag ein Modewort sein, doch letzten Endes wird davon unser Überleben abhängen", so Patel. Er entwarf das 585 Quadratmeter große Gebäude im Hinblick auf Solarenergie, natürliche Luftzirkulation, Ressourcenschonung und minimale Abfallmengen.

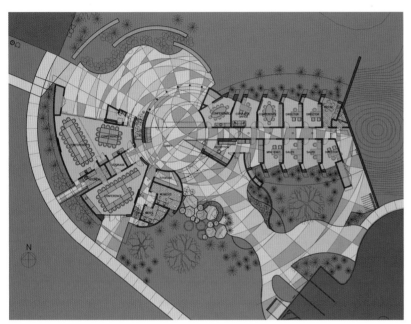

Cette salle polyvalente qui porte le nom de Randall Henderson, l'un des fondateurs de la ville de Palm Desert, est utilisée par la chambre de commerce locale et différentes associations des environs. Elle bénéficie du label écologique LEED Gold, tandis que le centre d'accueil des visiteurs construit à proximité a été le premier édifice de la ville à bénéficier du label LEED Silver. Narendra Patel, l'architecte responsable du projet, a déclaré: « L'écologie est certes à la mode aujourd'hui mais à terme, elle va devenir une nécessité pour survivre ». Il a conçu ce bâtiment d'environ 585 mètres carrés en accordant une importance particulière à l'énergie solaire, à la ventilation naturelle, à l'économie des ressources et à la minimisation des déchets.

left: Site plan_Entrance view_Exterior view. right: Entrance area_Building in landscape.
links: Lageplan_Eingangsansicht_Außenanaicht. rechts: Eingangsbereich_Landschaftsansicht.
à gauche: Plan de situation_Entrée_Le bâtiment dans son environnement. à droite: L'entrée la nuit_Autre vue du bâtiment dans son environnement.

left: Lobby. right: Sketch_Interior lobby_Glass façade_General view.
links: Eingangshalle. rechts: Skizze_Innenansicht der Eingangshalle_Glasfassade_Gesamtansicht.
à gauche: Hall d'entrée. à droite: Esquisse_Autre vue du hall d'entrée_Façade vitrée_Vue d'ensemble.

PASADENA_CA **THE DISNEY STORE HEADQUARTERS**

**ARCHITECTS:** CLIVE WILKINSON ARCHITECTS
**COMPLETION:** 2007_**TYPOLOGY:** OFFICE
**PHOTOS:** BENNY CHAN, FOTOWORKS

The original wood framed building is composed of three parts. The front portion is a 4.9-meter-high space with large timber trusses. The large rear portion is a double height wooden framed atrium space with a saw-tooth roof, creating dramatic clerestory lighting that spans the width of the space. These two portions are connected by a long interstitial brick walled structure, which inspired the creation of brick-like elements for the interior. These modular elements allude to children's block building games and remind staff of their role in creating products for children. The building also connects occupants to the exterior with a new landscaped courtyard at the front. This includes an ivy topiary of "Mickey Mouse ears".

Die originale Holzrahmenkonstruktion besteht aus drei Teilen: einem vorderen 4,9 Meter hohen Raum mit Holzträgern, einem hinteren zweigeschossigen Atrium mit Sheddach, dessen Lichtgaden den Raum überspannt, und einer langen Ziegelwandkonstruktion, die beide Teile miteinander verbindet. Diese modularen Elemente spielen auf die Bauklötze von Kindern an und erinnern die Mitarbeiter an ihre Aufgabe, Produkte für Kinder zu kreieren. Außer einem landschaftlich gestalteten Innenhof und durchgängig neuen Oberlichtern bietet das Gebäude auch eine Verbindung zu einem neuen Hof an der Vorderseite mit „Mickey Mouse-Ohren" aus Efeu.

Trois parties distinctes composent ce bâtiment original. La première est un espace à charpente en bois d'une hauteur de 4,90 mètres. La seconde, deux fois plus haute, présente un toit en dent de scie qui repose également sur une charpente en bois et dont les surfaces vitrées verticales assurent un excellent éclairage naturel. La troisième partie est un espace en brique qui assure la jonction entre les deux premières. Certaines cloisons, réalisées avec les cubes d'un jeu de construction surdimensionné, rappellent aux employés que leur rôle est d'élaborer des produits destinés aux enfants. Le bâtiment se complète à l'extérieur par une cour végétalisée agrémentée notamment par une structure recouverte de lierre dont la forme correspond à la silhouette de Mickey.

left: First floor plan_"Block conference room" – stacked_"Block conference room" – not stacked.
right: Workstations, "honeycomb conference room".
links: Grundriss Erdgeschoss_„Würfel-Konferenzraum" – aufgestapelt_„Würfel Konferenzraum"– nicht aufgestapelt. rechts: Arbeitsplätze, „Honigwaben-Konferenzraum".
à gauche: Plan du rez-de-chaussée_Salle de conférence avec cubes empilés_Salle de conférence avec cubes épars. à droite: Intérieur de la salle de conférence « Rayons de miel ».

REDONDO BEACH_CA **REDONDO BEACH CONTAINER HOUSE**

**ARCHITECTS:** DEMARIA DESIGN
**COMPLETION:** 2007_**TYPOLOGY:** LIVING
**PHOTOS:** ANDRE MOVSESYAN

The building structure is a family residence employing recycled cargo containers. Combined with technologies from the aerospace industry, these components have been brought together with traditional stick frame construction to create a "hybrid" home that is environmentally conscious and affordable. The use of materials and methods from other industries, non-related to residential construction, is part of the architect's philosophical approach. Features include airplane hangar doors, denim insulation, polyurethane insulated roof panels, tank less hot water heaters, greenhouse acrylic anels, and Formaldehyde-free plywood.

Der Baukörper des Einfamilienhauses besteht aus recycelten Frachtcontainern. In Kombination mit Techniken aus der Luft- und Raumfahrtindustrie und einer traditionellen Holzrahmenkonstruktion ergeben diese Komponenten ein umweltbewusstes und erschwingliches „Hybrid"-Haus. Die Verwendung von Materialien und Methoden aus anderen, nicht mit dem Wohnungsbau zusammenhängenden Industrien gehört zum philosophischen Ansatz des Architekten. Charakteristische Elemente sind Türen eines Flugzeughangars, eine Dämmung aus Denim, mit Polyurethan gedämmte Dachplatten, Durchlauferhitzer, Acrylpaneele von Gewächshäusern und formaldehydfreies Sperrholz.

Cette villa a été construite en utilisant des conteneurs recyclés, assemblés de manière traditionnelle et en utilisant des procédés empruntés à la technologie aéronautique, de manière à créer une maison « hybride » à fois respectueuse de l'environnement et n'engageant que de faible coûts de construction. L'utilisation de matériaux et de procédés inhabituels dans le BTP fait d'ailleurs partie intégrante du concept développé par les architectes. C'est ainsi que la « maison-conteneur » intègre des portes pour hangars d'avions, une isolation en toile de jean, des panneaux de toit en polyuréthane isolant, des chauffe-eau sans réservoir, des plaques acryliques pour serres et du contreplaqué sans formaldéhyde.

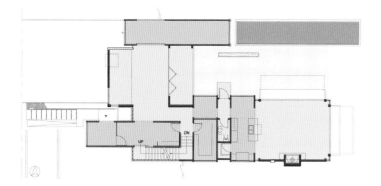

left: First floor plan_Exterior view_Interior view. right: Recycled cargo container_Exterior view at night_View from the garden to decks.
links: Grundriss erstes Obergeschoss_Außenansicht_Inneneinrichtung. rechts: Aufbereitete Cargo-Container_Außenansicht bei Nacht_Gartenansicht auf die Terrasse.
à gauche: Plan du rez-de-chaussée_Extérieur_Deux vues de l'intérieur. à droite: Villa en conteneurs industriels recyclés_La villa la nuit_La véranda vue du jardin.

RICHMOND_CA **CALIFORNIA DEPARTMENT OF HEALTH SERVICES**

**ARCHITECTS:** STUDIOS ARCHITECTURE
**COMPLETION:** 2005_**TYPOLOGY:** HEALTH
**PHOTOS:** TIM GRIFFITH

California's DHS wanted its new Richmond laboratory campus to project a less bureaucratic image. The designs for the initial two phases – consisting of research laboratory components – were constrained by security considerations. The Phase III office building however, provided the opportunity to create a structure that would serve as both the public "front door" and the communal "living room". The new building's design conveys DHS's commitment to innovation. The entry courtyard features a sculpture garden with a sunken grass court, while beyond the entryway, a central atrium feeds natural light into the building.

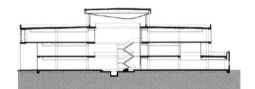

Der neue Laborkomplex des kalifornischen Department of Health Services (DHS) in Richmond sollte weniger verwaltungsmäßig erscheinen. Die Entwürfe für die ersten beiden Bauphasen – Bestandteile der Forschungslabore – waren von Sicherheitserwägungen eingeschränkt. Das Bürogebäude der dritten Phase hingegen bot Gelegenheit zu einem Bau, der als „öffentlicher Haupteingang" und gemeinschaftliches „Wohnzimmer" dienen würde. Die Gestaltung des Neubaus artikuliert DHS' Verpflichtung zur Innovation. Auf dem Vorplatz ist ein Skulpturengarten mit einem vertieften Grashof angelegt. Hinter der Zufahrt leitet ein zentrales Atrium natürliches Licht in das Gebäude.

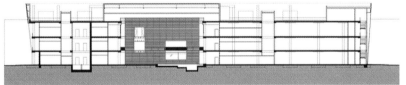

Lors de l'élaboration du centre médical de Richmond, les services de santé californiens ont demandé aux architectes de concevoir un bâtiment qui n'ait pas l'air « bureaucratique ». Alors que les laboratoires de recherche construits dans les deux premières phases du projet ont une apparence dominée par des considérations sécuritaires, le bâtiment présenté ici, construit dans la troisième phase, a bien été conçu comme une structure ouverte, une sorte de « salon communal ». Son apparence générale reflète l'intérêt des services de santé locaux pour l'innovation. La cour d'entrée présente une pelouse en contrebas et est ornée d'une sculpture, tandis que le grand puits de lumière central assure un bon éclairage naturel des espaces intérieurs.

left: Sections_Exit stair at west entry_Atrium_Central atrium. right: Entry east_Exterior stair Entrance area.
links: Schnitte_Außentreppe am Westeingang_Lichthof_Zentraler Lichthof. rechts: Osteingang_Außentreppe_Eingangsbereich.
à gauche: Deux vues en coupe_Escalier de secours du côté ouest_Puits de lumière_Autre vue du puits de lumière. à droite: Cour d'entrée _Escalier extérieur_Vue d'ensemble de l'esplanade d'entrée.

# SAN DIEGO_CA **ON GRAPE**

**ARCHITECTS:** SEBASTIAN MARISCAL STUDIO
**COMPLETION:** 2006_**TYPOLOGY:** LIVING
**PHOTOS:** HISAO SUZUKI

The approach for this urban infill project was to subdivide the land for two single-family residences, which maximizes the enclosed, narrow space. The design focused on planes of space, achieved by constructing continuous horizontal spaces between the properties and keeping the interior void open to the sky. The wood frame structure receives a floating exterior skin of engineered stone and Corten steel with an internal air chamber, providing thermal and acoustic insulation. Spatially, the residences offer a quiet respite within the city. Materially, dark stone, steel and Ipe wood accentuate San Diego's diverse urban fabric.

Bei dieser Lückenbebauung wurde das Grundstück für zwei Einfamilienhäuser geteilt und so der umschlossene, enge Raum maximal ausgenutzt. Die Gestaltung konzentriert sich auf räumliche Ebenen, die durch die Schaffung durchgehender horizontaler Räume zwischen den Immobilien und durch den inneren, zum Himmel offenen Luftraum entstehen. Die Holzrahmenkonstruktion ist von einer schwebenden Außenhülle aus Mauersteinen und Cortenstahl mit einer inneren Luftkammer umgeben, die für thermische und akustische Dämmung sorgt. Die Wohnhäuser bieten einen Ruhepol in der Stadt. Dunkler Stein, Stahl und Ipeholz akzentuieren die vielfältige Bebauungsstruktur in San Diego.

Le terrain disponible a été partagé de manière à construire deux maisons individuelles tout en optimisant l'utilisation de l'espace. Les deux bâtiments, construits côte à côte, s'élèvent sur plusieurs étages avec une spaceentre les eux. Ils se composent d'une structure porteuse en bois dotée d'une enveloppe en acier Corten, bois exotique et parement en pierres naturelles noires, doublée à l'intérieur par un vide d'air qui assure une bonne isolation thermique et acoustique. Le confort des logements permet aux utilisateurs de se ressourcer sans quitter la ville de San Diego.

left: Detail exterior_Bridge view into interior_Detail façade, view into interior. right: Bridge connecting the two spaces_Street side view_Interior garden.
links: Außendetail_Ansicht von der Brücke in den Innenbereich_Detail der Fassade, Blick in den Wohnraum. rechts: Brücke, die zwei Gebäudeteile verbindet_Straßenansicht_Innenhof.
à gauche: Détail de l'extérieur_Passerelle_Détail de la façade. à droite: Vue d'ensemble avec la passerelle qui relie les deux volumes_L'immeuble vu de la rue_Cour intérieure végétalisée.

# SAN FRANCISCO_CA **ALLEY RETREAT**

**ARCHITECTS:** CARY BERNSTEIN ARCHITECT
**COMPLETION:** 2008_**TYPOLOGY:** LIVING
**PHOTOS:** SHARON RISEDORPH PHOTOGRAPHY

The renovation of a dilapidated, detached garage at the back of a typical urban property transformed an uninhabitable foundation/storage area below the parking level into an active living space. This unusual structure, formed by the neighborhood's hilly topography, is accessed from a small, mid-block alley. The reconsideration of the garage-as-entry creates an "auto foyer" which complements the formal front door of the house. The new flexible space at the garden-level provides a retreat for both children and adults complete with washroom and wine cellar. The open façade of the building unites it with the house across the garden via a lush and green central courtyard.

Beim Umbau einer verfallenen freistehenden Garage auf der Rückseite eines typischen Stadthauses entstand aus einem Lagerschuppen unter der Parkebene ein neuer Wohnraum. Diese ungewöhnliche, von der umgebenden hügeligen Landschaft geformte Konstruktion wird über einen kleinen Durchgang in Blockmitte erschlossen. Die Garage wird zu einer „Auto-Eingangshalle" umfunktioniert und ergänzt den offiziellen Hauseingang. Der neue flexible Raum auf Gartenebene schafft einen Rückzugsort für Kinder und Erwachsene samt Toilette und Weinkeller. Die offene Fassade des Gebäudes ist mit dem Haus am anderen Ende des Gartens durch einen üppig begrünten Hof in der Mitte verbunden.

La tâche de l'architecte consistait à réaménager un débarras situé sous le garage d'une maison de banlieue typique. Le bâtiment étant construit sur une colline, l'espace en question est le résultat d'un décaissement. On y accède par une allée qui passe entre les parcelles, la maison disposant ainsi d'une entrée secondaire. L'espace nouvellement réaménagé se compose d'une cour intérieure à la végétation luxuriante, d'une chambre pour les enfants et d'un cave à vin.

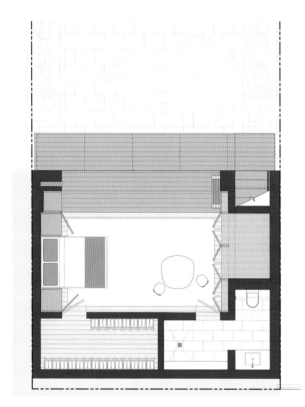

left: Ground floor plan with garden_Children's room_Stairs to garage. right: Patio_Alley view_Stairs to garden.
links: Grundriss mit Garten_Kinderzimmer_Treppe zur Garage. rechts: Innenhof_Durchgang_Treppen zum Garten.
à gauche: Plan du rez-de-chaussée et du jardin_Chambre des enfants_Escalier menant au garage.
à droite: Cour intérieure_Vue de l'allée_Escalier menant au jardin.

# SAN FRANCISCO_CA **1532 HOUSE**

**ARCHITECTS:** FOUGERON ARCHITECTURE
**COMPLETION:** 2003_**TYPOLOGY:** LIVING
**PHOTOS:** RICHARD BARNES

This new house includes a small front building with a garage on grade and a painting studio above and a three-story 2.500-square -foot house in the back with a courtyard between the two. The design plays with two sectional moves, one horizontally by introducing a courtyard in between the house and the painting studio and one vertically by digging the ground floor of the house the same level as the front street and garage. These two moves result in a creating a powerful interplay between inside and outside and between the different levels of the house and studio.

Der Neubau umfasst ein kleines Vorderhaus mit einer ebenerdigen Garage und einem darüber liegenden Maleratelier, an dessen Rückseite sich ein Hof und ein dreigeschossiges, 232 Quadratmeter großes Gebäude anschließen. Der Entwurf spielt mit dem Versetzen von Bauteilen. Eine horizontale Versetzung integriert einen Hof zwischen Gebäude und Maleratelier und eine vertikale senkt das Geländeniveau des Gebäudes auf die Ebene der Straße und der Garage ab. Beide Versetzungen ergeben eine kraftvolle Wechselwirkung zwischen Innen und Außen sowie zwischen den verschiedenen Ebenen des Gebäudes und des Ateliers.

Cette maison se compose d'un petit bâtiment sur rue avec un garage au rez-de-chaussée et un atelier de peintre au niveau supérieur, et d'un immeuble de deux étages dans la cour, offrant une surface habitable de 232 mètres carrés. L'ensemble joue sur deux plans différents: le premier horizontal, avec la cour qui s'étend entre les deux volumes ; le second vertical puisque le terrain a été décaissé de manière à mettre le rez-de-chaussée de l'immeuble sur cour au même niveau que celui de l'immeuble sur rue. Avec pour résultat un ensemble dynamisé par l'interaction entre l'intérieur et l'extérieur ainsi que par les différences de hauteur entre les deux volumes.

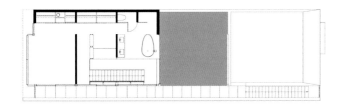
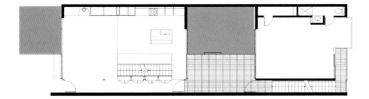
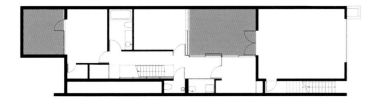

left: Plans_Courtyard entrance_Bridge towards bathroom_Stairs_Street side view right: Exterior at night.
links: Grundrisse_Hofeingang_Brücke mit Blick ins Badezimmer_Treppe_Straßenansicht. rechts: Außenansicht bei Nacht.
à gauche: Plans des différents niveaux_Entrée dans la cour_Passerelle menant à la salle de bain_Escalier_La maison vue de la rue. à droite: L'extérieur la nuit.

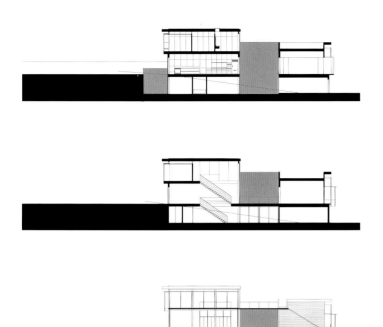

left: Exterior looking into interior. right: Sections_Kitchen and corridor_Master bedroom_Living room.
links: Blick ins Haus. rechts: Schnitte_Küche und Flur_Schlafzimmer_Wohnzimmer.
à gauche: Intérieur vu de l'extérieur. à droite: Trois vues en coupe_Cuisine et couloir_Chambre principale_Séjour.

SAN FRANCISCO_CA **TEHAMA GRASSHOPPER**

**ARCHITECTS:** FOUGERON ARCHITECTURE
**COMPLETION:** 2006_**TYPOLOGY:** LIVING
**PHOTOS:** RICHARD BARNES

A surprising integration of old and new elements, of competing urban forces, brings the remodeled warehouse alive. Three stories of interlocked spaces have distinct personalities and functions: office, main living area, and penthouse. The rigidity of the original concrete structure is broken down in a subtle interplay of light, surfaces, levels, and indoor and outdoor spaces – making the urban living experience as richly textured as the city itself. The second floor is the main living space for the young owners and their child. Its focus is a new courtyard, cut out from the existing floor plate that connects the building to the new penthouse above and to the sky.

Eine erstaunliche Einbindung von alten und neuen Elementen sowie von konkurrierenden städtischen Einflüssen lässt das umgestaltete Lagerhaus lebhaft wirken. Drei Geschosse mit verschachtelten Räumen verfügen über eine jeweils eigene Stimmung und Funktion: Büro, Hauptwohnbereich und Dachgeschoss. Die Originalkonstruktion aus Beton wird zu einem subtilen Zusammenspiel aus Licht, Oberflächen, Ebenen sowie Innen- und Außenräumen aufgebrochen, sodass die städtische Wohnerfahrung ebenso reich strukturiert ist wie die Stadt selbst. Mittelpunkt des zweiten Geschosses mit dem Hauptwohnraum der jungen Familie bildet ein aus der Geschossplatte herausgeschnittener Hof. Er vermittelt zwischen dem Gebäude und dem neuen Penthaus darüber.

Pour transformer un ancien entrepôt en logement, les architectes ont su intégrer l'ancien et le nouveau de manière surprenante afin de réaliser une synthèse des éléments urbains. Les trois niveaux interconnectés ont chacun une personalité et une fonction qui leur sont propres: bureau, séjour et pièces privées en duplex. La rigidité du béton de l'entrepôt a cédé la place à tout un jeu de lumières, de surfaces, de niveaux et d'espaces intérieurs/extérieurs, dont la richesse reflète la diversité de la ville elle-même. Les propriétaires (un jeune couple avec enfant) habitent au second niveau, où se trouve un puits de lumière aménagé en découpant une partie du plafond de manière à relier cet étage au niveau supérieur et à l'immensité du ciel.

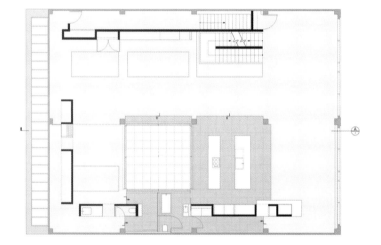

left: First floor plan_Deck_Penthouse. right: Dining area_Stairs_Courtyard.
links: Grundriss erstes Obergeschoss_Dachterrasse_Dachwohnung. rechts: Essbereich_Treppe_Innenhof.
à gauche: Plan du rez-de-chaussée_Terrasse_Véranda. à droite: Salle à manger_Escalier_Cour intérieure.

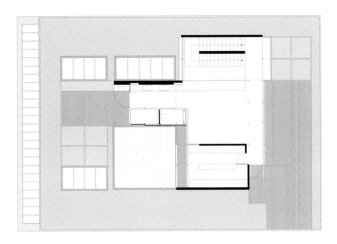

left: View into courtyard. right: Floor plan_Master bedroom towards bath area_Open kitchen, dining area_Master bedroom.
links: Blick in den Innenhof. rechts: Grundriss_Blick vom Schlafzimmer ins Badezimmer_Offene Küche, Essbereich_Schlafzimmer.
à gauche: Vue du séjour au travers des vitres de la cour intérieure. à droite: Plan_Chambre avec salle de bain_Cusine/Salle à manger_Chambre principale.

# SAN FRANCISCO_CA **CONTEMPORARY JEWISH MUSEUM**

**ARCHITECTS:** STUDIO DANIEL LIBESKIND
**COMPLETION:** 2008_**TYPOLOGY:** CULTURE
**PHOTOS:** BRUCE DAMONTE, MARK DARLEY (412 R., 414, 415)

With the opening of its new building, the Contemporary Jewish Museum will usher in a new chapter in its 20-plus year history of engaging audiences and artists in exploring contemporary perspectives on Jewish culture, history, art and ideas. The site of the CJM is an abandoned turn-of-the-century power station, which provides a complex urban locus and the necessary pressure for the emergence of a unique form and energy. The building will provide access to new spaces through the imposing Polk façade of the substation, which will be incorporated within the old structure and will articulate a close relationship to the new Millennium Tower and the pedestrian connector.

Mit dem neuen Gebäude eröffnet das Contemporary Jewish Museum ein neues Kapitel seiner 20-jährigen Geschichte. Das engagierte Publikum und Künstler können in dem Bau zeitgenössische Perspektiven auf jüdische Kultur, Geschichte und Kunst entdecken. Der Standort des Museums, das ehemalige Gelände eines Kraftwerks aus der Jahrhundertwende, bietet einen vielseitigen städtischen Raum und den nötigen Handlungszwang für das Entstehen einer durchschlagskräftigen Form. Das Gebäude ermöglicht einen Zugang zu Räumen durch die Polk-Fassade des Umspannwerks. Die neuen Räume werden in den Altbau eingebunden und eine enge Beziehung zum Millennium Tower und zur Fußgängerverbindung herstellen.

L'inauguration de l'annexe du Musée juif contemporain de San Francisco a marqué le début d'un nouveau chapitre dans l'histoire de cette institution fondée il y a plus de vingt ans et consacrée à la culture, l'histoire, les idées et la création artistique juives. L'annexe devant être installée dans une sous-station électrique désaffectée datant du début du XXᵉ siècle, il était nécessaire d'aménager le bâtiment en choisissant des formes à la fois énergiques et exceptionnelles. L'accès aux nouveaux espaces d'exposition se fait par un portail de l'imposante façade des années 1900, l'annexe assurant ainsi la transition entre le passé et la toute nouvelle Millennium Tower.

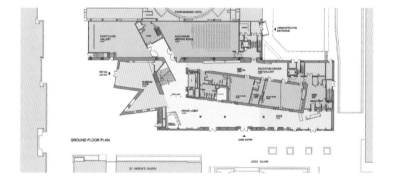

left: Ground floor plan_Detail façade_General view_Exterior view. right: Aerial view.
links: Grundriss Erdgeschoss_Fassadendetail_Gesamtansicht_Außenansicht. rechts: Luftbild.
à gauche: Plan du rez-de-chaussée_Trois vues de détail de la façade. à droite: vue aérienne.

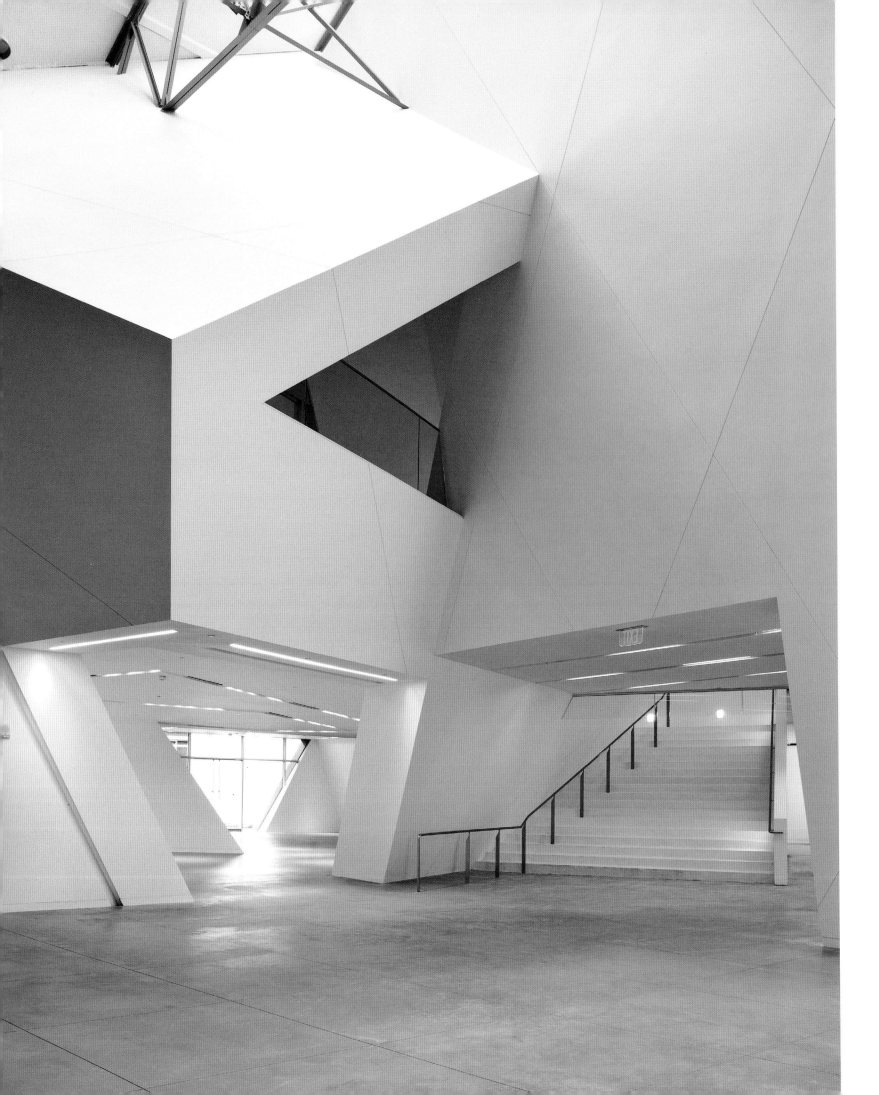

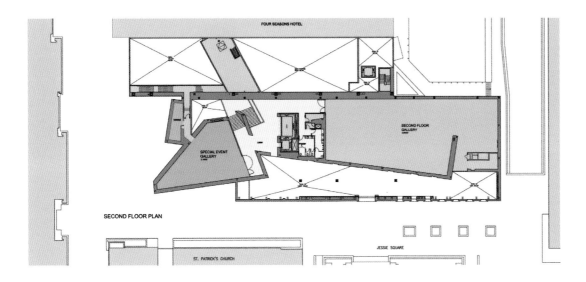

FOUR SEASONS HOTEL

SECOND FLOOR GALLERY

SPECIAL EVENT GALLERY

SECOND FLOOR PLAN

JESSIE SQUARE

ST. PATRICK'S CHURCH

left: Ground floor view. right: Second floor plan_Interior.
links: Ansicht Erdgeschoss. rechts: Grundriss zweites Obergeschoss_Interieur.
à gauche: Vue du rez-de-chaussée. à droite: Plan du premier étage_Intérieur.

# SAN FRANCISCO_CA **CALIFORNIA ACADEMY OF SCIENCES**

**ARCHITECTS:** RENZO PIANO BUILDING WORKSHOP
IN COLLABORATION WITH STANTEC
(FORMERLY CHONG PARTNERS ARCHITECTURE)
**COMPLETION:** 2008_**TYPOLOGY:** CULTURE / EDUCATION
**PHOTOS:** TIM GRIFFITH

The design unifies the Academy's original array of twelve buildings, which were built over eight decades, into a single modern landmark that places a visual and intellectual emphasis on the natural world. Topped with a 2.5-acre living roof the new California Academy of Sciences employs a wide range of energy-saving materials and technologies. The design was inspired by the concept of metaphorically lifting up a piece of the park and sliding the museum underneath. Steep undulations in the roofline roll over the Academy's domed planetarium, rainforest, and aquarium exhibits, echoing the topography of the building's setting and evoking the interdependence of biological and earth systems.

Der Entwurf vereinigt die elf, im Laufe von mehr als 80 Jahren entstandenen Bauten der Akademie in einem einzigen charakteristischen Bauwerk. Dieses hebt die natürliche Umwelt visuell und funktional hervor. Für das ein Hektar große Gründach der California Academy of Sciences wurde eine breite Palette energiesparender Materialien und Technologien verwendet. Inspiriert ist die Gestaltung von einer Metapher: Ein Stück des Parks wurde hochgehoben und das Museum darunter geschoben. Über den Kuppeln von Planetarium, Regenwald und Aquarium spiegeln die steilen Wellen der Dachsilhouette die Topografie in der Umgebung der Akademie wider. Sie erinnern an die wechselseitige Abhängigkeit des biologischen Systems und dem der Erde.

La tâche des architectes consistait ici à unifier douze bâtiments universitaires construits sur une période de quatre-vingts ans à l'aide d'une structure moderne qui mette la nature au premier plan, et cela au sens propre comme au figuré. Le nouveau toit végétalisé de l'Académie des sciences de Californie couvre une superficie de plus de dix mille mètres carrés et intègre tout un ensemble de matériaux et de technologies visant à économiser l'énergie. Son concept a été élaboré à partir d'une métaphore: soulever une partie du parc environnant et glisser les bâtiments en dessous. Le toit couvre un planétarium, un aquarium et une forêt tropicale artificielle. Ses ondulations font écho à la topographie du parc, l'ensemble suggérant l'interdépendance des écosystèmes.

left: Site plan_Glazed façade_Detail planted roof. right: Aerial view of exterior looking into interior.
links: Lageplan_Verglaste Fassade_Detailansicht vom bepflanzten Dach. rechts: Blick ins Interieur.
à gauche: Plan de situation_Façade vitrée_Détail du toit végétalisé. à droite: L'intérieur vu de l'extérieur la nuit.

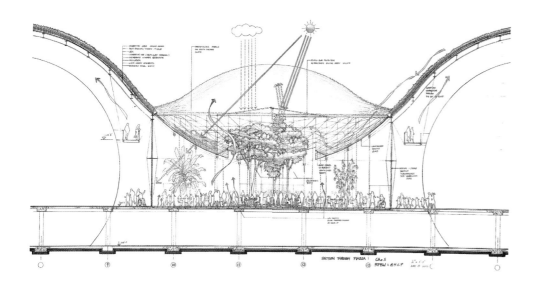

left: Entrance hall. right: Section_Planted courtyard_Glass ceiling_Aerial view.
links: Eingangshalle. rechts: Schnitt_Bepflanzter Innenhof_Glasdach_Luftbild.
à gauche: Hall d'entrée. à droite: Vue en coupe_Cour intérieure végétalisée_Verrière_Vue aérienne.

SAN FRANCISCO_CA **CONGREGATION BETH SHOLOM SYNAGOGUE**

**ARCHITECTS:** STANLEY SAITOWITZ | NATOMA ARCHITECTS
**COMPLETION:** 2008_**TYPOLOGY:** ECCLESIASTICAL
**PHOTOS:** RIEN VAN RIJTHOVEN

The two opposing forms of the Congregation Beth Sholom Synagogue – a windowless, bowllike half-cylinder and a zinc and glass-clad cube – make an audacious pair on a street lined with Victorian and faux-Victorian homes and dotted with old religious buildings. But the synagogue was designed from the inside out, focused on creating private, shared and interstitial spaces, carefully sequenced that would promote a fuller sense of communality. Lifted atop a single-story podium containing the daily chapel, a library, offices and meeting rooms, the sanctuary is a small marvel of design and construction.

Die beiden gegensätzlichen Formen der Congregation Beth Sholom Synagogue – ein fensterloser, schalenähnlicher Halbzylinder und ein mit Zink und Glas verkleideter Kubus – ergeben ein kühnes Gebäudepaar an der von Häusern im viktorianischen Stil und alten Sakralbauten gesäumten Straße. Allerdings ist die Synagoge von innen heraus entworfen, mit einem Augenmerk auf private, gemeinsame und überleitende Räume. Um den Gemeinschaftssinn zu fördern, reihen sich diese sorgfältig aneinander. Auf einem eingeschossigen Podest befinden sich die Kapelle für das tägliche Gebet, eine Bücherei, Büros und Besprechungsräume. Die Synagoge ist ein gestalterisches und architektonisches Wunderwerk.

Les deux volumes antagonistes qui composent cette synagogue — une arche sans fenêtres et un cube à l'enveloppe en zinc et verre — constituent un couple qui ne passe pas inaperçu dans une rue bordée majoritairement de villas en style victorien et de quelques bâtiments religieux des siècles passés. L'intérieur privilégie les interstices, les espaces privés et les zones communes de manière à favoriser la vie communautaire. Le sanctuaire, situé au-dessus d'un volume abritant la bibliothèque, plusieurs salles de réunion et la chapelle pour les prières de tous les jours, est une petite merveille tant en ce qui concerne le design que la réalisation.

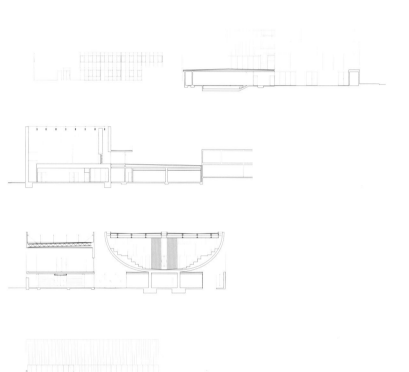

left: Sections_General view_Courtyard between the buildings. right: Entrance view.
links: Schnitte_Gesamtansicht_Hof zwischen den Gebäuden rechts: Eingangsansicht.
à gauche: Vues en coupe_Deux vues de la cour et du bâtiment. à droite: Entrée.

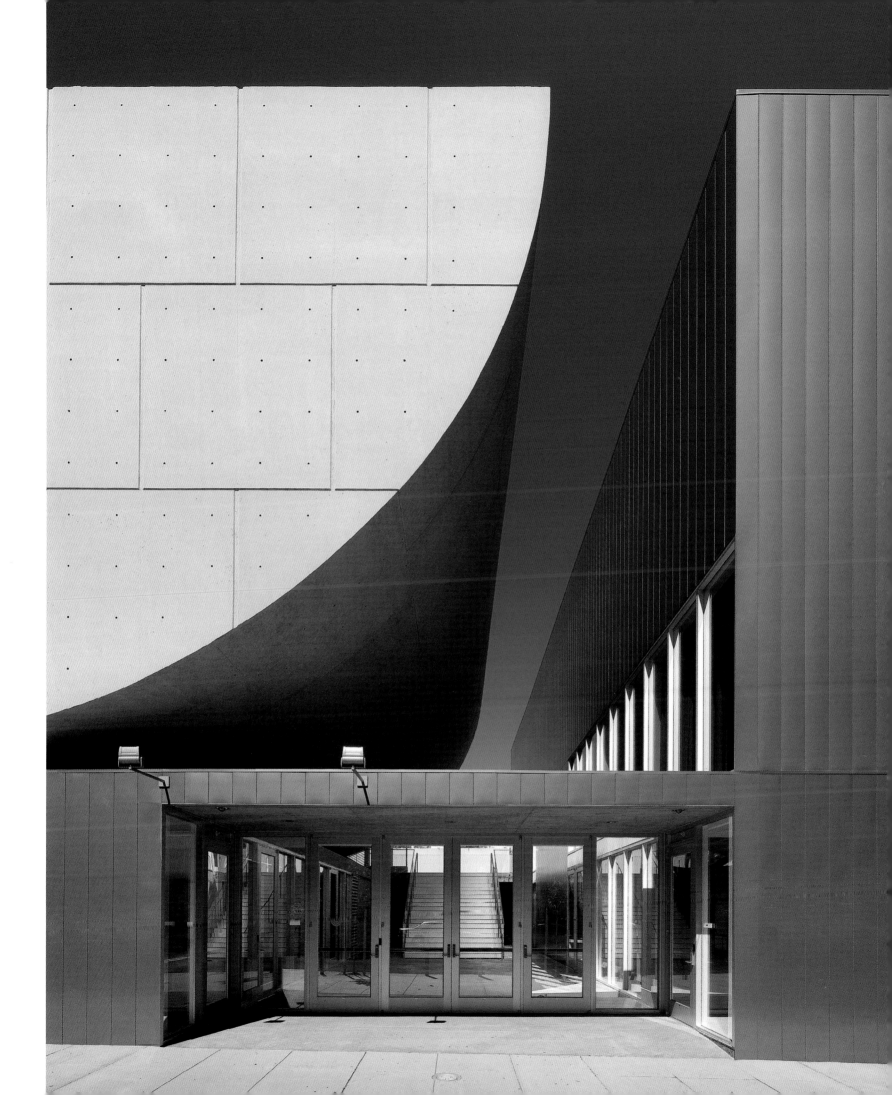

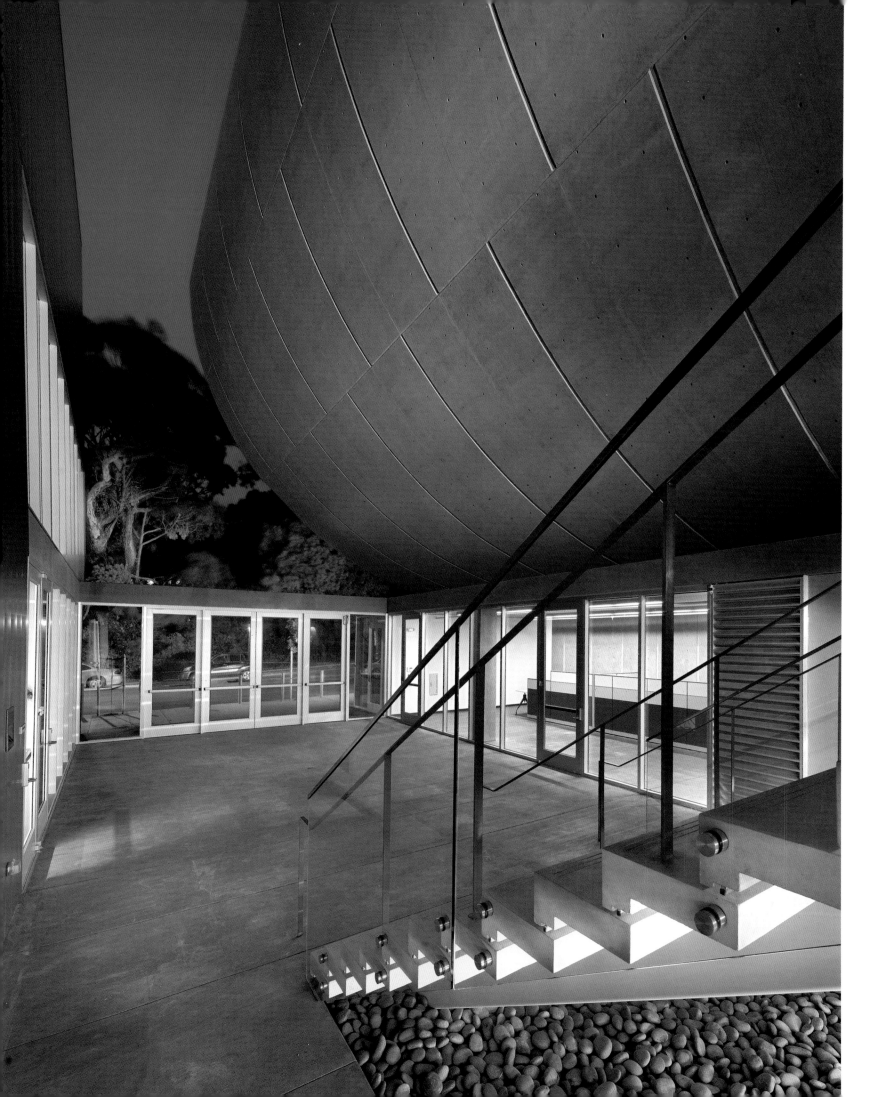

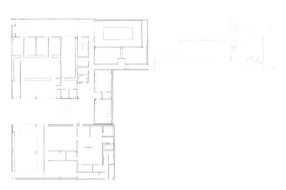

left: Lobby. right: Floor plans_View inside_Interior_Interior with wooden panels.
links: Eingangshalle. rechts: Grundrisse_Innenansicht_Inneneinrichtung mit Holzverkleidung.
à gauche: Hall d'entrée. à droite: Plans des différents niveaux_Vue vers l'intérieur_Deux vues de l'intérieur.

SANTA BARBARA_CA **STUDENT RESOURCE BUILDING AT THE UNIVERSITY OF CALIFORNIA SANTA BARBARA**

**ARCHITECTS:** SASAKI ASSOCIATES
**COMPLETION:** 2007_**TYPOLOGY:** EDUCATION
**PHOTOS:** ROBERT BENSON (424, 426, 427), GREG HURSLEY (425)

The Student Resource Building houses a diverse group of student-related organizations and offices. The entire building arrays around a central glazed space called The Forum. The Forum is the marketplace, the center of activity for students and is expressed on the exterior of the building as shaded glass volume. The organization draws people to each floor of the building, reinforcing the interaction between staff, faculty and students. A glass bridge traverses the space and also features clerestory windows and large glazed walls at either end that frame dramatic campus vistas. The Multi-Purpose Room is an oval shaped volume that has an angled roof and is also expressed visually on the building's exterior.

Im Student Resource Building sind verschiedene studentische Einrichtungen und Büros untergebracht. Der Gebäudekomplex reiht sich um einen verglasten Raum, das sogenannte Forum. Als Marktplatz und studentisches Aktionszentrum wird das Forum an seiner Außenseite von einem dunkelgetönten Glasvolumen artikuliert. Da das Wegesystem die Studenten in jedes Gebäudegeschoss führt, wird die Kommunikation zwischen Mitarbeitern, Dozenten und Studenten gefördert. Den Raum durchquert eine Glasbrücke mit Oberlichtern und gläsernen Wänden zu beiden Seiten, die spannungsvolle Aussichten auf den Campus rahmen. Auch der ovale Baukörper des Multi-Purpose Room mit seinem winkligen Dach kommt außen sichtbar zum Ausdruck.

Ce bâtiment abrite divers services et organismes en rapport avec la vie universitaire. Il est structuré autour du « forum », vaste espace abondamment vitré qui sert à la fois de marché et de lieu central d'activité pour tous les étudiants. La répartition des diverses fonctions sur plusieurs étages favorise l'interaction entre les professeurs, les étudiants et le personnel administratif. Une passerelle traverse le forum, bien éclairé par un clair-étage et de grandes baies qui offrent des vues panoramiques sur le campus. Citons encore la salle polyvalente, couverte par un toit en pointe et dont la forme ovale des détache par rapport au reste du bâtiment.

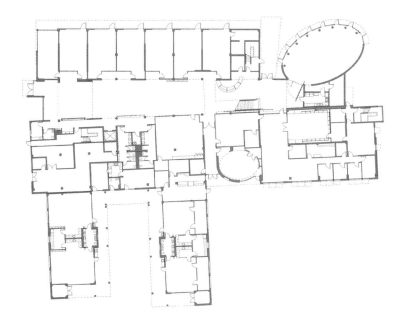

left: First floor plan_Side view_Lobby. right: Entrance view_General view.
links: Grundriss erstes Obergeschoss_Seitenansicht_Empfangshalle. rechts: Eingangsansicht Gesamtansicht.
à gauche: Plan du rez-de-chaussée_L'immeuble la nuit_Forum. à droite: Vue de l'entrée Vue générale.

left: Lobby. right: Interior_Multiple story interior_Atrium.
links: Eingangshalle. rechts: Interieur_Mehrstöckiges Interieur_Atrium.
à gauche: Forum. à droite: Intérieur_Vue des différents niveaux_Autre vue du forum.

# SANTA BARBARA _CA **MONTECITO RESIDENCE**

**ARCHITECTS:** SHUBIN + DONALDSON
**COMPLETION:** 2000_**TYPOLOGY:** LIVING
**PHOTOS:** TOM BONNER

This newly constructed residence is one of few contemporary designs in the area. It is distinctly organized with one main axis or spine that runs along the whole structure. The center of the building features the public areas with a shed roof over a long gallery for art. The open plan emphasizes space usage and contemporary living. A sculptural glass-and-steel fireplace separates the living area from the dining room. The far north-end block serves as the master bedroom and bath. The two-bedroom guest quarters are at the opposing end, and adjacent to a three-car garage. An exposed rafter system brings stability to the metal roof, while the walls of the house are plaster and glass.

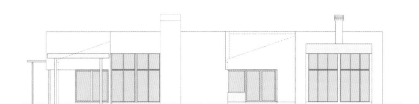

Das neue Wohnhaus ist eines der wenigen modernen Bauten in dem Gebiet. Es zeichnet sich durch eine Haupterschließungsachse entlang der gesamten Konstruktion aus. In der Gebäudemitte sind die gemeinschaftlichen Bereiche mit einem Sheddach über einer langen Galerie für Kunst angeordnet. Der offene Grundriss betont die Verwendung der Räume und den modernen Wohnstil. Ein plastischer Kamin aus Glas und Stahl trennt den Wohnbereich vom Esszimmer ab. Der Trakt am nördlichsten Ende enthält Hauptschlafzimmer und Bad. Ihm entgegengesetzt liegen die Gästewohnung mit zwei Betten und eine angrenzende Garage für drei Autos. Eine exponierte Sparrenlage stabilisiert das Metalldach, die Hauswände bestehen aus Putz und Glas.

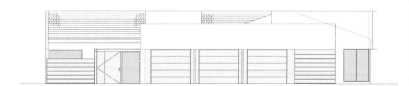

Cette villa agencée selon un axe longitudinal est un des rares bâtiments modernes dans la région où elle se trouve. Les espaces de séjour, situés au centre et couverts par un toit à une pente, incluent une longue galerie où sont exposées des œuvres d'art. Le plan ouvert optimise l'utilisation de l'espace et donne à l'intérieur un aspect contemporain. Une cheminée en verre et acier de qualité sculpturale sépare le séjour proprement dit de la salle à manger. La chambre principale et sa salle de bain se trouvent au nord. Deux chambres d'amis et un garage pour trois voitures sont leur pendant du côté sud. Des chevrons métalliques apparents assurent la stabilité du toit. Les murs, enduits, sont percés par de larges baies vitrées.

left: East and west elevation_Interior living space with glass fireplace_Exposed rafter system. right: Garden view_Entry with red beams_Garage.
links: Ost- und Westansicht_Wohnzimmer mit glasverkleidetem Kamin_Erweiterter Dachsparren für die Stabilität des Metalldachs. rechts: Gartenansicht_Hauseingang_Garage.
à gauche: Vues en élévation des façades est et ouest_Séjour avec insert_Chevrons métalliques apparents. à droite: La villa vue du jardin_Entrée avec poutrelles rouges_Garage.

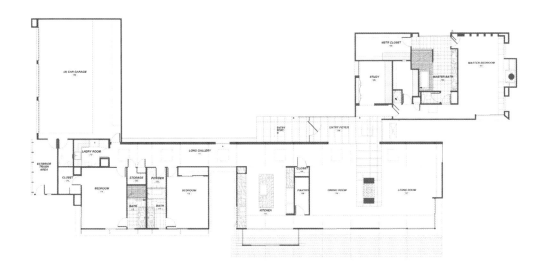

left: Gallery walls, metal roof. right: First floor plan_Red I-beam _Scuptural glass-and-steel fireplace.
links: Galeriewände, Metalldach. rechts: Grundriss erstes Obergeschoss_Roter Eisenträger im Kontrast zur weißen Wand_Kamin aus Glas und Stahl als Raumteiler.
à gauche: Couloir/galerie avec toit métallique. à droite: Plan du rez-de-chaussée_Poutres métalliques_Cheminée avec encadrement en verre.

SANTA BARBARA_CA **SANTA BARBARA RIVIERA RESIDENCE**

**ARCHITECTS:** SHUBIN + DONALDSON
**COMPLETION:** 2003_**TYPOLOGY:** LIVING
**PHOTOS:** CIRO COEHLO

Though not immediately obvious, this house embraces several characteristics of environmentally sustainable design. The basic design strategy is to site the house based on solar orientation, resulting in passive solar gains throughout the year. Photovoltaic power generates household electricity through a 2.8 kilowatt system (when power is not needed, it feeds back into the grid). A passive rooftop solar heating system provides for domestic hot water and a passive solar ground-level hot-water system is used to heat the pool. The natural flow of hot and cool air is fortified by the use of radiant hot-water floor heating and separate central air conditioning in the ceilings.

Auch wenn nicht sogleich erkennbar, besitzt das Haus mehrere Merkmale einer nachhaltigen Architektur. Die zugrundeliegende Entwurfsstrategie richtet das Haus zur Sonne aus, sodass ganzjährig passive Solargewinne erzielt werden. Eine 2,8 Kilowatt-Fotovoltaikanlage erzeugt den im Haushalt benötigten Strom (überschüssiger Strom wird ins Netz eingespeist). Für warmes Wasser sorgt ein Solarheizungssystem auf dem Dach, und zum Beheizen des Pools dient eine solare Wassererwärmung auf Geländeniveau. Die natürliche Strömung von warmer und kalter Luft wird durch eine Fußbodenheizung und eine separate zentrale Klimaanlage in den Decken verstärkt.

Il n'est pas évident au premier abord que cette villa a été construite selon les principes du développement durable. Pourtant, les architectes ont déterminé son orientation par rapport au soleil de manière à optimiser les économies d'énergie passives tout au long de l'année. De plus, l'alimentation en électricité est assurée par une installation photovoltaïque d'une puissance de 2,8 kW, de sorte que l'énergie en surplus peut être transférée au réseau public. Citons encore le chauffe-eau solaire installé sur le toit, ainsi que le dispositif passif utilisé pour réchauffer l'eau de la piscine. La villa dispose également d'un chauffage radiant par le sol et d'un système de climatisation intégré aux plafonds.

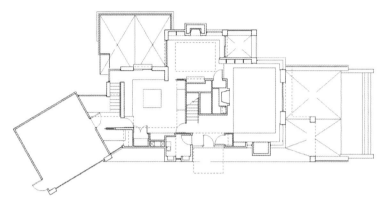

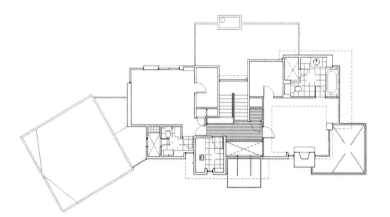

left: Floor plans_General view. right: Glazed entrance.
links: Grundrisse_Gesamtansicht. rechts: Verglaster Eingang.
à gauche: Plans_Vue d'ensemble. à droite: Entrée avec auvent en verre.

left: View into bathroom. right: Elevations_Bathtub with landscape view_Living room_Bedroom.
links: Blick ins Badezimmer. rechts: Ansichten_Badewanne mit Blick in die Landschaft_Wohnzimmer_Schlafzimmer.
à gauche: Vue du couloir et de la salle de bain. à droite: Vues en élévation_Salle de bain avec vue sur le paysage_Séjour_Chambre.

SANTA MONICA_CA **SANTA MONICA CIVIC CENTER PARKING STRUCTURE**

**ARCHITECTS:** MOORE RUBLE YUDELL ARCHITECTS AND PLANNERS
ASSOCIATE ARCHITECTS: INTERNATIONAL PARKING DESIGN
**COMPLETION:** 2007_**TYPOLOGY:** PUBLIC
**PHOTOS:** COURTESY OF THE ARCHITECTS

The new civic parking garage is part of the recently completed master plan for Santa Monica's Civic Center. The design brings a fresh perspective to a standard service amenity – the 298,786-square-foot structure includes 900 parking spaces on six levels above grade and two below grade – and takes it to a higher level that actually strengthens the urban fabric with street-level retail and café, spectacular views of the Pacific Ocean and the city, a garden, and a sense of personal safety.

Das neue Parkhaus gehört zum unlängst fertiggestellten Masterplan für das Verwaltungszentrum von Santa Monica. Die 27.758 Quadratmeter große Konstruktion bietet auf sechs überirdischen und zwei unterirdischen Ebenen 900 Parkplätze. Ihr Entwurf wertet einen durchschnittlichen Zweckbau auf und verbessert das Stadtbild durch einen Laden und Café auf Straßenebene sowie spektakulären Aussichten auf den Pazifischen Ozean und die Stadt, einem Garten und einer sicheren Umgebung.

Ce parking de neuf cents places d'une superficie totale de 27.758 mètres carrés sur huit niveaux — dont deux souterrains — a été construit à l'occasion du réaménagement récent du centre ville de Santa Monica. Il constitue une approche d'un nouveau type de ce genre de bâtiment, visant à renforcer le tissu urbain. Le parking intègre en effet un jardin ainsi que des cafés et boutiques situés au niveau de la rue. De plus, il offre des vues magnifiques sur la ville et l'océan Pacifique, tout en générant une sensation de sécurité à l'intérieur.

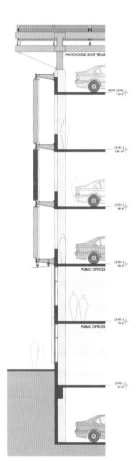

left: Section_Colored panels_ Street side view. right: Exterior.
links: Schnitt_Farbige Paneele_Außenansicht. rechts: Straßenansicht.
à gauche: Coupe _Vue entre les deux composantes de la façade_ La façade vue de la rue_La façade vue de la rue. à droite: La façade vue de la rue.

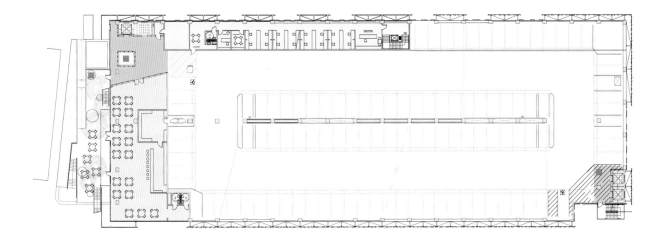

left: Exterior view. right: Floor plan_Detail exterior_Lighted panels_Street side view.
links: Außenansicht. rechts: Grundriss_Detail Außenansicht_Leuchtende Paneele_Straßenansicht.
à gauche: Extérieur. à droite: Plan_Panneaux multicolores_Façade la nuit_Deux vues d'ensemble.

SANTA MONICA_CA **THE ELI AND EDYTHE BROAD STAGE**

**ARCHITECTS:** RENZO ZECCHETTO ARCHITECTS
**COMPLETION:** 2005_**TYPOLOGY:** CULTURE
**PHOTOS:** BENNY CHAN/FOTOWORKS (440 L., 442), ROBERT BERGER
PHOTOGRAPHY 443 R.)

The Broad Stage is a state-of-the-art 540-seat theater in Santa Monica that provides a unique venue for the performing arts. A large, cantilevered overhang marks the entry plaza that serves as both gathering space and outdoor extension to the lobby. On the evening of a performance, the wood-clad shell of the house is illuminated like a softly glowing lantern. The space between the house shell and glass curtain wall forms a soaring lobby. In the auditorium, acoustical considerations inspired the use of convex plaster wall elements and sculpted mahogany panels that are arranged to both distribute the sound to the audience and to form layered pockets for lighting and box seating.

Das Broad Stage, ein modernes Theater mit 540 Sitzplätzen in Santa Monica, bietet den darstellenden Künsten einen einzigartigen Schauplatz. Eine große Auskragung prägt den Vorplatz, der als Treffpunkt dient und die Lobby nach draußen erweitert. An Abenden mit einer Aufführung erstrahlt der holzver-kleidete Baukörper wie eine Lampe in einem sanften Licht. Der Raum zwi-schen Baukörper und gläserner Vorhangwand ist als hoch aufragende Lobby ausgebildet. Wegen der Akustik wurden im Zuschauerraum konvexe verputzte Wandelemente und modellierte Mahagonipanecle verwendet. Diese sind so angeordnet, dass sie den Schall zu den Zuhörern leiten und geschichtete Fächer für Beleuchtung und Logenplätze bilden.

Cinq-cent-quarante places sont disponibles dans cette salle de spectacle ultramoderne au design exceptionnel. Le grand auvent en bois qui domine l'esplanade constitue une extension vers l'extérieur du hall d'entrée et permet aux spectateurs de se réunir avant ou après les représentations. Un éclairage tamisé donne au bâtiment l'apparence d'une gigantesque lanterne les soirs de spectacle. Le hall d'entrée s'élève sur plusieurs niveaux dans l'espace laissé libre entre l'enveloppe et un volume vitré. L'aménagement de la salle de spectacle inclut des éléments convexes en plâtre et en acajou qui remplissent plusieurs fonctions: assurer une bonne acoustique, masquer divers dispositifs d'éclairage et constituer des loges.

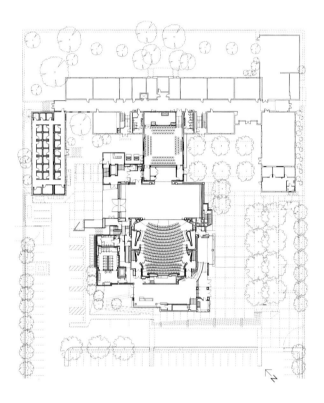

left: Site plan_General view_Street side view. right: Entrance view.
links: Lageplan_Gesamtansicht_Straßenansicht. rechts: Eingangsansicht.
à gauche: Plan de situation_Vue d'ensemble_Le bâtiment vu de la rue. à droite: Esplanade d'entrée.

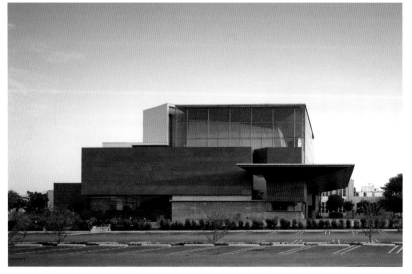

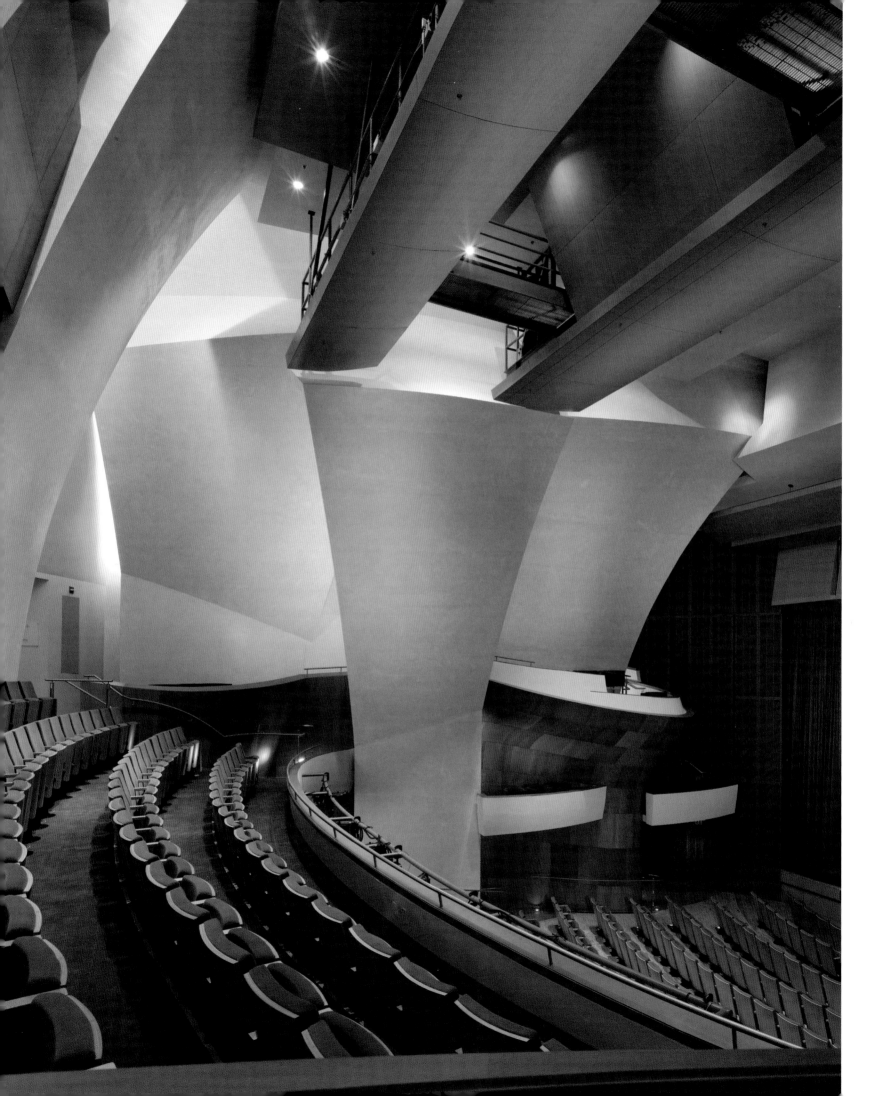

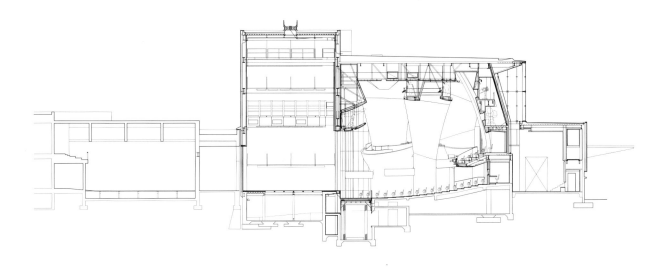

left: Auditorium. right: Section_Inner courtyard_Balcony_Detail interior.
links: Auditorium. rechts: Section_Innenhof_Balkon_Detail Interieur.
à gauche: Salle de spectacle. à droite: Vue en coupe_Cour intérieure_Balcon de l'auditorium
Détail de l'intérieur.

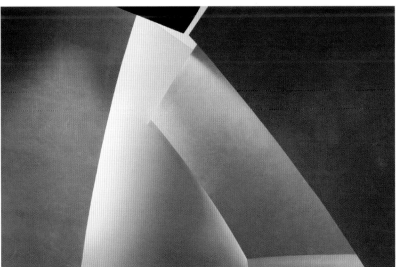

# SAUSALITO_CA **FINAL(LY) HOUSE**

**ARCHITECTS:** ROTHSCHILD SCHWARTZ ARCHITECTS
**COMPLETION:** 2008_**TYPOLOGY:** LIVING
**PHOTOS:** ROTHSCHILD SCHWARTZ ARCHITECTS

The house is located within great surroundings on Wolfback Ridge Road, in Sausalito, California. The south-facing ridge top site abuts the GGNRA, and is a gently sloping swale with panoramic views from east to west including the East Bay hills, the city of San Francisco, Golden Gate Bridge, Marin Headlands, and the Pacific Ocean. The site flows into the natural habitat, affording maximum solar exposure, while bracing maritime breezes and cloaking fogs. A sheltered courtyard is created by a double-walled retractable glass passageway, mediating the conflict between the expansive views and southern sun.

Das Haus liegt in der wunderbaren Umgebung an der Wolfback Ridge Road im kalifornischen Sausalito. Das Südgrundstück auf einem Gebirgskamm grenzt an das nationale Erholungsgebiet Golden Gate. Von seiner leicht abschüssigen, sumpfigen Senke bieten sich Panoramaaussichten von Osten nach Westen auf die Hügel der East Bay, San Francisco, die Golden Gate Bridge, die Küstenlandschaft Marin Headlands und den Pazifischen Ozean. Das Areal geht in den natürlichen Lebensraum über, ist maximal besonnt und profitiert gleichzeitig von erfrischenden Meeresbrisen und Nebelschleiern. Ein doppelwandiger einschiebbarer Durchgang aus Glas schafft einen geschützten Hof und löst den Konflikt zwischen Weitblick und Südsonne.

Ce bâtiment desservi par la Wolfback Ridge Road est situé sur une colline près de Sausalito, dans la réserve naturelle nationale du Golden Gate. Le cadre, magnifique, offre une vue panoramique sur les East Bay Hills, la ville de San Francisco, les piles du Golden Gate Bridge, les Marin Headlands et l'océan Pacifique. Parfaitement intégré à son environnement naturel, cet édifice qui bénéficie d'un ensoleillement maximal est rafraîchi par la brise du large et parfois perdu dans le brouillard marin. Une cour entourée de parois rétractables en double vitrage permet d'apprécier des vues panoramiques, sans pour autant subir les inconvénients liés à une exposition au sud.

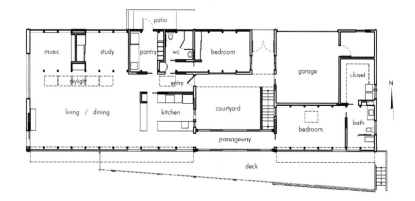

left: Floor plan_North façade with 100 year-old reclaimed redwood siding_Porous concrete and wood structure. right: Detail of south façade_Living roof with Golden Gate Bridge beyond_Roof-deck in the dry season.
links: Grundriss_Nordansicht mit 100-Jahre-alter Rotholz-Verkleidung_Offenporiger Beton und Holzkonstruktion. rechts: Detail der Südfassade_Begrüntes mit Blick auf die Golden Gate Bridge_Dachterasse in der Trockenzeit.
à gauche: Plan_Façade nord avec bardage en planches de bois rouge recyclées vieilles d'une centaine d'années_Intérieur en bois et béton poreux. à droite: Gros plan sur la façade sud_Toit végétalisé avec à l'arrière plan les piles du Golden Gate Bridge_Vue du toit à la saison sèche.

# VENICE_CA **HOTEL RAY**

**ARCHITECTS:** BELZBERG ARCHITECTS
**COMPLETION:** UNBUILT_**TYPOLOGY:** HOSPITALITY
**RENDERINGS:** BELZBERG ARCHITECTS

This 57-room green hotel stands on the site of the original Eames studio, introducing a new paradigm of ecotourism to the already diverse Venice tourist culture. While 'green' is typically associated with engineering feats of new hybrid materials, energy generation and carbon reduction, Belzberg Architects took their cue from the research and production methodologies of the Eames' and capitalized their interest in digital design techniques, combining with the affordances of new hybrid materials to generate novel effects. Subterranean cogeneration plants and cooling systems free the roof for multiple activities and amenity.

Dieses nachhaltige Hotel mit 57 Zimmern steht auf dem Grundstück des ehemaligen Studios von Ray und Charles Eames und ist in der vielfältigen Touristenkultur von Venice ein neues Beispiel für Ökotourismus. Normalerweise wird Nachhaltigkeit mit den technischen Großleistungen neuer Hybridwerkstoffe, der Energiegewinnung und Kohlendioxidreduktion assoziiert. Belzberg Architects hingegen ließen sich von den Forschungs- und Produktionsmethoden der Eames' inspirieren und erzielten mit digitalen Entwurfstechniken und modernen Hybridwerkstoffen ungewöhnliche Effekte. Unterirdische Anlagen mit Kraft-Wärme-Kopplung und Kühlsysteme halten das Dach für diverse Aktivitäten und Einrichtungen frei.

Cet hôtel « vert » de cinquante-sept chambres a été construit à l'emplacement des anciens studios Eames, ouvrant ainsi une nouvelle dimension d'écotourisme dans la région déjà très diversifiée de Venice. Alors que les bâtiments écologiques se contentent habituellement d'incorporer des matériaux hybrides et de réduire la consommation d'énergie et la production de dioxyde de carbone, celui-ci s'inspire des méthodes de recherche et de production élaborées par Eames, tout en capitalisant l'intérêt des architectes pour la conception digitalisée de manière à générer de nouveaux effets. L'installation en souterrain des équipements de cogénération et de climatisation libère de l'espace sur le toit, qui est ainsi disponible pour toutes une série d'activités de loisirs.

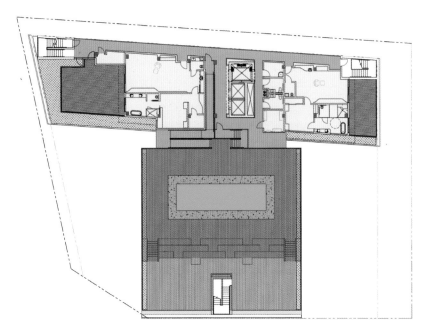

left: Upper floor plan_General view_Structural and window detail. right: View from the street Exterior.
links: Grundriss Obergeschoss_Gesamtansicht_Gebäude- und Fensterdetail. rechts: Straßenansicht_Außenansicht.
à gauche: Plan du niveau supérieur_Vue d'ensemble_Gros plan sur la façade. à droite: L'hôtel vu de la rue_Autre vue d'ensemble.

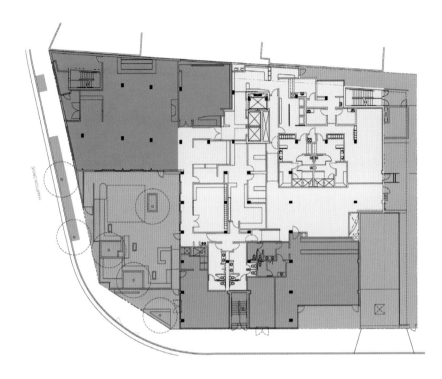

left: Exterior. right: Floor plan_Detail.
links: Außenansicht. rechts: Grundriss_Detail.
à gauche: Extérieur. à droite: Plan_Détail.

# VENICE_CA **ONE WINDOW HOUSE**

**ARCHITECTS:** TOURAINE RICHMOND ARCHITECTS
**COMPLETION:** 2006_**TYPOLOGY:** LIVING
**PHOTOS:** BENNY CHAN, FOTOWORKS

As housing prices soar in Los Angeles due to a low inventory of available housing, urban neighborhoods are becoming increasingly dense by Los Angeles standards. By going up instead of out, this 1,500-square-foot house has views of the city and mountains and proposes a new model for meeting zoning requirements while leaving plenty of open space on the tight urban lot. The house is "zoned" by level and creates a seamless flow from front to back yards through the ground level living space. The volume is clad with corrugated, galvanized metal; other materials include cellular plastic glazing and sanded OSB.

Da in Los Angeles wenige Häuser auf dem Markt sind, schnellen die Immobilienpreise in die Höhe. Bezeichnend ist auch eine für dortige Verhältnisse zusehends dichtere Bebauung. Indem sich das 139 Quadratmeter große Haus nach oben und nicht zu den Seiten entwickelt, bietet es Aussichten auf Stadt und Berge. Als neues Vorbild für die Einhaltung von Bebauungsvorschriften lässt es auf dem winzigen Stadtgrundstück reichlich Freiraum. Das geschossweise in Zonen aufgeteilte Haus schafft in dem ebenerdigen Wohnbereich einen nahtlosen Übergang vom Vor- zum Hintergarten. Sein Baukörper ist mit verzinktem Wellblech verkleidet. Weitere Materialien sind Schaumstoffabdeckungen und geschliffene OSB-Platten.

La crise du logement à Los Angeles a eu pour résultat une envolée des prix de l'immobilier et un accroissement de la densité urbaine. Cette maison de 139 mètres carrés sur plusieurs niveaux, avec vue sur la ville et les montagnes environnantes, propose une solution novatrice pour satisfaire aux exigences du zonage tout en laissant des espaces libres sur le terrain dans ce quartier où le tissu urbain est très dense. Le bâtiment structure les différents niveaux en « zones » distinctes et propose un séjour au rez-de-chaussée qui assure une liaison progressive entre la rue et l'arrière-cour. Parmi les matériaux utilisés, citons les panneaux de polycarbonate, la tôle ondulée galvanisée et les plaques OSB passées au jet de sable.

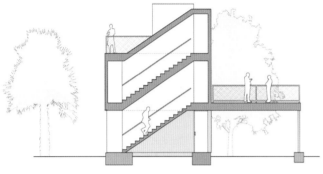

left: Sections_Corrugated, galvanized metal façade_Exterior_Living space_Closet space. right: Street view.
links: Schnitte_Geriffelte und verzinkte Metallfassade_Außenansicht_Wohnraum_Schrank und Flur rechts: Straßenansicht.
à gauche: Vues en coupe_Façade en tôle ondulée galvanisée_Extérieur_Séjour_Couloir. à droite: Le bâtiment vu de la rue.

# VENTURA_CA **MUSSEL SHOALS HOUSE**

**ARCHITECTS:** DESIGNARC
**COMPLETION:** 2005_**TYPOLOGY:** LIVING
**PHOTOS:** BENNY CHAN, FOTOWORKS

Located at a critical juncture of the California coastline between Los Angeles and Santa Barbara, the project responds to the significant constraints of a paucity of budget and a requirement to secure the house against storm and absence. The result is a confident and self-effacing home that defers to the repose and tranquility of the sea while providing a place of quiet respite for the client. The introduction of rolling sunshades and storm doors complete the house's protective layering, fending off the depredations of sun, salt air, and rogue surfers, while allowing variability in living space based on weather conditions.

An einem kritischen Streckenabschnitt der kalifornischen Küste zwischen Los Angeles und Santa Barbara gelegen, reagiert das Projekt auf die beachtlichen Beschränkungen durch ein knappes Budget und die Notwendigkeit, das Haus gegen Unwetter und bei Abwesenheit zu schützen. Das Ergebnis ist ein überzeugender und zurückhaltender Bau, der sich dem Frieden und der Stille des Meeres unterordnet, während er dem Bauherrn einen ruhigen Rückzugsort bietet. Sonnenrollläden und Windfangtüren vervollständigen die Schutzschicht des Hauses, indem sie das Eindringen von Sonne, salziger Luft und kriminellen Surfern abwehren und dabei variable, auf die Wetterverhältnisse abgestimmte Wohnräume schaffen.

Cette villa située sur la côte californienne entre Los Angeles et Santa Barbara se devait de concilier deux antagonismes: un budget très restreint et de hautes exigences en matière de sécurité face aux tempêtes et aux absences prolongées des propriétaires. Les architectes ont donc choisi un style à la fois discret et ferme, réalisant ainsi une maison où l'on peut se retirer pour savourer le calme et la tranquillité qui émanent de l'océan. Ils l'ont équipée de stores enroulables et de portes anti-tempêtes qui présentent un double avantage, puisque ces équipements permettent à la fois de faire face aux agressions pouvant être causées par le soleil, les embruns et les voyous, et d'ouvrir largement la villa sur l'extérieur lorsque le temps s'y prête.

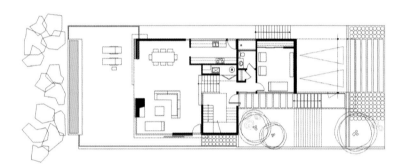

left: Floor plan main level and upper level_Interior with view of ocean_View from street. right: Rear façade with sunshades and storm doors.
links: Grundriss Erdgeschoss und Obergeschoss_Wohnzimmer mit Meerblick_Straßenansicht.
rechts: Rückansicht mit Sonnenschultz und Windfangtüren.
à gauche: Plans_Intérieur avec vue sur l'océan_La villa vue de la rue. à droite: Face arrière avec stores et portes anti-tempêtes.

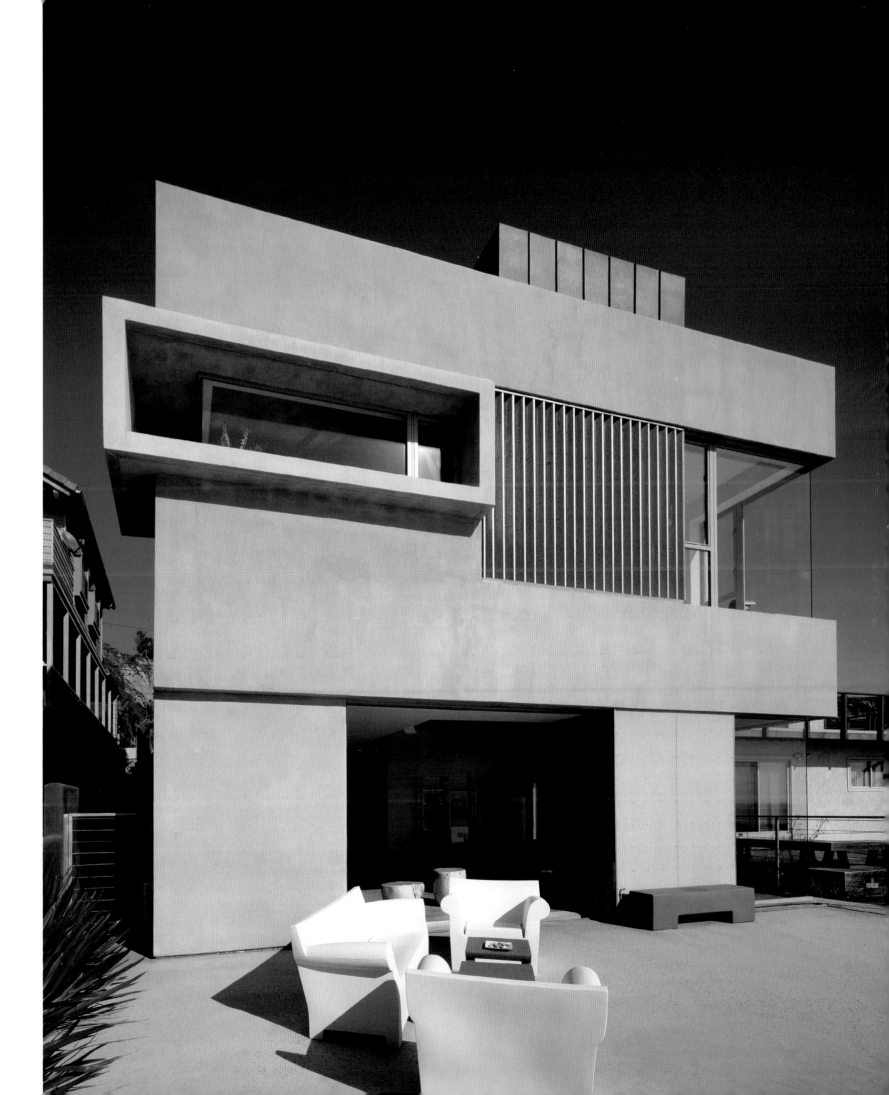

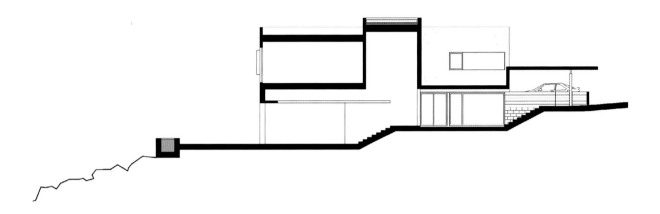

left: Stepped entry. right: Section_Master bedroom with ocean view.
links: Eingang. rechts: Schnitt_Schlafzimmer mit Meerblick.
à gauche: Extérieur. à droite: Vue en coupe_Séjour avec vue sur l'océan.

# WEST HOLLYWOOD_CA **FORMOSA 1140**

**ARCHITECTS:** LOHA (LORCAN O'HERLIHY ARCHITECTS)
**COMPLETION:** 2008_**TYPOLOGY:** LIVING
**PHOTOS:** LAWRENCE ANDERSON/ESTO

Located in the heart of West Hollywood, this new eleven-unit housing project emphasizes the central importance of shared open space for the residents and the community. Formosa takes what would be the internalized open space of the courtyard and moves it to the exterior of the building to create a park which occupies approximately one third (4,600 square feet) of the project site. As a result of shifting the common open space to the exterior and pushing the building to one side, units are organized linearly allowing for 'park frontage' and cross-ventilation for every unit.

Mitten in West Hollywood gelegen, unterstreicht dieses neue Mehrfamilienhaus mit elf Wohneinheiten die Bedeutung gemeinsam genutzter Freiräume für Bewohner und Gemeinde. Das Formosa-Konzept verlegt einen innenliegenden offenen Hofraum an die Außenseite des Gebäudes, sodass ein Park entsteht, der fast ein Drittel (427 Quadratmeter) des Grundstücks einnimmt. Indem die Gemeinschaftsflächen nach außen verlagert werden und das Gebäude an die Seite des Grundstücks rückt, lassen sich die Wohneinheiten linear an der „Parkfront" anordnen und mit Querlüftung versorgen.

Ce bâtiment de onze logements situé à West Hollywood accorde une grande importance aux espaces de plein air mis à la disposition de tous les occupants. La cour intérieure traditionnelle est remplacée par un jardin extérieur de 427 mètres carrés, soit environ un tiers de la surface totale du terrain. Cette « externalisation » des espaces communs, couplée à la construction du bâtiment en bordure de la rue, a pour résultat une organisation linéaire des logements le long du jardin et une ventilation croisée de tous les appartements.

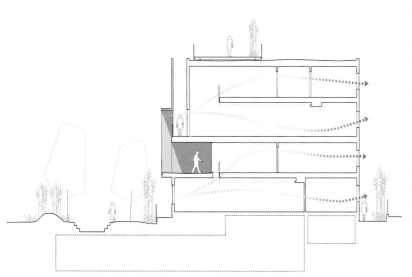

left: Section_Interior bedroom and bath_South elevation facing the park. right: West street elevation_Fourth floor roof deck.
links: Schnitt_Schlafzimmer und Badezimmer_Südansicht gegenüber Park. rechts: Westansicht Viertes Obergeschoss, Dachterrasse.
à gauche: Vue en coupe_Chambre avec salle de bain_Façade sur le jardin côté sud. à droite: Façade sur rue côté ouest_Toit en terrasse.

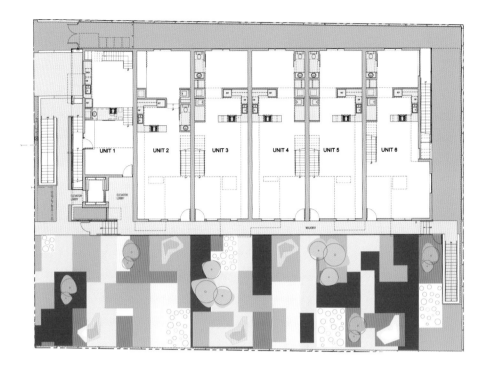

left: South elevation façade detail. right:Floor plan_Corridor_Detail.
links: Südeansicht, Fassadendetail. rechts: Grundriss_Korridor_Detail.
à gauche: Détail de la façade sud. à droite: Plan_Passerelle_Détail.

# WEST HOLLYWOOD_CA **GARDNER 1050**

**ARCHITECTS:** LOHA (LORCAN O'HERLIHY ARCHITECTS)
**COMPLETION:** 2006_**TYPOLOGY:** LIVING
**PHOTOS:** LAWRENCE ANDERSON/ESTO

Located in the city of West Hollywood, California Gardner 1050 is the result of a series of studies into how various housing typologies can be re-invigorated to create new opportunities for living within the extremely tight economic and spatial parameters of the speculative housing market. As a model of court-yard housing developments, the project utilizes a variety of design strategies to elevate it above the mundane infill developments typical of speculative housing.

Das Projekt in der kalifornischen Stadt West Hollywood ist das Ergebnis einer Reihe von Untersuchungen über die Wiederbelebung verschiedener Gebäude-typen, um unter den extremen wirtschaftlichen und räumlichen Randbedin-gungen des spekulativen Häusermarkts neue Möglichkeiten für das Wohnen zu schaffen. Als Modell für die Bebauung mit Hofhäusern nutzt das Projekt vielfältige Entwurfsstrategien und hebt sich so von den typischen banalen Nachverdichtungen des spekulativen Häuserbaus ab.

Ce complexe situé à West Hollywood, en Californie, a été conçu sur la base de diverses études visant à déterminer dans quelle mesure il est possible de construire un nouveau type d'immeubles résidentiels dans un contexte économique et spatial déterminé par une forte spéculation immobilière. Les bâtiments qui composent l'ensemble Gardner 1050, regroupés autour d'une cour, utilisent ainsi diverses stratégies stylistiques pour s'affirmer face aux projets « mondains » qui caractérisent l'immobilier spéculatif.

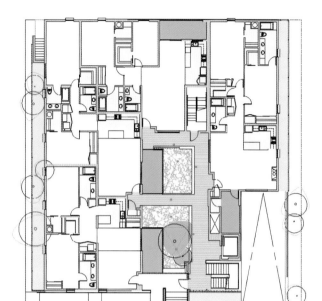

left: First floor plan_Exterior view from street_Bridges connecting units. right: Looking down into interior.
links: Grundriss Erdgeschoss_Straßenansicht_Brücken verbinden die Bauelemente. rechts: Blick ins Erdgeschoss.
à gauche: Plan du rez-de-chaussée_Immeubles vus de la rue_Passerelles entre les appartements. à droite: Intérieur vu de haut.

# WEST HOLLYWOOD_CA **HABITAT 825**

**ARCHITECTS:** LOHA (LORCAN O'HERLIHY ARCHITECTS)
**COMPLETION:** 2007_**TYPOLOGY:** LIVING
**PHOTOS:** LAWRENCE ANDERSON/ESTO

The units are organized around light wells that filter light down into the dwelling units from roof gardens above. All units are single loaded allowing for cross-ventilation and light to enter from multiple sides. The strategic use of black on the southern vertical volume grounds the building, rendering a heavy silhouette as an architectural proclamation. The choice of a lime green rhymes with nature and embodies both the horizontal and vertical landscape concepts of the Schindler House. Materials are a combination of non-combustible cement board and Local forest managed dark stained Redwood siding.

PM

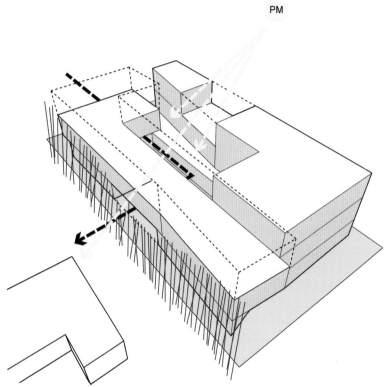

Die Wohneinheiten sind um Lichtschächte organisiert, welche die Helligkeit von den Dachgärten in die Wohnungen darunter filtern. Da alle hofseitig zu erschließen sind, werden Querlüftung und Lichteinfall von mehreren Seiten ermöglicht. Strategisch eingesetztes Schwarz am südlichen vertikalen Baukörper verortet das Gebäude und macht seine strenge Silhouette zu einer architektonischen Aussage. Lindgrün greift die Natur auf und symbolisiert die horizontalen und vertikalen Landschaftskonzepte des angrenzenden Schindler Hauses. An Materialien finden sich eine Kombination aus Zementbauplatten und dunkel gebeizten Schalungsbrettern aus Rotholz der lokalen Forstwirtschaft.

Les appartements de cet immeuble s'organisent autour de puits de lumière aménagés par le percement des toits en terrasse. Tous les logements disposent d'une ventilation croisée et d'un éclairage naturel arrivant de tous les côtés. L'usage du noir sur la façade sud est le résultat d'un choix stratégique qui vise à alourdir la silhouette afin d'affirmer l'identité architecturale du bâtiment. Quant à l'usage du vert citron sur les autres façades, il rime non seulement avec la nature, mais aussi avec le paysage horizontal et vertical de la Schindler House voisine. À ces deux couleurs correspondent deux matériaux différents: du bois rouge d'origine locale traité avec une lasure sombre, et des plaques de béton ignifugées.

left: Project massing study_Interior courtyard at night_Wooden façade, balconies_Detail exterior.
right: View of entry_Detail of courtyard and columns_Open kitchen and light well.
links: Studie der Baumasse_Innenhof bei Nacht_Hölzerne Fassade, Balkone_Detail. rechts: Eingangsansicht_Innenhof und Pfeiler_Offene Küche und Lichtschacht.
à gauche: Étude des volumes_Cour intérieure la nuit_Balcons sur la façade en bois noir_Détail de l'extérieur. à droite: Zone d'entrée_Gros plan sur les colonnes dans la cour_Cuisine ouverte et puits de lumière.

WESTMINSTER_CA **WESTMINSTER ROSE CENTER**

**ARCHITECTS:** CO ARCHITECTS
**COMPLETION:** 2006_**TYPOLOGY:** CIVIC
**PHOTOS:** BENNY CHAN, FOTOWORKS

The city needed a facility to accommodate multiple civic and cultural functions, including banquets, performances, awards ceremonies, galleries, and meeting spaces. Thus, the principal components of the Rose Center are a banquet hall, a theater with 400 seats, and a sequence of multiple-use foyer spaces. Taking advantage of a benign climate, the center also includes an outdoor landscape with a 600-foot-long entry plaza garden, and a public function courtyard. Sited to face the city hall across the street, the center establishes its presence through the innovative use of glazing on the front façade.

Die Stadt benötigte eine Einrichtung für die Aufnahme verschiedener kommunaler und kultureller Funktionen darunter Festessen, Aufführungen, Preisverleihungen, Galerien und Besprechungsräume. Zu den Hauptkomponenten des Rose Center zählen daher ein Bankettsaal, ein Theater mit 400 Sitzplätzen und eine Reihe vielseitig nutzbarer Foyers. Das Center nutzt das milde Klima für einen 183 Meter langen, gärtnerisch gestalteten Vorplatz im Freien sowie einen öffentlichen Hof. Auf der gegenüberliegenden Straßenseite des Rathauses gelegen, bekundet es seine Präsenz mit einer innovativ verglasten Vorderfassade.

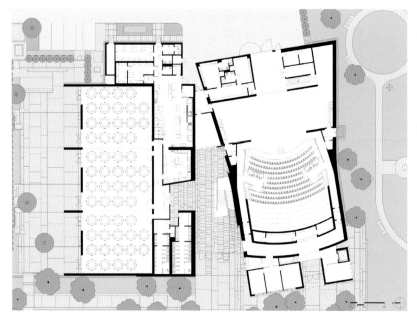

La municipalité de Westminster avait besoin d'un centre polyvalent pour l'organisation de manifestations diverses telles que les banquets, les spectacles, les remises de prix, les expositions et les congrès. Les architectes ont donc conçu un bâtiment qui abrite une salle de banquet, un auditorium de quatre cents places et divers espaces polyvalents. Ils ont aussi prévu une cour de service accessible au public, ainsi qu'un jardin qui s'étire sur 182 mètres de long devant l'entrée et tire profit de la douceur du climat. Situé juste en face de l'hôtel de ville qui se dresse de l'autre côté de la rue, le nouveau bâtiment affirme son caractère novateur par une façade entièrement vitrée.

left: Site plan_General view_Detail façade. right: Entrance view, fully glazed façade.
links: Lageplan_Gesamtansicht_Fassadendetail. rechts: Eingangsansicht, verglaste Fassade.
à gauche: Plan de situation_Vue d'ensemble_Détail de la façade. à droite: Façade et hall d'entrée.

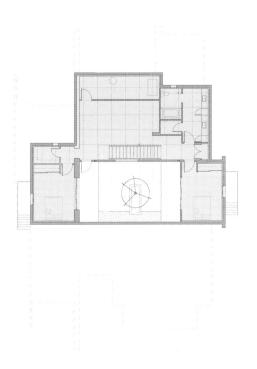

left: View of central void. right: Lower floor plan_Interior.
links: Blick in den Innenraum. rechts: Grundriss Untergeschoss_Interieur.
à gauche: Vue de la cour intérieur. à droite: Plan de niveau supérieur_L'intérieur.

# PORTLAND_OR **SKYBOX**

**ARCHITECTS:** STEFAN ANDREN / KROWN LAB
**COMPLETION:** 2005_**TYPOLOGY:** LIVING
**PHOTOS:** STEFAN ANDREN / KROWN LAB

Perched atop a steep hillside surrounded by green space, Skybox is designed to encompass more loft-like qualities than those of a traditional house. Decks and terraces are created within the dwelling itself, leaving its surroundings untouched and allowing it to better blend in with the natural environment. The house has an open, flowing floor plan, which allows one space to stream into the next, creating a flexible and space efficient dwelling. Rather than the use of walls and doors, shifts in ceiling heights and floor levels are used to emphasize division of space.

Auf einem steilen Abhang von Grün umgeben soll Skybox mehr einem Loft als einem traditionellen Haus gleichen. Die Terrassen entstehen innerhalb des Wohnbereichs, sodass die Umgebung unberührt bleibt und eine bessere Einbindung in das natürliche Umfeld erfolgt. Eine offene, fließende Raumanordnung schafft ineinander übergehende Räume und ein flexibles, räumlich effizientes Wohnhaus. Statt Wänden und Türen sorgen unterschiedliche Deckenhöhen und Geschossebenen für die Raumaufteilung.

Perchée sur une colline boisée, la Skybox offre un espace domestique qui rappelle plus un loft qu'une maison traditionnelle. Les architectes ont aménagé des plates-formes et des vérandas à l'intérieur de manière à minimiser l'impact du bâtiment sur son environnement et à favoriser son intégration dans la nature. Le plan ouvert et fluide génère une interpénétration des pièces et optimise l'utilisation de la surface disponible. La division de l'espace se fait moins par des cloisons et des portes que par des variations de la hauteur des plafonds et des du niveau du sol.

left: Floor plans_View from sleeping room to deck_Living space_Shower. right: Exterior view_Kitchen_Alternative view of exterior.
links: Grundrisse_Ansicht vom Schlafzimmer_Wohnraum_Dusche. rechts: Außenansicht_Küche_Außenansicht.
à gauche: Plan des différents étages_Chambre_Séjour_Douche. à droite: Extérieur_Cuisine_Le bâtiment vu au travers des arbres.

# PORTLAND_OR **FENNELL RESIDENCE**

**ARCHITECTS:** ROBERT HARVEY OSHATZ ARCHITECT
**COMPLETION:** 2005_**TYPOLOGY:** LIVING
**PHOTOS:** CAMERON NEILSON

The Fennell Residence, a floating house on the Willamette River, just outside Portland, Oregon presents a unique opportunity for design. Curved glue lam beams of Douglas fir seem to ebb and flow over the structure in sympathy with the ripples along the river's surface, bringing a sense of fluidity through-out the home. The loft style residence with the master suite on the second floor and the living areas below is punctuated at its western end by an expansive glass wall that allows sweeping views of the river and a physical connection to the water via a sliding door and a wooden deck.

Die Fennell Residence, ein schwimmendes Haus auf dem Fluss Willamette gleich außerhalb von Portland in Oregon, präsentiert eine einzigartige Gestaltung. Gebogene brettschichtverleimte Träger aus Douglasie scheinen sich im Einklang mit der Kräuselung auf der Flussoberfläche über der Konstruktion zu heben und zu senken, wodurch im gesamten Haus ein fließender Eindruck entsteht. Das im Loftstil gestaltete Haus mit dem Elternschlafzimmer in der ersten Etage und den Wohnbereichen darunter, wird an seinem westlichen Kopfende von einer großzügigen Glaswand akzentuiert. Diese gestattet weite Aussichten auf den Fluss und über eine Schiebetür und ein Holzterrasse auch eine räumlich-bauliche Verbindung zum Wasser.

Cette maison qui flotte sur la Willamette River, près de Portland dans l'Oregon, est un chef-d'œuvre du design. Ses toits, soutenus par une charpente en lamellé-collé à base de pin Doublas, semblent onduler au rythme des vagues à la surface de l'eau, donnant ainsi un caractère particulièrement dynamique à l'ensemble du bâtiment. L'intérieur, de type « loft », se compose de chambres à l'étage et d'espaces de séjour au rez-de-chaussée. La grande baie vitrée qui occupe toute l'extrémité ouest offre une vue panoramique sur la rivière. Elle s'ouvre par une porte coulissante qui permet d'accéder à une grande terrasse en bois qui s'étend juste au-dessus de la surface des eaux.

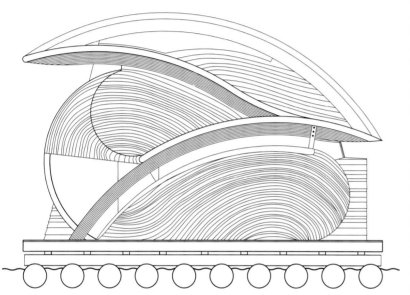

left: Elevation_Exterior_Detail of façade. right: Interior view, living area.
links: Ansicht_Außenansicht_Detail der Fassade. rechts: Innenansicht, Wohnzimmer.
à gauche: Vue en élévation_Extérieur_Autre vue de l'extérieur. à droite: Séjour.

FENNELL RESIDENCE

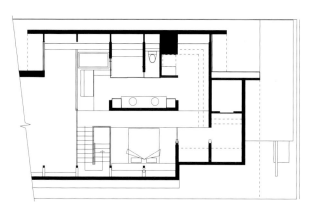

left: Interior view, master suite. right: Floor plans_Exterior view from the deck to the glass wall.
links: Innenansicht, Zimmerflucht. rechts: Grundrisse_Außenansicht von der Terrasse auf die verglaste Fassade.
à gauche: Chambre. à droite: Plans_Intérieur vue de la terrasse.

PORTLAND_OR **WILKINSON RESIDENCE**

**ARCHITECTS:** ROBERT HARVEY OSHATZ ARCHITECT
**COMPLETION:** 2004_**TYPOLOGY:** LIVING
**PHOTOS:** CAMERON NEILSON

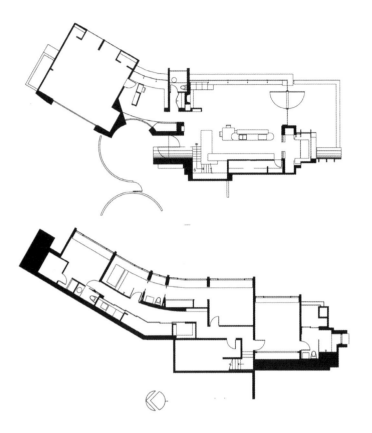

The flag lot and a fast sloping grade provided the opportunity to bring the main level of the house into the tree canopy to evoke the feeling of being in a tree house. This house evades the mechanics of the camera, which makes it difficult to grasp the spaces as they flow inside and out. One has to actually stroll through the house to capture its complexities and its connection to the exterior. Being part of the landscape, a natural wood ceiling floating on curving laminated wood beams passes through a generous glass wall, which wraps around the main living room.

Auf einem schmalen Grundstück bot ein steiles Gefälle die Gelegenheit, die Hauptebene des Hauses unter einem Blätterdach zu platzieren, sodass innen der Eindruck eines Baumhauses entstand. Bei dem schwer zu fotografierenden Haus sind die Übergänge zwischen Innen und Außen fließend. Man muss das Haus durchschreiten, um seine komplexen Verbindungen mit dem Außenraum zu erfassen. Als Teil der Landschaft führt eine Naturholzdecke auf gebogenen Schichtholzträgern durch eine großzügige, den Hauptwohnraum umschließende Glaswand.

Un terrain en forte pente a inspiré les architectes à construire une maison qui donne aux occupants l'impression d'habiter dans une cabane dans les arbres. Le bâtiment est difficile à saisir avec un appareil photo, tant l'intérieur semble se fondre ici avec l'extérieur. Il faut absolument le découvrir par soi-même pour saisir toute sa complexité et l'intensité de ses liens avec l'environnement. Le toit en bois aux formes ondulantes fait partie du paysage et flotte sur une charpente en lamellé-collé. On l'apprécie au mieux à l'intérieur dans le grand séjour, qui se prolonge par une terrasse couverte au-delà d'une grande cloison vitrée.

left: Floor plans_Detail exterior_Rear view. right: Exterior view of wood beams and pivotal glass entry door.
links: Grundrisse_Detail der Außenansicht_Rückansicht. rechts: Rückansicht der Holzbalken und der Glasfassade.
à gauche: Plans des différents niveaux_Détail de l'extérieur_Détail de la face arrière. à droite: Face arrière avec poutre en bois et porte d'entrée pivotante en verre.

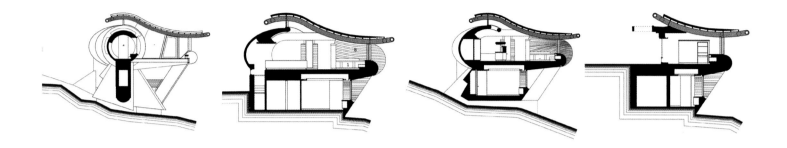

left: Interior view of entry. right: Sections_Kitchen.
links: Eingangsansicht. rechts: Schnitte_Küche.
à gauche: Vestibule. à droite: Quatre vues en coupe_Cuisine.

LOGAN_UT **THE MANON CAINE RUSSELL AND KATHRYN CAINE WANLASS PERFORMANCE HALL**

**ARCHITECTS:** SASAKI ASSOCIATES
**COMPLETION:** 2006_**TYPOLOGY:** CULTURE
**PHOTOS:** ROBERT BENSON

This 420-seat project is a play of geometries of both acoustical and contextual significance, featuring sculpted, geometric forms that evoke the look of the surrounding mountains. An orthogonal concrete shell with thick concrete walls enclose the main performance space whose height, shape and materials were carefully considered for optimum sound qualities. The contrasting zinc panel-coated entrance pavilion has origami-like folded volumes that suggest a melding of the man-made and the natural. By day, triangular skylights angle light into interior spaces and by night the pavilion faces a dramatically lit outdoor piazza.

Das Projekt mit 420 Sitzplätzen ist ein Spiel mit Geometrien von akustischer wie kontextualer Bedeutung. Seine modellierten, geometrischen Formen erinnern an das Bild der umgebenden Berge. Eine orthogonale Betonschale mit dicken Wänden umschließt den Hauptaufführungsraum, dessen Höhe, Gestalt und Materialien sorgfältig nach optimalen Akustikeigenschaften bestimmt wurden. Die wie eine Origamiarbeit gefalteten Baukörper der mit kontrastierenden Zinkplatten verkleideten Eingangspavillons lassen an ein Verschmelzen des von Menschenhand Geschaffenen mit dem Natürlichen denken. Tagsüber sorgen dreieckige Oberlichter für Helligkeit in den Innenräumen. Am Abend wird die Piazza gegenüber dem Pavillon spannungsvoll beleuchtet.

La géométrie de cette salle de concert de 420 places répond à des impératifs non seulement acoustiques mais aussi contextuels, puisque ses formes évoquent les montagnes qui se dressent à l'horizon. La forme, le poids et le matériau de l'enveloppe orthogonale ont été choisis afin d'optimiser l'acoustique dans la salle principale. Les éléments en zinc du pavillon d'entrée contrastent avec le béton de l'enveloppe et composent un origami qui suggère une synthèse entre nature et architecture. Ses châssis triangulaires assurent un bon éclairage naturel durant la journée. La nuit venue, le pavillon apparaît au bout d'une grande esplanade richement illuminée.

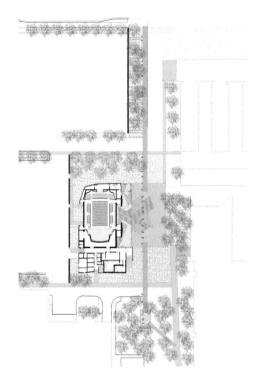

left: Site plan_Concert hall_Triangular skylights_Zinc panel-coatedd façade. right: Approach to hall_Aerial view.
links: Lageplan_Konzerthalle_Dreieckiges Oberlicht_Fassade aus Zinkpaneelen. rechts: Eingangsansicht_Luftbild.
à gauche: Plan de situation_Salle de concert_Ouvertures triangulaires_Façade en verre et panneaux de zinc. à droite: Vue d'ensemble_Le bâtiment vu de haut.

# SALT LAKE CITY_UT **UTAH MUSEUM OF FINE ARTS**

**ARCHITECTS:** MACHADO AND SILVETTI ARCHITECTS
**COMPLETION:** 2000_**TYPOLOGY:** CULTURE
**PHOTOS:** MICHAEL MORAN

This project required that the architecture of the new museum acknowledge and exploit its privileged location at the terminus of the campus mall and its unique condition as a free-standing artifact seen against the spectacular backdrop of the Wasatch Mountain Range. Given the museum's stated programmatic intentions, the decision was made to make the proposed Grand Gallery the centerpiece of the project. Inside, the visitor is drawn into a dynamic play of volumes and light by the tension developed between the easy and well-scaled circulation system that follows the organization of the galleries.

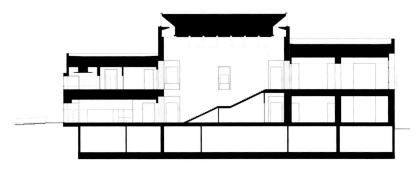

Bei diesem Projekt musste die Architektur des neuen Museums die bevorzugte Lage würdigen und nutzen. Am Ende des Wegs durch den Campus erscheint der Bau vor dem spektakulären Hintergrund der Gebirgskette Wasatch als einzigartiges freistehendes Artefakt. Aufgrund des festgelegten musealen Programms wurde beschlossen, die große Galerie zum Herzstück des Projekts zu machen. Innen wird der Besucher von einem dynamischen Spiel aus Baukörpern und Licht angezogen. Es entwickelt sich aus der spannungsvollen, an der Organisation der Galerien ausgerichteten Wegeführung.

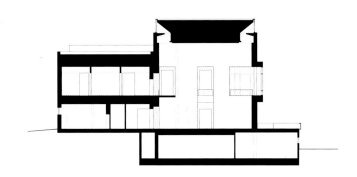

La tâche des architectes consistait ici à construire un musée qui tire profit de son emplacement privilégié à une extrémité du domaine universitaire, dans un site magnifique dominé par la chaîne de montagnes de Wasatch. Ils ont donc conçu un ensemble de bâtiments organisés autour d'un grand espace central d'exposition. À l'intérieur du musée, un système de circulation simple et bien proportionné guide les visiteurs au travers des espaces d'exposition annexes agencés en fonction de l'interaction dynamique des volumes et de la lumière.

left: East and West sections_Gallery_Stair access to gallery_Exterior_Window detail. right: Front entrance_Exterior.
links: Ost- und Westschnitt_Galerie_Treppenaufgang zur Galerie_Außenansicht_Fensterdetail. rechts: Vordereingang_Außenansicht.
à gauche: Vue en coupe des façades est et ouest_Salle d'exposition_Escalier menant à la salle du niveau supérieur_Extérieur_Façade avec oriel. à droite: Esplanade d'entrée_Vue d'ensemble.

# WOODLAND_UT **MONTE-SILO**

**ARCHITECTS:** GIGAPLEX
**COMPLETION:** 2006_**TYPOLOGY:** LIVING
**PHOTOS:** SCOTT ZIMMERMAN

The charge was to design a house that is both homelike in scale and yet comfortable for weekend guests. Two linked corrugated metal grain silos are the structural basis for this building. They are so arranged as to allow the most proximate visual and aural access to the adjacent Provo River. The metal grating provides shading during the summer month, while the southern exposure ensures passive solar heat gain during the winter. An electric mesh is embedded into the slabs of the lower floor as a first auxiliary heat source, and a propane-burning stove provides the back up.

Zu entwerfen war ein Haus, das von der Größe her gemütlich und für Wochenendgäste dennoch bequem sein sollte. Zwei miteinander verbundene Getreidesilos aus Wellblech bilden die konstruktive Basis für dieses Gebäude. Sie sind so angeordnet, dass sie visuell und akustisch möglichst nah zum angrenzenden Fluss Provo liegen. Der metallene Gitterrost sorgt für Sonnenschutz in den Sommermonaten, während die Südlage passive Solargewinne im Winter gewährleistet. Als erste zusätzliche Wärmequelle sind elektrische Heizschlangen in die Platten des Untergeschosses integriert, als Reserveheizung dient ein Propangasofen.

L'objectif était de construire une maison de week-end de taille modeste mais néanmoins confortable. Les architectes ont juxtaposé deux silos à grains en tôle ondulée, les disposant de manière à offrir une vue sur la rivière Provo qui coule à proximité. Du côté sud, un balcon en grille métallique procure de l'ombre en été, tandis que l'exposition au soleil assure des gains calorifiques passifs en hiver. Le chauffage actif est fourni par un réseau de fils électriques intégré au sol du rez-de-chaussée et par un poêle à propane.

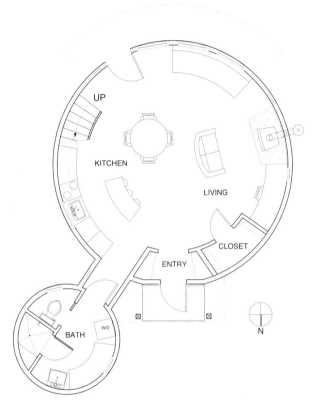

left: First floor plan_Interior_Bedroom_Exterior. right: Exterior view at night.
links: Grundriss erstes Obergeschoss_Inneneinrichtung_Schlafzimmer_Außenansicht. rechts: Außenansicht bei Nacht.
à gauche: Plan du rez-de-chaussée_Intérieur_Chambre_Extérieur. à droite: Le bâtiment au crépuscule.

# CLYDE HILL_WA **HINOKI HOUSE**

**ARCHITECTS:** REX HOHLBEIN ARCHITECTS
**COMPLETION:** 2008_**TYPOLOGY:** LIVING
**PHOTOS:** CATHERINE TIGHE

The Hinoki House is a single-family residence designed for a family of four. The clients were interested in living in an open modern plan, but one with a clear separation between public and private zones. This led to the development of two separated boxes, the cooking/dining box and the sleeping/bathing box; one transparent and open to arriving guests and daily life, and the other sequestered and quiet, with intimate family spaces. The client's love of gardens instigated the idea of connecting the two separated boxes with in-between green spaces, defined with transparency and intersecting stone garden walls, and covered with flat green living roofs which echo the courtyard landscape.

Den Bauherren des Einfamilienhauses war an einem modernen offenen Grundriss gelegen, der allerdings deutlich zwischen öffentlichen und privaten Zonen unterscheiden sollte. Daher wurden zwei separate Kuben entwickelt, von denen einer zum Kochen und Essen und der andere zum Schlafen und Baden dient. Ersterer ist transparent und für Gäste und Alltagsaktivitäten offen, der zweite abgeschottet, ruhig und mit intimen Räumen für die Familie ausgestattet. Die Freude des Bauherrn an Gärten führte zur Verbindung der separaten Kuben durch begrünte Freiflächen. Diese einsehbaren Bereiche werden von sich kreuzenden Gartenmauern aus Naturstein bestimmt. Ihre flachen Gründächer spiegeln die Landschaft des Grundstücks wider.

Les clients — une famille de quatre personnes — souhaitaient habiter dans une maison moderne qui établisse une claire distinction entre les pièces de séjour et les espaces privés. Les architectes ont répondu à cette exigence en concevant deux volumes distincts: le premier, transparent et ouvert sur l'extérieur, réservé à la cuisine et au séjour/salle à manger ; le second, plus calme et intimiste, abritant les chambres et les salles de bain. Le goût des clients pour les jardins a incité les architectes à aménager entre les deux volumes séparés un miniparc paysager qui se caractérise par sa transparence et ses pierres disposées dans la végétation.

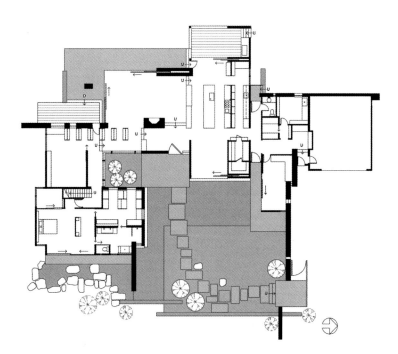

left: Main floor plan_Master bathroom_Kitchen_Office from entry bridge_View of pool. right: East elevation_Entry to office with pool view_Living room terrace.
links: Grundriss Erdgeschoss_Badezimmer_Küche_Büroansicht vom Eingang_Blick auf den Teich.
rechts: Ostansicht_Büroeingang mit Blick auf den Teich.
à gauche: Plan du rez-de-chaussée_Salle de bain principale_Cuisine_Deux vues du bassin. à droite:
Côté est_Vue du bassin et du bureau_Terrasse du séjour.

# MAZAMA_WA **DELTA SHELTER**

**ARCHITECTS:** TOM KUNDIG/OLSON
SUNDBERG KUNDIG ALLEN ARCHITECTS
**COMPLETION:** 2005_**TYPOLOGY:** LIVING
**PHOTOS:** COURTESY OF THE ARCHITECTS

Set on a slight rise within a one-hundred-year flood plain in an alpine river valley, this 1,000 square-foot weekend cabin is essentially a steel-clad box on stilts that can be completely shuttered when the owner is away. Raised above the ground to minimize potential flood damage and to take in 360-degree views of the surrounding forest and mountains, the cabin was conceived as a low-tech, virtually indestructible weekend house.

Das Wochenend-Haus, ein Kasten aus Stahl auf Stützpfeilern in einer Fluss-Aue, kann bei Abwesenheit komplett abgeschottet werden. Der Bau ist als quasi nicht zerstörbare low-tech Konstruktion angelegt. Durch die Hochstellung des Gebäudes wird die Überflutungsgefahr eingedämmt und ein 360° Panoramablick ermöglicht.

Cette maison de week-end de trois cents mètres carrés est construite sur un terrain en pente situé dans une plaine inondable. Revêtue de plaques d'acier, elle est posée sur pilotis et peut être entièrement fermée quand le propriétaire est absent. La position surélevée met l'intérieur à l'abri des inondations et garantit une vue panoramique sur les forêts et montagnes environnantes. Il s'agit d'un bâtiment « low-tech » pratiquement indestructible.

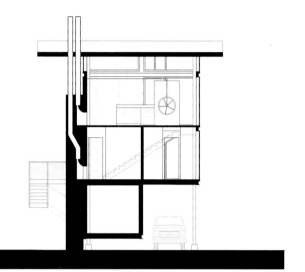

left: Section_Interior, living room_Entrance. right: Exterior in the fall.
links: Schnitt_Innenansicht, Wohnzimmer_Eingang. rechts: Ansicht im Herbst.
à gauche: Vue en coupe_Séjour_Zone d'entrée. à droite: Vue d'ensemble_La maison en hiver_La maison en automne.

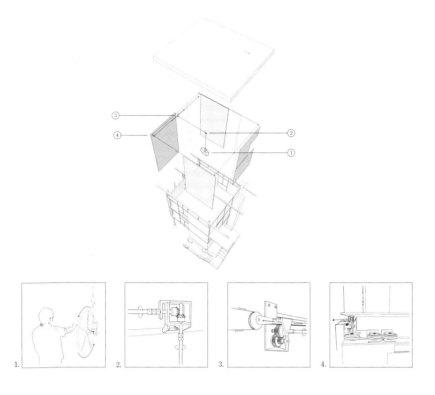

1.  2.  3.  4.

left: Exterior in the winter. right: Exploded view_Exterior.
links: Ansicht im Winter. rechts: Auseinandergezogene Darstellung_Außenansicht.
à gauche: Vue des bungalows. à droite: Vue en éclaté_L'eterieur.

# MAZAMA_WA **ROLLING HUTS**

**ARCHITECTS:** TOM KUNDIG/OLSON SUNDBERG KUNDIG ALLEN ARCHITECTS
**COMPLETION:** 2008_**TYPOLOGY:** LIVING
**PHOTOS:** COURTESY OF THE ARCHITECTS

Rolling huts was created in response to the owner's need and desire for space to house family and friends. The chosen site is a licensed campground for sixteen licensed RVs, where the huts evoke originally populated RVs and traveling caravans. The structures of these unconventional huts are lifted slightly on the site, a flood plain meadow in an alpine river valley, providing an unobstructed view of the surrounding mountains.

Rolling Huts wurde entsprechend den Anforderungen des Besitzers an Unterkunftsmöglichkeiten für Familie und Freunde errichtet. Der Baugrund ist Teil eines offiziellen Campingplatz mit sechzehn Stellplätzen, wobei bereits die Hütten selbst an Wohnmobile erinnern. Die auf der Aue eines Flusstales gelegenen unkonventionellen Hütten wurden leicht angehoben und bieten so einen ungehinderten Blick auf die umgebenden Berge.

Les « Rolling Huts » sont de bungalows qui servent à loger la famille et les amis du propriétaire d'un terrain prévu pour accueillir seize camping-cars ou mobile-homes — ce qui explique leur forme particulière. Ces bâtiments qui sortent de l'ordinaire ont été placés sur pilotis car le terrain, situé près d'une rivière, est facilement inondable. La position surélevée présente de plus l'avantage d'offrir une vue panoramique sur les montagnes environnantes.

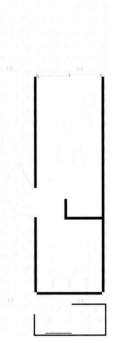

left: Floor plan_Exterior view_Living space. right: Exterior wooden construction.
links: Grundriss_Außenansicht_Wohnraum. rechts: Außenansicht der Holzkonstruktion.
à gauche: Plan_Vue des bungalows_Séjour. à droite: Bungalow avec toit en bois.

# INDEX

## ARCHITECTS ARCHITEKTEN ARCHITECTES

# TYPOLOGY TYPOLOGIE TYPOLOGIE

# PROJECTS PROJEKTE PROJETS